T0319544

Robert McNamara's Other War

POLITICS AND CULTURE IN MODERN AMERICA

Series Editors: Margot Canaday, Glenda Gilmore,
Michael Kazin, Stephen Pitti, Thomas J. Sugrue

Volumes in the series narrate and analyze political and social
change in the broadest dimensions from 1865 to the present,
including ideas about the ways people have sought and wielded
power in the public sphere and the language and institutions of
politics at all levels—local, national, and transnational. The series
is motivated by a desire to reverse the fragmentation of modern
U.S. history and to encourage synthetic perspectives on social
movements and the state, on gender, race, and labor, and on
intellectual history and popular culture.

Robert McNamara's
Other War

The World Bank
and International Development

Patrick Allan Sharma

PENN

UNIVERSITY OF PENNSYLVANIA PRESS

PHILADELPHIA

Copyright © 2017 University of Pennsylvania Press

Published by
University of Pennsylvania Press
Philadelphia, Pennsylvania 19104-4112
www.upenn.edu/pennpress

Printed in the United States of America
on acid-free paper

1 3 5 7 9 10 8 6 4 2

Library of Congress Cataloging-in-Publication Data
ISBN 978-0-8122-4906-4

For Bitta

CONTENTS

Introduction

On February 28, 1968, in a ceremony in the East Room of the White House, Lyndon Baines Johnson awarded Robert Strange McNamara the Presidential Medal of Freedom. It was a bittersweet moment for the outgoing secretary of defense. On one hand, the president spoke glowingly of McNamara's seven years of public service, especially his transformation of the nation's military establishment. On the other hand, even though nobody mentioned it, the Vietnam War was on everyone's mind, and the honoree, who had played a key role in guiding U.S. strategy, looked like a broken man. When it came time for McNamara to address the audience, tears welled in his eyes. A few years earlier, he had been considered one of the most capable officials in Washington. Now, battered by criticism and gnawed by doubt, he stood silent, failure personified.[1]

Nevertheless, Johnson sounded a positive note for the future. Although Medal of Freedom recipients were usually at the end of their careers, the president announced that McNamara's most important work lay ahead. Johnson had recently appointed his outgoing defense secretary to the presidency of the World Bank, a Washington-based intergovernmental organization dedicated to promoting global development. In this role, Johnson told the White House audience, McNamara would be able to "attack the root causes of violence and turmoil: poverty, disease, ignorance, and hopelessness" and thereby "win the most important war of all . . . promot[ing] freedom throughout the world." Then, as if to convince those who doubted that one of the architects of the Vietnam War could succeed in his new fight, Johnson made a bold prediction. Many years hence, he declared, people would look back and say that a "revolution of achievement in the developing nations began with the appointment of Robert S. McNamara to the World Bank."[2]

Despite this claim, Robert McNamara soon faded into obscurity. After the ceremony, the man who came to prominence as one of the "Whiz Kids" who saved the Ford Motor Company from bankruptcy in the 1950s departed the U.S. government for good. McNamara did not reemerge on the American public scene until three decades later, when he acknowledged that he and others in the Kennedy and Johnson administrations had been "terribly wrong" about the Vietnam War.[3]

But McNamara never went away. For thirteen years following that day in the White House—nearly twice the time he spent at the U.S. Department of Defense—he continued to put his stamp on history while presiding over the World Bank. Across the Potomac from the Pentagon, the former defense secretary went from prosecuting a war in Vietnam to fighting poverty around the globe. In the process, he transformed the World Bank and the field of international development in important and lasting ways.

This book tells this story. Drawing on a wide range of materials, including previously untapped World Bank documents, it details a largely unexplored chapter in the history of one of the world's most important international organizations and in the life of one of the twentieth century's most enigmatic figures.[4] In so doing, it offers a window onto the international politics of the 1970s, the roots of globalization, and the origins of today's development landscape.

*   *   *

Robert McNamara assumed the presidency of the World Bank on April 1, 1968, a little over one month after he tearfully departed the Johnson administration. The Vietnam War had taken an immense toll on him. As a result, few expected much of his time at the Bank. McNamara had other plans. Instead of fading away, the man whose fondness for quantitative analysis once led Senator Barry Goldwater to refer to him an "IBM machine with legs" immediately set out to reprogram the institution.[5]

Governments led by the United States had created the World Bank alongside the International Monetary Fund (IMF) in the waning days of World War II to ensure that the world economy would not break down and cause World War III. The Bank's role was to promote economic expansion by making low-interest loans to governments. The idea was simple. The Bank would finance development projects in cash-strapped countries. This would propel growth, stimulate private investment, and improve living standards.

Despite these ambitious goals, the Bank was a conservative financial institution at heart. It raised most of its money by selling its bonds to private investors, rather than from government contributions. Consequently, the Bank avoided doing things that might jeopardize its creditworthiness. For many years, it did not lend to the world's poorest countries because it believed that they would be unable to repay. Instead, the Bank lent mainly to governments in better-off nations in Asia, Latin America, and Europe. The Bank also did not fund projects in education, health, or other social sectors. Rather, it directed the bulk of its resources to energy and transportation projects, which Bank officials considered more productive or "bankable." The Bank's traditionalism was reflected in the composition of its staff, which in its early years was drawn almost entirely from the United States and Great Britain.

This approach did not suit McNamara. He had managed sprawling organizations at Ford and the Pentagon, and he found the Bank's smallness unacceptable. Moreover, he viewed international development as a critically important issue. Like many at the time, he saw global poverty as both a humanitarian problem and a source of political conflict. McNamara wanted the Bank to expand its activities to address this set of challenges. "I have always regarded the World Bank as something more than a Bank, as a development agency," he stated in his first speech as president. "I [am] determined on one thing: that the Bank can and will act."[6]

McNamara pushed the World Bank in a number of new directions upon his arrival. He centralized decision-making authority in the Bank presidency and used this power to expand the organization's borrowing and lending portfolios, staff size, and research program. At the same time, he broadened the organization's focus from promoting the economic growth of developing countries to alleviating poverty within their borders. The vigor with which he sought to remake the Bank underscored his belief in the importance of development and made clear that he viewed the Bank presidency as a way to redeem himself after Vietnam.

It was a challenging time to be working in development. The belief that poor countries could, with the right mix of capital and expertise, accelerate their transformation into wealthier societies was widely shared in the postwar decades.[7] When McNamara arrived at the Bank, however, many people had come to question whether development was possible or even desirable. Although the economies of many poor countries had grown impressively in the postwar decades, living standards often had not improved accordingly. Such findings contributed to a growing sense that foreign aid impeded, rather than encouraged, development. In the late 1960s, the longstanding belief in government's ability to manage the economy also began to come under significant challenge. Meanwhile, nascent environmental, human rights, and feminist movements highlighted ways that economic growth exacerbated ecological, political, and social problems. As British economist E. F. Schumacher wrote in 1970, "development has gone ahead in many places, but the people, the poor, the great majority, have been bypassed and left out."[8]

And then there was Vietnam.

When McNamara assumed the presidency of the Bank, it was becoming clear the war was a lost cause, at least from the U.S. perspective. This fact contributed to the mounting sense that foreign aid was ineffective and that nation-building efforts were doomed to failure. Yet, despite his own doubts about the war, McNamara clung to the belief that well-intentioned outsiders could engineer progress in the developing world. To McNamara, the tragedy of Vietnam was not that the United States had gotten involved in another country's civil war. Rather, the problem was that military intervention had been necessary in the first place. In order to prevent similar conflicts from erupting elsewhere, McNamara the World Banker insisted that the Western world involve itself more extensively in the affairs of developing countries.

McNamara used his bully pulpit at the Bank to make this point, even as he dodged questions about Vietnam by claiming that his status as an international civil servant prevented him from addressing "political" issues. Whether he was speaking to the press at the Bank's headquarters in Washington or visiting a Bank-financed project in a developing country, he insisted that development—defined to mean faster economic growth and better living standards—was the singular issue of the day. Previous World Bank presidents had sounded this theme, but McNamara brought unparalleled energy to the job. He continually lobbied Western governments to channel more money to the Bank, prodded officials in developing countries to reform their economic policies along lines the Bank recommended, and encouraged the Bank's staff to deepen their engagement with issues the organization had previously ignored.

Coming at the same time that the foreign aid budgets of many Western countries were shrinking, McNamara's activism thrust the World Bank into a leadership role in the international development field. Although Vietnam continued to haunt him, the former defense secretary soon gained a reputation as an antipoverty crusader, and the World Bank quickly emerged as the most powerful force in development.

* * *

But McNamara was no more able to escape the perils of his vision at the Bank than at the Department of Defense. Although he increased the organization's stature and achieved some personal redemption during his thirteen years as its president, McNamara led the Bank to behave in ways that undermined its goals of promoting growth and alleviating poverty in the developing world. McNamara's drive to increase the size and scope of the Bank's lending contributed to a decline in the quality of projects that it funded. The Bank's encouragement of expanded private lending to developing countries following the 1973–74 oil crisis also exacerbated the sovereign debt problems that started to plague many of these countries as the decade progressed. McNamara's remedy for these problems, structural adjustment lending, made matters worse, as these loans obligated borrowing governments to adopt austerity policies that did little to promote growth or reduce debt.

In its most basic sense, Robert McNamara's presidency of the World Bank is a story about good intentions gone awry. This is a common theme in the history of development.[9] It also serves as a sequel to his tenure as secretary of defense. McNamara's leadership of the Pentagon, particularly his management of the Vietnam War, has long been criticized for its focus on quantitative analysis and its prioritization of bureaucratic requirements over operational needs. As journalist David Halberstam put it, Secretary of Defense McNamara was "the quantifier trying to quantify the unquantifiable."[10] Similar dynamics characterized McNamara's time at the Bank. McNamara's primary goal at the organization was to increase its power. His focus on maximizing the Bank's influence diverted attention from ensuring that its projects were worthwhile and that borrowing governments could afford its loans.

Yet McNamara's greatest legacy at the Bank lies less in the organization's particular failures and successes during the time than in his transformation of the organization. In many ways, Robert McNamara made the World Bank into what it is today. Although he was not the first Bank president to recognize that promoting development involved more than financing infrastructure projects, he was the first to insist that the organization devote significant resources to other sectors. Similarly, although McNamara was not the first Bank president to realize that the organization's fundamental strength lay in its ability to advance ideas about development, he was the first to turn the Bank into an intellectual leader. And while the Bank had previously attached conditions to its loans to encourage governments to reform their economic policies, McNamara made conditionality a central feature of the organization's work.

McNamara's ability to move the Bank in these directions was as attributable to the force of his personality as it was to changes in the international
political economy. The 1970s was a transformative decade in contemporary
history.[11] Among other developments, U.S.-Soviet tensions eased, countries
in the global South sought to assert their economic independence, and transnational flows of goods, people, and capital—"globalization"—accelerated. The
1970s were also an important time for development, a practice that originated
in the colonial era to become a centerpiece of world affairs as the United
States and the Soviet Union battled for global influence in the postwar years.
Over the course of the decade, the development agenda broadened from promoting the economic growth of developing countries to alleviating poverty
within their borders. International and nongovernmental organizations also
became centers of development thinking and practice. In addition, the preferred means of promoting development shifted from financing infrastructure projects to, on one hand, making "bottom-up" investments in human
capital and, on the other hand, encouraging "top-down" policy reform.[12]

Robert McNamara's World Bank was a key part of this history. Through
his personal advocacy and his efforts to alter the Bank's priorities, the former defense secretary was pivotal in placing poverty alleviation onto the development agenda. And by encouraging Western governments to channel
their foreign aid through the Bank, he helped make multilateral lending a
preferred vehicle for development finance. McNamara's presidency of the
Bank thus demonstrates the important role that international organizations
have played in world affairs and the influence that particular individuals
have had on history.[13]

CHAPTER 1

An Unlikely World Banker

Many people in the Bank were worried when Lyndon Johnson announced Robert McNamara's appointment to the Bank presidency.[1] McNamara was, to say the least, a strange choice to head the organization. The former defense secretary's role as an architect of the Vietnam War made him unpopular around the globe and demonstrated his limited understanding of at least one part of the developing world. McNamara also lacked experience in finance and development, the main components of the Bank's work. This dual role was a product of a complex history that shaped the organization's activities before, during, and after McNamara's tenure.

The Bank Before McNamara

The World Bank was conceived in early 1942, shortly after the Japanese attack on Pearl Harbor, when U.S. treasury secretary Henry Morgenthau, Jr., asked Harry Dexter White, his chief international advisor, to draw up plans for a postwar system that would prevent a repeat of the economic conditions that had led to world war. White, a committed internationalist (who was later discovered to have passed secrets to the Soviet Union during the war) responded by suggesting the creation of two intergovernmental organizations. The first would bail out countries experiencing balance of payments difficulties and coordinate international monetary activity, thereby preventing a repeat of the currency wars of the 1930s. This organization would become the International Monetary Fund (IMF). The second organization would, in White's words, "supply the huge volume of capital that will be needed virtually throughout the world for reconstruction, for relief, and for economic recovery."[2] This would become the International Bank for Reconstruction and Development (IBRD), or World Bank for short.

White's ideas found favor in Washington, and over the next two years he led a team of U.S. officials in refining the plans. The proposal for the World Bank almost never got off the ground, however. While the Allies were interested in the international stabilization fund, the proposal for the Bank drew little attention. When preparations for an international conference to discuss the plans began in earnest in 1944, so few nations had shown interest in the Bank that U.S. officials feared the organization might never come into existence.[3]

The inattention that greeted the proposal for the Bank was due in part to the organization's limited mandate. Although White envisioned a broad role for the Bank as a coordinator of postwar relief efforts, other administration officials believed this would engender opposition in Congress.[4] Thus, the plan for the Bank that the United States circulated to other governments outlined a limited role for the organization. With start-up capital provided by member countries, the Bank would raise money through the sale of its bonds and use these funds to make long-term, low-interest loans to governments for specific development projects. In so doing, the organization would help restore international lending, which had collapsed in the interwar period. As Morgenthau noted in 1943, "the primary aim of such an agency should be to encourage private capital to go abroad for productive investment by sharing the risks of private investors in large ventures."[5] The Allies were also disinterested because the Bank would privilege U.S. interests. Although any country could be a member, voting power would depend on how much money a country provided. In practice, this meant that the United States, the only nation capable of making a significant contribution, would control the Bank.[6]

John Maynard Keynes, the famed British economist, was particularly lukewarm about the proposal. Like White, Keynes viewed expanded international trade, the stabilization of exchange rates, and the revival of foreign investment as necessary conditions for peace. However, he was worried about U.S. dominance of the world economy and argued against the proposals. Rather than have the dollar serve as the world's reserve currency, Keynes suggested the creation of a new international currency to prevent large trade imbalances.[7] Though he supported an organization for postwar reconstruction, he also disagreed with the specifics of the Bank, particularly the idea that countries whose resources had been drained by the war, including the United Kingdom, contribute to its funding.[8]

Nevertheless, Keynes recognized the reality of U.S. power and, once it became clear that the United States would insist on seeing its plans through, dropped his resistance.[9] He acceded to the U.S. proposals onboard the streamliner that carried European delegations across the Atlantic to the United Nations Monetary and Financial Conference in Bretton Woods, New Hampshire, in the summer of 1944.[10] Even then, the Bank's fate remained uncertain. Although delegates to preparatory meetings in Atlantic City, New Jersey, managed to come up with a general outline for the Bank, delegates made no mention of the organization during the first week of the conference at Bretton Woods. Officials only agreed to take time form the monetary deliberations to discuss the Bank at the insistence of a handful of representatives from Latin America and Europe, who were interested in obtaining low-interest loans for their countries.[11]

The ensuing negotiations resulted in an organization fairly similar to the initial U.S. proposal. The Bank's founders wanted to avoid the reckless foreign lending of the 1920s and sought to ensure that the organization operate conservatively. Accordingly, the Bank's Articles of Agreement mandated that funds would finance only clearly defined projects, rather than be provided directly to governments to use as they pleased. The Articles also required that the value of the Bank's liabilities remain less than its reserves, that it would lend to central governments only if no alternative sources of capital were available on reasonable terms, and that countries that wanted to join the Bank would have to become members of the IMF, which would have the power to monitor their economic affairs.[12]

Wartime conditions further constrained the Bank's structure. European countries convinced the United States to limit the amount of money governments would contribute directly to the organization. Instead of the U.S. plan, which called for governments to contribute at least 20 percent of the total amount of the Bank's funding, with that percentage increasing over time, the Articles capped direct contributions at 20 percent. The remainder was to take the form of assurances from national governments that could be used as collateral for the Bank's borrowing. The agreement to accept this level of callable as opposed to paid-in capital meant that the organization would have less money on hand and that demand for its bonds would be lower.[13]

The United States was, however, able to ensure that it would control the Bank. The capital contributions of member countries determined voting power, which meant that the United States would wield the most power within the organization. To assuage the Soviet Union's concern that the Bank would serve as an instrument of U.S. foreign policy, the Articles prohibited the Bank and its officers from interfering in the "political affairs" of the organization's members and from taking the "political character" of countries into account when making lending decisions.[14]

The delegates at Bretton Woods could not help but marvel at their strange creation. Keynes, who presided over the negotiations, noted that the restrictions on the Bank's lending meant that it would operate like a fund, while the IMF would be more like a bank.[15] Although the Bank's Articles allowed for nonproject loans in special circumstances, neither the conditions for nor the content of these activities were clear. In addition, while the Bank was to operate only on the basis of economic considerations, nobody was sure how it would remain apolitical. The relationship between the Bank's president, staff, and representatives of its member countries was also undetermined. The peculiarity of the Bank so struck Georges Theunis, a member of the Belgian delegation, that he later observed, "It was accidentally born with the name Bank, and Bank it remains, mainly because no satisfactory name could be found in the dictionary for this unprecedented institution."[16]

The Bank's founders were correct in emphasizing the organization's uniqueness. Never before had so many governments pledged to pool their resources to promote reconstruction and development. Indeed, until Bretton Woods, international organizations had concerned themselves primarily with political, rather than economic, issues.[17] Despite its limitations, the Bank thus represented an unparalleled experiment in global governance.

To be sure, there was some precedent for the Bank. The idea of a public international development bank had been around since the nineteenth century, and calls for a multilateral investment agency circulated in the interwar period.[18] In the years before Bretton Woods, the United States had also sought to institutionalize international economic cooperation. In 1930, U.S. officials and private bankers spearheaded the creation of the Bank for International Settlements (BIS) to manage the repayment of World War I debts.[19] And the following decade, the U.S. government attempted to establish an organization that would serve as a lender-of-last resort, guarantor and supplier of investment capital, and coordinator of monetary policy for nations in the Western hemisphere.[20] These efforts not only demonstrated the U.S. government's reliance on public-private cooperation but also formed part of a longer American tradition of promoting the global expansion of capitalism.[21]

While the creation of the Bank marked the culmination of certain long-term trends, it also represented a break from tradition. In order to counter the tendency of nation-states to compete against each other, the postwar planners sought to institutionalize multilateral decision-making. The shared experiences of depression and war, as well as memories of the failed World War I peace agreement, created unique conditions for this ambitious endeavor, and U.S. leadership ensured that these plans were realized. The Roosevelt administration recognized that World War II presented an opportunity to transform the international system in much the same way that the Great Depression had enabled it to recast domestic policy. Indeed, the principle that animated the New Deal—that government could productively intervene in the economy—drove the proceedings at Bretton Woods. As Roosevelt put it in describing the plans for the IMF and World Bank, the postwar order would bring about "expanded production, employment, exchange and consumption—in other words, more goods produced, more jobs, more trade and a higher standard of living for us all."[22] In this respect, Bretton Woods formed part of an unprecedented U.S.-led effort to promote global peace and prosperity through international organizations, which the historian Elizabeth Borgwardt has termed a "new deal for the world."[23]

One of the most significant aspects of the postwar order was the way it crystallized understandings of the proper relationship between the public and private sectors. Although they disagreed on the specific form the system should take, the postwar planners believed in the need to strengthen economic ties between countries and, at the same time, improve conditions within them. This was no easy task: the breakdown of the world economy in the interwar period had shown how difficult it was to maintain both an open global economy and robust welfare states. The postwar planners thus faced a dilemma: how to reconstitute international trade and investment while ensuring that countries remained protected from the vicissitudes of the world market. What emerged was a shared understanding that governments should be free to maintain domestic policy autonomy while integrating into the international economy on their own terms, a process of managed globalization that political scientist John Ruggie has termed "embedded liberalism."[24] The faith in government's ability to control economic forces informed the creation of the Bank. As much as they viewed the revival of global capital as vital to the postwar recovery, the postwar planners understood the need for public oversight of the private market. Viewed through this lens, the constraints on the Bank's lending operations reflected a keen understanding of the perils of unregulated finance.[25]

Despite the consensus that globalization needed to be managed, international cooperation remained elusive following Bretton Woods. The Soviet Union rejected the agreement after failing to secure a reconstruction loan from the United States. The UK also balked at signing on to the plans in the hopes that it could convince the United States to ease the terms of postwar aid. Support for Bretton Woods was uncertain even in the United States, where the Roosevelt administration struggled to convince Congress to accede to the proposals.[26]

The delay in ratification delayed the Bank's opening to 1946.[27] That March, the inaugural meeting of the Bank and IMF's Board of Governors, which consisted of the finance ministers of the organizations' member countries, took place in Savannah, Georgia. At this meeting, officials decided to place the headquarters of the two institutions in Washington, D.C. The Bank commenced operations a few months later and the following year approved its first loan of $250 million to the government of France for postwar reconstruction. Over the subsequent months, the Bank made other reconstruction loans to the governments of the Netherlands, Denmark, and Luxembourg.[28]

Although they formed a brief chapter in the organization's history, the Bank's postwar reconstruction loans were significant for a few reasons. For one, as the primary supplier of capital to Western Europe in the immediate aftermath of the war, the Bank played an important role in meeting the region's financial needs before the onset of the Marshall Plan.[29] More important as far as the Bank is concerned, the loans highlighted a recurring tension between "program" and "project" lending. Upon receiving requests for postwar aid, a struggle broke out in the Bank over the precise form that this assistance should take. The Bank's economists argued in favor of loans that would provide general budgetary support, program loans, while the Bank's bankers and lawyers thought that funds should be earmarked for specific projects, as directed by the Bank's Articles of Agreement.[30] The Bank's economists felt that the organization's resources would be better utilized through program loans, both because these gave borrowing governments greater flexibility and because project financing would, since money is fungible, simply supplement borrowers' budgets. The Bank's bankers and lawyers, on the other hand, favored project lending because they thought such loans would provide a better means of ensuring that the Bank was repaid, which was important given the organization's need to establish its creditworthiness in the eyes of private investors.[31] The Bank's economists carried the day, in part because postwar conditions necessitated fast-disbursing budgetary support loans, but the tension between program and project lending would persist throughout the organization's history.[32]

The Bank's reconstruction loans further demonstrated the extent of U.S. influence over the organization. Just weeks before the Bank opened, Harry Truman announced that the United States would begin providing financial assistance to the noncommunist governments of Greece and Turkey. If the Soviet refusal to sign on to Bretton Woods had not already done so, the Truman Doctrine put the final nail in the coffin of the international cooperation hopefully envisioned by postwar planners. The onset of the Cold War had immediate ramifications for the Bank. U.S. officials pressured the organization's management to increase the volume and speed the disbursement of its reconstruction loans as a way to bolster the noncommunist governments of Western Europe. Shortly thereafter, the Bank acceded to U.S. demands by rejecting loan applications from the communist governments of Poland and Czechoslovakia.[33]

The United States exerted its greatest influence on the World Bank when it decided to bypass the organization and create the European Recovery Program in the summer of 1947. As the U.S. government's preferred means of facilitating postwar reconstruction, the Marshall Plan displaced the Bank in Western Europe. As a result, the organization turned to development. It made its first loan to a "less developed" country in 1948, a $13.5 million loan to the government of Chile for the construction of hydroelectric dams. The following year, it dispatched a team of economists and industrial and agricultural experts to Colombia on its first major "country mission."[34]

"Development" had a strange history at the Bank. Interestingly, Harry Dexter White had not included the term in his initial proposal for the Bank. Instead, one of White's assistants appended it to the Bank's official title shortly before presenting the original plan to the Allies in 1943. White appears to have been unconcerned by the addition. Although he was focused mainly on postwar reconstruction, he had no objections to the proposed Bank lending for other reasons. Indeed, by giving the Bank a mandate beyond reconstruction, "development" provided a broader basis upon which the organization could encourage the revival of global capital flows.[35]

That White disregarded "development" in initial plans for the Bank was partially due to the meaning of the term at the time. To mid-century officials, development was synonymous with industrialization. Accordingly, promoting development meant providing resources to capital-scarce countries, the same activity the Bank would undertake with respect to postwar reconstruction. This made geography the characteristic that distinguished development from reconstruction—the former focused primarily on Latin America, the latter mainly on Europe—and led to some tension at Bretton Woods. While delegates from Europe and the United States were concerned with the Bank's reconstruction work, Latin American countries sought to place development at the forefront of the organization's agenda. The result was a compromise in which both roles featured equally. Accordingly, Article I of the Bank's charter reads, the Bank's mission is to "assist in the reconstruction and development of territories of members."[36]

Even so, it was clear that development would eventually surpass reconstruction as the Bank's primary focus. As Keynes predicted in his opening address to the Bretton Woods conference:

> The field of reconstruction from the consequences of war will mainly occupy the proposed Bank in its early days. But, as soon as possible, and with increasing emphasis as time goes on, there is a second primary duty laid upon it, namely to develop the resources and productive capacity of the world, with special attention to the less developed countries.[37]

What Keynes did not appreciate was that the number of less developed countries would increase significantly over the coming years—and how intertwined were development and colonialism. The interwar period had witnessed not only the emergence of the United States as the world's main economic power but also a dramatic change in colonial relations. During this time, European nations began to rely on a new form of interventionism to preserve their increasingly tenuous grip on their colonies. Whereas colonial powers had long focused on extracting the maximum amount of resources from their territories, in the 1930s they embarked on programs designed to improve the living standards of their colonial subjects as a means to quell nascent anticolonial movements.[38] In so doing, they pioneered the practice of international development.[39]

The dawning of the development age had mixed implications for the Bank. On one hand, the organization benefited from the support that countries were giving to development. The Bank drew much of its initial staff from the former colonial bureaus of Europe and partnered with Western countries' foreign aid agencies in financing various development projects. On the other hand, the Bank played a decidedly secondary role in the nascent field of development. During the organization's first decades, its lending remained significantly smaller and less attractive than grants and other concessional forms of assistance provided by Western nations. In addition, because the Bank could only lend to central governments, it was unable to operate in regions that remained under colonial control.[40]

The Bank was further constrained by its reliance on private funding. Because it raised most of its capital by selling its bonds on the private market, the Bank's overriding priority during its initial years was to establish its creditworthiness.[41] This was a main reason why, after issuing program loans to European governments for postwar reconstruction, the Bank focused almost exclusively on project lending. Beginning in the late 1940s, the vast majority of its funds went toward financing the construction of power and transportation infrastructure. Building dams, power plants, ports, and highways provided measurable rates of return that ensured borrowing governments could repay the Bank.[42] The Bank's internal dynamics reflected this change, as the proportion of engineers to economists in the organization increased in the 1950s.[43]

Despite its slow start, the Bank expanded significantly in the 1950s and 1960s. On the borrowing side, in 1959 IBRD bonds received a AAA credit rating, and shortly thereafter the Bank started to raise funds in Western Europe.[44] With respect to lending, the Bank stimulated demand for its loans by marketing them to borrowers and helping to establish planning agencies in developing countries.[45] Bank operations increased significantly as a result. Whereas in 1948, the Bank's Board approved five loans totaling $24 million, in 1961 it made 49 loans totaling $878 million.[46]

The Bank's structure expanded accordingly. In 1955, it established the Economic Development Institute (EDI), a program that brought developing country officials to the organization's headquarters for training in economic policy. A year later, member countries founded the International Finance Corporation (IFC) as an affiliate body to make equity investments in private enterprises in developing countries.[47] And in 1960, it created the International Development Association (IDA), which raised funds from governments and provided long-term, low-interest loans, "credits," to nations too poor to qualify for IBRD loans.[48]

IDA enabled the Bank to broaden its geographical focus and, because its charter stipulated that credits go toward "specific projects of high developmental priority," expand its lending criteria beyond solely financial considerations.[49] In this way, IDA marked the Bank's full-fledged entry into development. Yet IDA had its limits. A U.S. initiative meant to undercut developing country efforts to create a concessional lending affiliate in the United Nations, whose one country-one vote principle would ensure that they had a greater voice, the creation of IDA demonstrated how the U.S. government continued to view the Bank as a foreign policy instrument.[50] The United States and its allies also designed IDA to be weak. Unlike the IBRD, IDA did not have the power to borrow on the private market or, like the IFC, profit from its investments. Instead, it obtained funds from triennial contributions from member countries, meaning that its survival depended on patronage from wealthy nations.

Although external forces defined the parameters in which the Bank evolved, its development was also contingent on the preferences of its management. Aside from IDA, the Bank was not dependent on regular government contributions. As a result, the Bank's management exercised considerable sway over the organization.[51] At the top of this hierarchy sat the World Bank president, appointed to five-year terms by the U.S. government pursuant to an informal agreement between the United States and Western European nations. The power of the Bank president was a legacy of John J. McCloy, the Bank's second president. A prominent Washington lawyer who would go on to head the Central Intelligence Agency, McCloy assumed the Bank presidency in March 1947 after the brief tenure of Eugene Meyer, former chairman of the U.S. Federal Reserve and publisher of the *Washington Post*. As a condition for accepting the post, McCloy demanded that the power of the Bank's Board of Executive Directors, the representatives of the organization's member-states who formally approved loans, be curbed. To this end, he ensured that the Bank's president—not the representatives of its member-countries—had full authority over staffing decisions and borrowing and lending negotiations.[52]

Eugene Black, a former executive at Chase National Bank who took over from McCloy in 1949, used these powers to guide the Bank's maturation during his fourteen years as president. Black focused the Bank's operations on funding projects with a high rate of return. This increased the Bank's creditworthiness, which enabled it to expand its borrowing and lending operations.[53] Black also recognized that the Bank could, because of its relative independence from governments, play a role as an international arbitrator. Accordingly, during his tenure the organization mediated a dispute between the governments of India and Pakistan over rights to water from the Indus

River. He also tried to use the organization as a vehicle to settle claims aris-
ing from the Egyptian government's nationalization of the Suez Canal.[54]

George Woods, who succeeded Black in 1963, put a different stamp on
the Bank. Like Black, Woods, came to the Bank from Wall Street. But while
Black had sought to limit Bank funding to large infrastructure projects
in creditworthy nations, Woods directed more resources to governments in
Africa and Asia and for education and agriculture projects. Woods also increased the role of economists in the Bank and established ties with other
international organizations.[55] Woods's expansionary efforts came at a cost.
The Bank struggled to sell its bonds and briefly stopped lending in the
mid-1960s.[56] The organization also damaged its relationship with its largest
borrower when it pressured the government of India to devalue the rupee
and lift import controls.[57] By the time Robert McNamara succeeded Woods
in 1968, the Bank's role as a development financier was in some doubt.

McNamara Before the Bank

Even before he stepped foot in the World Bank, Robert McNamara was one
of the most important figures in modern history. McNamara spent the seven
years before coming to the Bank as a highly influential U.S. secretary of defense. In the words of Pentagon historians, he "put his mark on the Department of Defense with deeper impression than any secretary in the twentieth
century before or after him."[58] McNamara's legacy was wide-ranging. Among
other things, he instituted budgeting systems that continue to shape Department planning and reorganized the agency's intelligence efforts. Yet Mc-
Namara remains best known as one of the primary architects of the U.S. war
in Vietnam. His role in the conflict—including his efforts to hide details about
it from the public and his long-term struggle to come to grips with it—has
long defined him in popular memory.[59]

Before Vietnam, McNamara's life was characterized by ambition and
achievement. Born on June 9, 1916, in San Francisco, California, he made his
way from a middle-class upbringing in Oakland, California, to the University of California at Berkeley, where he studied economics, participated in
student government, and met his wife Margaret.[60] After college, he enrolled
in the Harvard Business School. While there, he was captivated by a branch
of management variously termed statistical accounting, financial control,
management control, and control accounting. This approach attempted to

improve the efficiency of businesses through numerical analysis: first by collecting facts about a company's operations, then by quantifying this data, and finally by using this information to allocate resources across the firm. Du Pont and General Motors pioneered the practice in the first decades of the twentieth century, and by the time McNamara arrived at Harvard in 1937 it was beginning to be deployed across a range of industries.

Using statistics to manage large organizations fascinated McNamara, who had developed a love of numbers in high school. The prospect of being able to impose order on the world in this way also meshed with his desire to exert control over himself and his environment. Since he was young, McNamara had sought to structure his affairs a highly ordered way. In seeking to distinguish himself in school, for instance, he carefully planned his academic and social calendars with the goal of outworking his colleagues.[61] McNamara was also drawn to scientific management because it promised a path to professional achievement. For most of McNamara's youth, the U.S. was mired in the Great Depression. The idea that effective management could increase a business's profitability and, in so doing, save the economy attracted him. He distinguished himself at Harvard and joined the business school faculty after graduation.[62]

McNamara's teaching career did not last long. During World War II, the military enlisted him to teach Army Air Force officers how to apply statistics to war planning. The analyses proved so important that McNamara soon found himself traveling to Allied bases in Europe and Asia to conduct the research himself. McNamara threw himself into this work. He spent long hours examining flight patterns, helped develop a system for the Air Force's internal reviews, and made a name for himself when he brought to the attention of his superiors an ineffective plan to arm Chinese forces by way of India. In 1944, McNamara found himself advising General Curtis LeMay on Allied operations in the Pacific, including the devastating firebombing of Japan.[63]

After the war, McNamara and nine other Army Air Force officers, nicknamed the "Whiz Kids," landed jobs at the Ford Motor Company. The legendary carmaker had been losing ground to General Motors and Chrysler since the 1920s and was then in a state of crisis. Henry Ford, the founder, was in his eighties. Edsel, his son and designated successor, had passed away. And Henry II, Edsel's son and the new president of the company, had spent most of the previous years in the military. Although government contracts boosted Ford's profits during World War II, by 1945 it was on its last legs. "The company was not only dying," remembered a former executive, "it was already dead."[64]

McNamara was placed in Ford's finance department. No sooner had he set about straightening the company's books than he discovered that practically nothing had been subject to strict oversight. Balance sheets were determined by weighing stacks of invoices and receipts, and no one knew precisely what it cost to build a car. Frustrated by the disorder but confident in his methods, McNamara developed an accounting system for the company and helped decentralize Ford's operations along the lines adopted by General Motors in the previous years.[65]

McNamara came to embody scientific management during this time. His earnest demeanor took physical form when he traded his Harvard tweed and Air Force blue for the charcoal gray suits of Detroit. He strode around Ford headquarters with account book and pencil in hand, hair slicked back and eyes poring over numbers from behind wire-rimmed glasses. He was often the first to arrive and the last to leave, and he developed a knack for impressing his superiors with his grasp of statistics. As other Whiz Kids departed, McNamara rose up the ranks, and in 1960 Henry II named him president of the company. McNamara, just forty-four at the time, was the first president to come from outside the Ford family.[66]

His time in the automobile industry would soon come to an end, however. Less than a month after being appointed president of Ford, Robert Lovett, President Truman's secretary of defense and one of McNamara's superiors during World War II, recommended McNamara as a potential cabinet member to president-elect John F. Kennedy. Kennedy was eager to have a businessman in his cabinet and asked McNamara to be his secretary of the treasury. McNamara declined, reportedly saying he would have more power over the U.S. economy at Ford, but accepted Kennedy's counteroffer to become defense secretary.[67]

Kennedy charged McNamara with the formidable task of bringing the U.S. Department of Defense, a sprawling complex of agencies that operated with little civilian oversight, under centralized control.[68] Despite his lack of political experience, McNamara was able to make significant progress toward this goal. He surrounded himself with energetic staffers and used a version of control accounting known as planning, programming, and budgeting to increase his power over the institution. In the process, McNamara made quantitative analysis a more important part of Pentagon operations and shifted authority from the generals to the civilian leadership.[69]

McNamara's administration of the Pentagon won him few friends among the military brass but many admirers elsewhere. He became one of Kennedy's most trusted cabinet officials, earned the respect of members of Congress for his methodical responses to their questions, and awed journalists with his ability to synthesize vast amounts of data. Before long, people began to view McNamara as a human computer who, through intelligence and hard work, brought about significant improvements in government.[70]

There was some truth to this image. McNamara was a bright and devoted public servant, and his leadership of the Pentagon demonstrated the applicability of modern management to public administration. Nevertheless, this picture belied a more complex reality. At the same time that he was transforming the Department of Defense, McNamara was advising the president on U.S. foreign policy. His strategic vision was wanting. He encouraged Kennedy to undertake the failed Bay of Pigs invasion in April 1961 and, during the Cuban Missile Crisis that October, initially supported a naval blockade, only to backpedal and argue for an air strike against Cuba.[71] In both cases, McNamara showed himself to be a firm believer in the use of military power, something he and others in the Kennedy administration believed should play a greater role in U.S. foreign policy.[72]

Nowhere was this more evident than in the administration's stance toward Vietnam, a focus of U.S. interest ever since it began a protracted war of independence against the French colonial government in the 1940s. In the early 1960s Kennedy expanded U.S. efforts to assist the government of South Vietnam in its war against the communist North. Within a year of taking office, he dispatched U.S. military advisors to South Vietnam and created a formal military command for the country.[73] Although Kennedy resisted calls to send U.S. ground forces to the country, the U.S. commitment increased significantly under his watch. By the end of 1963, there were over 16,000 U.S. military personnel in South Vietnam.[74]

Having exerted greater control over the Pentagon and solidified his influence in Kennedy's cabinet, McNamara played a key role in formulating U.S. policy toward Vietnam. In 1961, he and secretary of state Dean Rusk urged Kennedy to deploy forces to the region.[75] McNamara's influence increased after Kennedy's assassination in 1963. Lyndon Johnson inherited Kennedy's foreign policy team, and McNamara soon emerged as one of the new president's chief advisors. McNamara continued to advocate strengthening the U.S. commitment to South Vietnam. In 1964, after he informed Johnson that the North Vietnamese had attacked U.S. warships in the Gulf of Tonkin (a report that turned out to be false), Johnson obtained Congress's permission to expand the war.[76] In 1965, the United States began bombing North Vietnam, and Johnson followed McNamara's advice in deploying 50,000 troops to South Vietnam.[77]

True to form, McNamara used quantitative analysis to manage the war. Yet techniques that had previously served him well failed in Vietnam. Indicators that the Pentagon used to determine the progress of the war provided an incomplete picture of conditions on the ground and led U.S. policymakers to deploy ever-greater commitments of troops and materiel. Evidence of the folly of McNamara's management of the war, such as his determination of North Vietnamese capabilities through estimates of enemy body counts, soon became notorious. His bureaucratic mindset also prevented him from absorbing information that came from outside the chain of command or that contravened the official line, problems that contributed to the U.S. military's failure to achieve its objectives despite its continued escalation of the conflict.[78]

The aura that had surrounded McNamara soon began to fade, and domestic and international criticism mounted. In 1965, an antiwar activist immolated himself outside McNamara's Pentagon window. His public appearances soon became sites of protest. His congressional testimonies turned combative. And his press briefings became exercises in statistical doublethink. Even to his dwindling group of supporters, the man who had come to Washington to exert rationality and control over the U.S. defense establishment had become indistinguishable from the war he was mismanaging.[79]

It was understandable, then, that most people expected to hear about Vietnam when McNamara delivered a speech to the American Association of Newspaper Editors in Montreal in 1966. Surprisingly, he did not mention the war once. Instead, McNamara used the occasion to draw attention to what he claimed was a broader and far more significant set of issues. If one examined patterns of armed conflict around the world, he declared, three facts jumped out. One, most instances of organized violence were civil wars. Two, almost all these conflicts took place in developing countries. Three, their intensity and frequency were increasing. Far from being isolated, distant events, McNamara argued, these conflicts posed a direct threat to the United States. As he put it, "violence anywhere in a taut world threatens the security and stability of nations half a globe away." In order to deal more effectively with these challenges, McNamara argued that the definition of national security had to change. Peace could not be purchased through "military hardware," "military force," or "military activity." Rather, Western nations needed to eliminate potential sources of conflict by improving the "standards of living" for people in developing countries. "The essence of security," McNamara concluded, "means development."[80]

The audience was shocked. Although many knew McNamara to be a supporter of the U.S. foreign aid program, his rejection of military force as the central component of national security ran counter to U.S. policy in Vietnam. Journalist James Reston, who had accused McNamara in print of lying about the war, gushed that the defense secretary had reached "beyond the draft, beyond the Pentagon, beyond administration policy, beyond the present, even beyond the concept of sovereign nation states, and certainly beyond Vietnam" in search for a "unifying principle" to govern international relations.[81] To some, McNamara's words confirmed that, despite his reputation, the defense chief was a humanitarian. The speech had revealed "the real Robert McNamara," a columnist wrote, "lofty and far ranging and liberal beyond any dogmas."[82] As Reston put it, McNamara "is a philosophical computer, and the philosopher in him is stronger than the computer."[83]

McNamara's words reflected many of his core beliefs. Like many who came of age during the Great Depression, he had witnessed poverty and unemployment firsthand, and he believed that without government intervention such conditions would have led to significant social and political unrest. "Had President Roosevelt not done some of the things he did," McNamara later told the filmmaker Errol Morris, referring to the New Deal, conditions "could have become far more violent."[84] McNamara's faith in the ability to solve seemingly intractable problems like poverty also reflected his managerial background, which led him to view organizations of varying complexity, whether a business, government agency, or entire country, as entities that could be controlled with modern management techniques. As he famously put it during his time at the Pentagon, "management is the gate through which social, political, economic, technological change, indeed change in every dimension, is rationally spread through society."[85]

McNamara also had strong missionary tendencies. As a young man, he once remarked to a friend that his life's goal would be to "help the largest number," and he viewed his efforts to reform the organizations he led as emblematic of an abiding desire to serve the public good. Long after he left Ford, for example, McNamara boasted of how he had been the first automobile executive to try to institute safety features in cars. (He neglected to mention that he dropped these plans when pressured by his fellow executives.) And as secretary of defense he had tried to promote progress in domestic race relations by creating a program entitled "Project 100,000" that lowered the educational standards for military induction. McNamara billed this as a means to assist poor youth to achieve a better future while downplaying the fact that it increased the number of minorities deployed to Vietnam.[86] Even McNamara's initial support for the war meshed with his humanistic proclivities. Like many others, McNamara saw U.S. intervention not simply as a means to contain communism but as an opportunity to promote the economic, social, and political progress of a postcolonial nation.[87]

McNamara's speech also reflected basic principles of U.S. foreign policy. The notion that the economic development of poor countries was vital to U.S. security had been part of the country's strategic thinking since 1949, when President Truman established the U.S. foreign aid program.[88] Although the stated purpose was to promote "the improvement and growth of underdeveloped areas," officials intended foreign aid as means of ensuring a successful resolution of the Cold War.[89] Development became even more of a strategic priority in the 1960s. Worried that newly independent countries would turn toward the Soviet Union and convinced that poverty bred political instability, President Kennedy declared the 1960s the "Decade of Development," requested large increases in U.S. foreign aid levels, and created the U.S. Agency for International Development (USAID) to manage the country's foreign assistance programs.[90]

Both the U.S. military intervention in Vietnam and the U.S. foreign aid program were predicated on a belief in the ability of U.S. officials to control events in the developing world. Consequently, failure in Vietnam undermined the popularity of foreign aid.[91] Although it would take some time for this to become clear, McNamara had an idea what was coming. At the time he delivered his speech in Montreal, he had come to doubt the possibility of a U.S. victory. In early 1965, months before encouraging Johnson to make the fateful decision to commit ground troops, he began to suspect the war could not be won. By the following summer, he had grown concerned that further escalation would damage other U.S. foreign policy objectives.[92] As the war intensified, McNamara's suspicions were confirmed. Soon he was presiding over a war he knew was unwinnable.[93]

McNamara's sense of loyalty prevented him from directly confronting Johnson or resigning. Nevertheless, his concerns continued to grow. In May 1967, he made his reservations known by calling for a restriction on U.S. bombings and a limit on future commitments of ground forces.[94] As he told the president, "the picture of the world's greatest superpower killing or seriously injuring 1,000 non-combatants a week, while trying to pound a tiny, backward nation into submission, is not a pretty one."[95]

McNamara's position angered Johnson. Discontent over the war had made the president intolerant of dissent within his inner circle. The fact that McNamara, of all people, was questioning U.S. strategy was particularly irritating.[96] The apostasy of his once-hawkish secretary of defense so exasperated Johnson that he complained to a senator that McNamara had "gone dovish on me."[97]

Relations between Johnson and McNamara continued to deteriorate over the coming months. As the president struggled with his own doubts about Vietnam, McNamara insisted privately that the war needed to be wound down. Yet even as he encouraged Johnson to deescalate, he continued to maintain in public that the United States and South Vietnam were winning.[98] These lies took their toll. McNamara grew estranged from his son. His wife was hospitalized with ulcers. He began to waver in his congressional testimonies. And his behavior became erratic. Members of the administration soon started to worry about his mental state.[99]

A secretary of defense on the verge of a nervous breakdown was bad enough. One who was rumored to have shared his discontent over the war with Robert Kennedy, Johnson's main rival for the upcoming Democratic nomination for the presidency, presented Johnson with an untenable situation. On one hand, Johnson understood that dissent in his cabinet not only hampered effective policymaking but also might, if it became known, doom his chances for reelection. But removing McNamara would confirm rumors of internal strife and allow critics to argue that the administration was hiding the truth about the war from the public. Even worse, relieving McNamara of his duties might cause him to criticize the war in public.[100]

Johnson decided to neutralize McNamara by sending him to the World Bank. In early 1967, George Woods, whose five-year term as Bank president was coming to an end, had recommended to Johnson that he take advantage of the U.S. government's prerogative to appoint the Bank president to select McNamara as his replacement. McNamara's "essence of security" speech had impressed Woods, who was leaving the Bank because of health issues, and he thought the defense secretary's managerial skills would serve the Bank well.[101] Woods discussed the idea with McNamara separately, and McNamara, looking for a way out of the Pentagon, mentioned the possibility to Johnson in passing.[102]

At first, nothing came of these discussions. McNamara's name was not among an initial list of potential World Bank presidents circulated by the Treasury Department, which handled U.S. policy toward the Bank.[103] Rather, the administration's main goal was to find someone who had a background in finance and development, neither of which described McNamara.[104]

However, after McNamara broke with Johnson over the escalation of bombing in North Vietnam in November, the president rethought Woods's suggestion. He informed Treasury Secretary Henry Fowler of his desire to appoint McNamara to the Bank presidency and on the second to last day of the month announced to nearly everyone's surprise, including McNamara's, that his secretary of defense would be leaving the Pentagon for the World Bank in the coming months.[105]

Johnson's decision to appoint McNamara to the Bank presidency was shrewd. Because the Bank's Articles of Agreement prevented the organization's officers from commenting on the political affairs of member countries, McNamara would have to remain silent on Vietnam if he wanted to keep his job. Aware of this possibility, upon learning of the appointment Robert Kennedy rushed to the Pentagon and urged McNamara to decline Johnson's offer. McNamara refused, and on November 29, immediately after the Bank's member countries approved his appointment, told reporters he would be leaving the Department of Defense for the World Bank in the spring.[106]

Yet while it was politically expedient, Johnson's relegation of McNamara to the Bank was also a craven act. That the president was willing to place McNamara, who had overseen a war that killed thousands of Vietnamese civilians, in charge of an organization tasked with promoting the development of poor countries testified to the remarkably narrow vision Johnson had for the Bank. Just as troubling was the fact that McNamara, knowing that the war was a lost cause and that his public criticism might help end it, was willing to go quietly.

Nevertheless, McNamara's appointment seemed to hold mixed implications for the "unprecedented institution" whose headquarters were just down the street from the White House and across the river from the Pentagon. The Bank was getting an experienced manager, but one whose best days seemed far behind him.

CHAPTER 2

Modernizing the Bank

Rainer Steckhan must have thought someone was playing an April Fool's joke on him. For the past two years, the young German had served as George Woods's personal assistant at the World Bank. Woods's tenure had just ended, and today, April 1, 1968, was the beginning of the new president's term. Eager to get a head start, Steckhan arrived at the Bank headquarters in downtown Washington early that morning. He had barely sat down at his desk when someone burst into his office. The visitor thrust out his right hand and introduced himself as Robert McNamara, the new president of the World Bank. Steckhan was startled. His old boss had never behaved so informally, and none of the Bank's senior managers arrived to work this early.[1]

This was not how Steckhan expected to meet Robert McNamara, of all people. The Bank's seven hundred professional staff members had been bracing for their new boss's arrival for months. Since Lyndon Johnson announced the former defense secretary's appointment to the Bank presidency the previous November, rumors of McNamara's hard-driving management style, his obsession with numbers, and the prospect that he would shake up the World Bank as he had the Ford Motor Company and the U.S. Department of Defense had circulated throughout the organization.[2] Despite McNamara's reputation, no one was sure exactly what type of leader he would make. Some imagined that he would treat the Bank presidency as a sinecure from which to recover from the Pentagon, biding his time until he could land another job in government or the private sector. Others thought McNamara would use the Bank to continue the fight against communism, winning the allegiance of foreigners through dollars instead of guns. Or maybe McNamara would view the Bank as a means to do penance for Vietnam, promoting development as atonement for the war.[3] At the very least, most believed that McNamara's history would hamper him. Not only was he, at fifty-one, the youngest president in the Bank's history and the first to come to the organization without a background in finance, but he was one of the primary architects of the Vietnam War, had recently been overseeing one of the largest militaries in human history, and had cut his teeth as an automobile executive.[4]

Steckhan was pleasantly surprised to find his new boss personally engaging and eager to get to work the morning of April 1. The previous evening, Lyndon Johnson had appeared on U.S. television to announce that he was forgoing his bid for reelection and ordering a partial halt to the bombing of North Vietnam, the very policy McNamara had lobbied for over the past year and a half. McNamara made no mention of the news happening down the street at the White House. Instead, after having Steckhan show him around the spacious presidential office on the twelfth floor of the Bank's headquarters, McNamara convened the President's Council, a group of the organization's senior managers who met every week to advise the Bank president on policy and administrative issues. McNamara used the occasion to dispel some of the concerns management might have had about their new leader. After introducing himself as "a new boy who need[ed] to learn" about the Bank, he listened patiently to their descriptions of the Bank's work.[5] No one dared bring up Vietnam, but McNamara seemed nothing like the anticommunist warmonger or overbearing executive that many made him out to be.[6]

Nevertheless, McNamara already had some idea of what he wanted to accomplish. Since arriving in Washington in 1961, he had been a strong supporter of international development. Like other Kennedy and Johnson officials, McNamara saw foreign assistance as an important tool in the U.S. strategic arsenal. During his tenure as secretary of defense, for instance, he had argued for increasing U.S. aid to South Asia by stating that "everything we have done in Vietnam won't count for a thing if Indian democracy goes down the drain."[7] As noted earlier, McNamara's support for development also had personal roots. As a young man, he told a friend of his intent to "help the largest number." His managerial background led him to view entire countries as susceptible to rational planning and control. And his upbringing during the Great Depression sensitized him to poverty while imparting in him a belief in the power of government intervention.

Vietnam did not disabuse McNamara of these views. On the contrary, McNamara's experience during the war strengthened his faith in development. Viewed in the context of his growing doubts about the war, McNamara's 1966 "essence of security" speech—in which he declared that development was the key to world peace—reflected a change in his view of the type of power that should be deployed to create a better world, rather than in whether such power should be used. McNamara saw the World Bank presidency as an opportunity to continue down a lifelong path of public service, finally freed from the constraints of politics, militarism, and the profit motive.

Nevertheless, McNamara quickly realized that his new position had its own limits. Upon entering office, he was surprised to learn of the Bank's modest reach in the developing world. William Clark, a former aide to British Prime Minister Anthony Eden who had started working at the Bank at the end of George Woods's tenure, recalled that McNamara found the Bank's lending program "small and patchy" compared to the "obvious need." He was particularly troubled by the fact that the Bank had made "no loans to such critical areas as Indonesia or Egypt, nor to the great majority of the very poorest countries in Africa."[8]

McNamara voiced these concerns three days after arriving at the Bank. In a scene that augured the transformation that was about to come over the organization, he reconvened the President's Council and asked them why the Bank was not lending to more countries. Bank officials responded by highlighting the organization's political and financial constraints. The Bank was not lending to the nationalist government of Gamal Nasser in Egypt, for instance, because doing so might upset members of the U.S. Congress and thus jeopardize International Development Agency funding. The Bank also avoided operating in sub-Saharan Africa because countries in the region were too poor to quality for the Bank's regular loans and lacked the capacity to make productive use of IDA funds.[9]

During the meeting, the sky outside suddenly grew dark. McNamara listened patiently to the President's Council members and as soon as they were done ordered them to prepare a "list of all the projects or programs that [they] would wish to see the Bank carry out if there were no financial constraints" on the Bank's ability to lend or the capacity of developing countries to borrow. The group was stunned.[10] Although the Bank had expanded its lending under George Woods, management prioritized financial considerations when making lending decisions. Moreover, the organization tended to receive requests for loans rather than seek out lending opportunities. According to one former World Banker, "no one knew how to respond" to McNamara's unusual request.[11] News from outside amplified their shock. As the President's Council members filed out of the meeting, they learned that the cause of the preternaturally dark sky was smoke from the rioting that followed the assassination of Martin Luther King, Jr.[12]

The Bank and the world around it were entering a new age.[13] As protests raged around the globe, international politics and economics were changing in profound ways. For the Bank, the critical issue was declining support in the West for international development. The relaxation of tensions between the United States and Soviet Union, the gradual end of the postwar economic boom, and disappointment with the results of previous nation-building efforts raised questions about development and contributed to a significant decline in the foreign aid programs of many Western countries. U.S. foreign aid commitments declined from $3.6 billion in 1963 to $3.3 billion in 1968.[14] French foreign aid fell from $1 billion in 1962 to $850 million in 1968. And British aid, which averaged $500 million annually between 1964 and 1967, dropped to $430 million in 1968.[15]

Waning support for development presented a significant challenge to the Bank. Although the Bank did not directly rely on government contributions, a lack of support might place too great a strain on its shoulders or undermine its efforts in other ways. The United States was already dragging its feet in contributing to IDA, and demand for IBRD bonds on Wall Street had begun to decline. Lower foreign aid levels also spelled trouble for developing countries, which needed these funds not just for domestic investment but also to service mounting debt obligations.[16] The pressing capital needs of developing countries combined with the growing unpopularity of foreign assistance led observers to speak about a "crisis in aid."[17]

In moving from the Pentagon to the World Bank, then, Robert McNamara exchanged one set of global problems for another. Moreover, McNamara recognized that the Bank as he inherited it was incapable of addressing its challenges. Its small lending portfolio was just the tip of the iceberg. The organization's entire approach was too restrained. If the Bank was to contribute to solving the development problems of the coming years, McNamara felt that it had to change in fundamental ways. The Bank needed to focus more squarely on promoting development, and its capacity for achieving this goal had to be greatly increased.

McNamara outlined his initial objectives as Bank president in a detailed agenda that he drew up for himself shortly after entering office. In characteristically detailed fashion, he listed for himself ninety-eight goals for his first months. These included expanding the Bank's borrowing and lending programs, recruiting more professional economists to the organization, forging ties with other international organizations, establishing long-term lending targets for each of the Bank's borrowing countries, and personally monitoring the progress of some of the organization's development projects.[18]

McNamara's agenda demonstrated the hyperactivity that would come to mark his presidency. The man who seemed so thoroughly defeated when he left the Pentagon threw himself into his new work. He divided his long days into tightly scheduled 15-minute blocks and, in a symbol of his desire to rejuvenate himself, jogged up the twelve flights of stairs to his office early each morning. When he was not at the Bank's headquarters in Washington, the former Ford executive traversed the globe, visiting first world capitals and third world slums in a near constant effort to expand the Bank's activities. McNamara buttressed his energetic management of the Bank with influential speeches on development issues. In the process, he gained a reputation as a pioneering development thinker outside the Bank at the same time that staff came to know him as a hardnosed boss. Indeed, McNamara's drive was so great and the scope of his activities so encompassing that at times it seemed that his primary motivation was to keep himself busy.

But McNamara's leadership represented something else. The goal that occupied the majority of his time and which proved to be his most lasting mark on the Bank was to increase the organization's size, sophistication, and reach. His own efforts and favorable circumstances allowed him to go a long ways toward increasing the Bank's power, and within a few years he had turned the organization into the world's preeminent development institution.

Expansion

His first task was to increase the Bank's size. McNamara had managed extremely large organizations at the Ford Motor Company and the U.S. Department of Defense. Now, as president of the World Bank, he found himself in charge of an organization whose total borrowings over the previous year were less than what the United States spent every month in Vietnam. According to one former Bank staffer, McNamara was so disoriented that "at first he kept talking in billions" about the organization's borrowing and lending programs, then "would correct himself and say, 'I meant millions.'"[19]

Increasing the Bank's size meant raising more money. The Bank obtained its funds from a handful of sources, including direct contributions from its members as well as interest payments on its loans. The largest portion, about 34 percent in 1968, came from the sale of its bonds on the private market, and the Bank raised about 40 percent of these funds in the United States.[20] While this reflected the dominant role of the United States in the world economy, it also increased the riskiness of the Bank's portfolio and prevented it from capitalizing on alternate markets. Accordingly, on McNamara's first day in office he informed his senior staff of his desire to diversity the organization's borrowings by selling more bonds in other countries.[21]

Robert Cavanaugh, the Bank's treasurer, thought that expanding the organization's borrowings too quickly would jeopardize its credit rating and make it more difficult to borrow at favorable rates.[22] Yet the Bank's bond placements proceeded with a great deal of success, and by the time McNamara delivered his inaugural address at the World Bank and IMF annual meetings in September 1968 he was able to report that over the previous three months the organization had "raised more funds by borrowing than in the whole of any single calendar year in its history."[23]

Cavanaugh resigned. In his place, McNamara hired Eugene Rotberg, a young lawyer at the U.S. Securities and Exchange Commission (SEC). Rotberg was only thirty-nine at the time and had no experience in finance or development. Nevertheless, he possessed two key qualities McNamara wanted for the Bank: quantitative proficiency (Rotberg had gained a reputation for sophisticated market analyses during his time at the SEC) and an expansive understanding of development. Rotberg later recalled that when interviewing him McNamara did not seem to mind his inexperience. When McNamara asked whether he had studied finance or economics in college, Rotberg responded that he had majored in history. What did he think about world poverty? Rotberg said it was a problem he would be willing to spend his life trying to solve. And what were his impressions of bankers? Rotberg told McNamara that at the SEC he was trying to throw most of them in jail. In fact, Rotberg's lack of Wall Street connections seemed to attract McNamara. As he later remembered, McNamara tapped him because he "was not beholden to Wall Street" and would thus have no allegiances beyond the Bank.[24]

When Rotberg began in November 1968, McNamara instructed him to increase the Bank's borrowing portfolio in any way he could.[25] Rotberg achieved this goal by broadening the range of securities the Bank offered and cultivating investors around the globe, including in the emerging markets of Western Europe, Japan, and the Middle East.[26] Rotberg's success at the Bank earned him praise as "the world's greatest borrower." Upon his retirement in 1987, he had raised over a trillion dollars for the organization.[27]

Although Rotberg managed the specifics, McNamara played a hands-on role in fundraising.[28] Whereas Rotberg focused mainly on facilitating the private placement of Bank bonds, McNamara concentrated on lobbying government officials in wealthy countries to increase their contributions to IDA and to purchase more of the organization's bonds directly. What McNamara lacked in financial experience, he made up for with his energy. Ever eager to increase the Bank's coffers, at one point he admitted that locating new funding sources made him "very anxious."[29]

McNamara's efforts almost ended before they began. A few weeks after assuming the Bank presidency, he appeared in a television commercial reading a statement supporting Robert Kennedy's role in the Cuban Missile Crisis.[30] Kennedy had recently announced his candidacy for the Democratic nomination for the presidency of the United States, and in order to address concerns about his lack of foreign policy experience had enlisted officials from his brother John's administration to testify on his behalf.[31] Despite McNamara's denials that he was campaigning for his friend, observers considered the appearance a violation of the rule preventing Bank officials from interfering in the political affairs of the organization's members.[32] The *New York Times* editorialized that McNamara had "displayed poor judgment and poorer taste" in appearing in the commercial, and Republican senators called on him to resign from the Bank.[33] McNamara apologized and escaped further censure, but the affair demonstrated that he remained an intensely polarizing figure even in his new post.

It also complicated the Bank's efforts to secure U.S. funding for the International Development Agency. Although the United States had been instrumental in creating IDA in 1960, its support for the Bank's concessional lending affiliate had always been tenuous. As noted earlier, IDA was created as a means to undermine developing country demands for the creation of a UN-managed agency that would issue loans on favorable terms to the world's poorest countries. By 1964, the United States had reduced its share of IDA from the 45 percent of total funds it provided toward initial capitalization to 42 percent.[34] The U.S. desire to reduce its share of IDA funding resurfaced during the IDA II negotiations that began in 1967, as U.S. negotiators balked at George Woods's proposal for a $2.4 billion replenishment.[35] In order to win U.S. support, the Bank's management agreed to reduce the U.S. contribution to 40 percent of the total.[36] Nevertheless, funding legislation stalled in Congress, and as other nations waited for the U.S. to take action before releasing their contributions, IDA began to run out of funds in 1968.[37]

Although Congress approved the appropriation the following spring, these difficulties strengthened McNamara's resolve to diversify the Bank's funding.[38] West Germany was one of his main targets. Despite experiencing slower growth than during the "miracle" years of the 1950s, the West German economy continued to grow at an impressive rate in the 1960s, and by the end of the decade the country was running trade surpluses.[39] Recognizing that German officials were eager to avoid inflation, McNamara marketed World Bank bonds as a way to invest the country's excess funds.[40] In the summer of 1968, he traveled to Frankfurt to discuss the Bank's borrowing prospects with West German bankers. He then went to Bonn, where he obtained the permission of Finance Minister Franz Strauss to undertake a series of bond offerings in the country and convinced Karl Schiller, West Germany's minister of economic affairs, to increase West Germany's contribution to IDA.[41] Later that day, the Bank borrowed 400 million Deutschmarks from a consortium of West German banks. The following month, the Bank sold another $100 million of its bonds in West Germany. This was the largest foreign bond placement in the country's history and increased the Bank's annual borrowings in West Germany to $295 million.[42] That December, eager to capitalize still further on what one Bank official called the "tremendous pool of capital in Germany which could be put to use for development purposes," McNamara called on his staff to develop a "yearly borrowing program" for West Germany "covering all lenders."[43]

News from the United States tempered McNamara's excitement. At a meeting in West Germany in June, he learned that an assassin had killed Robert Kennedy while he was campaigning in Los Angeles. After concluding the meeting, McNamara rushed back to Washington. Television reporters stopped him on the sidewalk outside the Bank's headquarters. As tears streamed down his face, he expressed dismay before ducking into the building. For McNamara, like many others, Bobby's death triggered memories of his brother John's murder five years earlier. The assassination was especially difficult for McNamara given his fondness for Bobby, whom he continued to consider a close friend. Bobby was also McNamara's last tie to the Kennedy administration, and his candidacy remained the best hope that McNamara had of reentering U.S. politics. McNamara had done everything in his power to put the previous years behind him during his first months at the World Bank. The assassination thrust him back into despair. His close friends took note of his moodiness and drinking. His wife, Margaret, voiced concerns about his emotional state.[44]

Yet McNamara's personal struggles did not deter him from his mission at the Bank. In the wake of Bobby's death, he redoubled his efforts to expand the Bank's funding. In August, the organization raised $42 million in Kuwait in the Bank's first public bond offering in the Middle East, and the following spring he directed Rotberg to increase the Bank's non-U.S. bond placements still further.[45] To assist with these efforts, McNamara recruited capital markets experts to the Bank and had the organization's research staff, which spent most of its time studying conditions in developing countries, conduct analyses of borrowing prospects in wealthy countries.[46]

McNamara also dispatched William Clark, whom he had appointed as the Bank's head of public relations, to Tokyo to determine the prospects for Bank fundraising in Japan. Japan's impressive postwar recovery—during the 1960s, the country experienced annual growth rates of over 10 percent—had resulted in its recent "graduation" from Bank borrowing.[47] As with West Germany, McNamara considered Japan a potentially lucrative funding source. However, Japanese officials were reluctant to increase their support of the Bank. While the government was looking to expand its foreign aid program, Clark reported that there was "a widespread feeling in Japan that the World Bank was dominated by the United States."[48] Japanese officials reiterated this message to McNamara at the World Bank-IMF annual meetings in Washington a few months later when they indicated that they were planning to channel more of their foreign aid through the Asian Development Bank (ADB), a regional development lender, rather than the World Bank.[49]

McNamara refused to take "no" for an answer. In a meeting with Japanese Prime Minister Eisaku Sato in Washington, he attempted to assuage concerns about U.S. dominance of the Bank by noting that if Japan increased its contribution it would became one of the organization's five largest shareholders and, as provided by the Bank's Articles of Agreement, gain a permanent seat on its Board. McNamara also promised that the Bank would devote more attention to Japan's regional interests over the coming years. "The World Bank Group would play an increasingly active part in meeting the needs for economic assistance of other countries in Southeast Asia," McNamara pledged, including "assistance for reconstruction in that region once the war in Vietnam was over." Although this message might have sounded strange coming from one of the chief architects of the war, McNamara was undaunted. "It was one of the unfortunate consequences of the war in Vietnam that the American people were now less willing than before to accept foreign commitments," McNamara noted, and this directly threatened the Japanese economy. "Serious debt service problems were confronting countries in southeast Asia, not only in Indonesia, but also in India, Pakistan and Korea," he warned. "Unless assistance was given to these countries on soft terms it would be difficult for private investors and exporters . . . in Japan . . . to continue to operate in those countries."[50]

McNamara's sales pitch struck a chord. Like their West German counterparts, Japanese officials were eager to invest their country's surpluses abroad, and they saw Bank bonds as a useful means toward this end. In February 1970, the Bank announced its first borrowings in Japan. That fall, the Bank opened a Tokyo office to, in McNamara's words, "maintain close contact with the appropriate organs of the Japanese Government, with the Bank of Japan, and with Japanese banks and other financial institutions." A few months later, the Japanese government purchased $30 million of Bank bonds, and shortly thereafter Japan displaced India as the organization's fifth largest shareholder. In 1972, the Bank of Japan lent the Bank 100 billion yen, which at the time constituted the largest single borrowing in the Bank's history.[51]

In addition to increasing the Bank's fundraising in Japan and West Germany, McNamara shored up the Bank's financial position in the United States. Soon after assuming the Bank presidency, he flew to New York to meet with the organization's underwriters to determine the prospects for future bond placements in the United States. A few months later, he requested permission from U.S. treasury secretary Henry Fowler to undertake a round of borrowings in the country. Aware of mounting concerns about the U.S. balance of payments, McNamara assured Fowler that the Bank would focus on maximizing its non-U.S. borrowings in the years ahead.[52] Fowler agreed to McNamara's request, and in September the Bank sold $250 million of bonds to U.S. investors, a major turnaround given that the Bank had struggled to borrow in the United States over the previous years.[53] In order to further solidify private support for the Bank, McNamara gave a speech to the Bond Club of New York in which he sought to assuage concerns about the Bank's expansion by reaffirming that the organization was "not a philanthropic organization and not a social welfare agency."[54]

The Bank continued to enjoy significant fundraising success—both in terms of overall borrowings and in terms of diversification—in the coming years.[55] The organization's borrowings nearly doubled between 1968 and 1971, and by 1974 U.S. investors held less than a quarter of its bonds.[56] IDA's resources also grew more than twelvefold over the course of McNamara's presidency. As one contemporary observer put it, "non-banker McNamara has demonstrated an uncanny shrewdness and aptitude for the craft."[57]

When he was not raising money, McNamara looked for ways to spend it. As with his fundraising drive, this effort compelled McNamara abroad. During his first years, he devoted a significant amount of time to visiting developing countries. McNamara was no stranger to overseas travel. As secretary of defense, he had gone to Vietnam on a regular basis. Although intended to assess conditions on the ground, these trips had been of limited effectiveness. Largely confined to Saigon and a handful of military bases, McNamara rarely spoke with anybody outside the chain of command, a fact that led observers like David Halberstam to conclude that he was unwilling to come to grips with the realities of the war.[58]

It is not clear what lessons McNamara gleaned from these experiences, but as president of the Bank he expanded his horizons. Accompanied by his wife and a handful of assistants, he not only traveled to many African, Asian, and Latin American countries for the first time but also made a point, then unheard of for a Bank president, to venture outside capital cities to visit urban slums and rural villages. As he noted before a trip to the Ivory Coast in 1969, "learn[ing] . . . about the country" required not just meeting with senior officials but "driving around [and] . . . see[ing] particular development projects" firsthand.[59]

McNamara's travels demonstrated his newfound freedom. At the Pentagon, he was subordinate to the president, something his protracted struggle with Lyndon Johnson over U.S. strategy in Vietnam made clear. As the head of the World Bank, however, McNamara not only was able to engage in what he considered a pleasurable line of work—"it beats the hell out of selling automobiles," he said shortly after entering the Bank—but also was freer to set his agenda.[60]

But while the Bank liberated McNamara from earlier constraints, his mindset remained similar to that which had marked his time at the Pentagon. In his efforts to turn the Bank into a more global institution, he drew the organization into closer alliance with governments that were pursuing

Figure 1. Visiting Bengal on a 1976 trip to India. Courtesy of the World Bank Group Archives.

heavy-handed development strategies. While it would be going too far to state that McNamara demonstrated a preference for authoritarian regimes, and while the prevalence of such governments at the time meant that it would have been difficult for the Bank to avoid working with them, McNamara believed that democracy could impede the adoption of policies that he considered necessary for development. For instance, he believed that Japan's rapid

Figure 2. Visiting Calcutta on a 1976 trip to India. Courtesy of the World Bank Group Archives.

post-World War II development would not have been possible without the U.S. occupation. As he told filmmaker Errol Morris:

> Japan, by 1968 when I went to the World Bank, was an example of a country that had been totally devastated by World War II and yet had fantastic development [that] . . . was a function of MacArthur being a proconsul. MacArthur was a dictator and he dictated that Japan should focus on education and agriculture, and he brought some very radical people in.[61]

The Bank's relationship with Indonesia is one of the more prominent examples of the way the organization worked with authoritarian regimes during the McNamara era. Although Indonesia joined the Bank in 1954, it left in 1965 having never received a loan.[62] The country rejoined the Bank two years later, but by the time McNamara arrived at the Bank in 1968 no new loans had been made.

McNamara found this situation unacceptable. Indonesia was one of the world's most populous developing countries and had been a geopolitical hotspot since achieving its independence from the Netherlands in the late 1940s. Indonesia had long occupied a central place in McNamara's thinking, as well. As secretary of defense, he had observed that its "resources, territory . . . and strategic location" made it "the greatest prize of all" in Southeast Asia, and while at the Pentagon he helped develop U.S. policy toward the country during the decisive middle years of the decade.[63] In 1964, McNamara lobbied members of Congress to reduce U.S. aid to the nationalist Sukarno government, and under his watch the Department of Defense channeled financial and technical assistance to the Indonesian military, which under the leadership of Suharto deposed Sukarno in a bloody coup in 1966.[64]

Upon assuming the Bank presidency, McNamara immediately set about accelerating Indonesia's reentry into the organization. Soon after taking office, he persuaded Bernard Bell, a longtime Bank staffer who had led the organization's efforts to liberalize the Indian economy in the mid-1960s, to head a new "resident mission" in Jakarta.[65] McNamara envisioned the Bank's Jakarta office, the first of its kind, coordinating the organization's lending in Indonesia and advising government officials on economic policy. The Indonesian government agreed to the proposal, and in June McNamara flew to Jakarta to finalize the plans.

McNamara found a receptive audience. After meeting with Indonesia's new economic ministers, many of whom had attended McNamara's alma mater, the University of California, Berkeley, he sat down with Suharto. The Indonesian president, perhaps seeking to find common ground with a man who until recently had been managing a war against the communist government of North Vietnam, boasted of his efforts to eradicate communism in Indonesia. Before Suharto had a chance to finish, McNamara asked him how his government planned to integrate into the economy the country's ethnic Chinese, who Suharto had targeted in anticommunist purges that killed over half a million people.[66]

McNamara was clearly more than the zealous anticommunist Suharto had expected. Yet this was as far as McNamara was willing to push his host. McNamara did not consider the Indonesian government's abuses a reason to withhold or condition lending to the country. Rather, upon departing from Indonesia, he declared that he was "fully satisfied that the government is following the right lines of policy."[67]

Over the coming years, the Bank played a key role in helping to shape Indonesia's development. Bank funding helped the Suharto regime expand ties with the West and consolidate power.[68] The Bank's relationship with Indonesia also exemplified McNamara's interest in having the organization play a more active role in policy advising. Although McNamara was keen to increase the Bank's lending to Indonesia, he saw advising as a more important function. As he explained to Bank officials, the Bank's "technical assistance and the stamp of approval," rather than its loans, were unique resources that would be most helpful to the government.[69]

McNamara received a less friendly welcome during a trip to India a few months later. India was the Bank's largest borrower, but memories of the organization's ill-fated campaign to force the government to adopt a package of liberalization measures remained fresh on people's minds when McNamara visited in November 1968. The Vietnam War was also highly unpopular. Upon his arrival in Calcutta, McNamara was greeted by protests so large that he had to flee the city by helicopter.[70]

McNamara had become accustomed to criticism, however, and the event had little impact on him. Over the coming years, he continued to spend considerable time in developing countries, some of which had only recently gained independence and become members of the Bank. As a result, his reputation began to change. Whereas many had been skeptical of the former defense secretary's appointment to the Bank, his travels to the Bank's borrowing nations demonstrated his commitment to international development and seemed to mark a break with his controversial past. McNamara tended to impress his hosts with his knowledge of their country's economic conditions and his promises to deliver more loans.[71] As William Clark, who often accompanied him on these trips, put it, developing country leaders were "delighted to discover that McNamara is human."[72] While much of the praise was ceremonial, developing country leaders appear to have been sincere in their approval. For example, Senegalese President Leopold Senghor took time out from a White House meeting with Richard Nixon to declare that he considered McNamara "a friend," and in 1972 developing countries unanimously supported his appointment to a second five-year term as Bank president.[73]

McNamara's travels signified a tremendous expansion in Bank lending. McNamara was determined to increase the organization's development operations. Specifically, he wanted to direct more funds to poorer countries and to finance new types of projects. To this effect, in his inaugural address at the World Bank-International Monetary Fund annual meetings in September 1968, he announced his desire to multiply the amount of overall Bank lending, to direct more IBRD loans and IDA credits to countries in Africa and Latin America, and to have the Bank increase its support for agriculture and education projects.[74] Under McNamara, the Bank met these goals. IBRD loan commitments increased from $847 million in 1968 to $8.8 billion in 1981, while IDA credit commitments grew from $107 million to $3.5 billion during the time. The composition of Bank lending also changed. In McNamara's first five years, the organization directed twice the amount of funds for agriculture, three times the amount for telecommunications, and four times the amount for education than it had lent to each of these sectors in the Bank's entire history. All the while, the organization continued to provide significant support for transportation and energy projects.[75]

Although McNamara was the primary impetus, the Bank's expansion also dovetailed with changes in U.S. foreign policy. In the late 1960s, budgetary pressures convinced American officials to channel an increasing share of U.S. foreign assistance through multilateral channels.[76] Whereas 3 percent of U.S. foreign assistance was channeled through international organizations from 1964 to 1966, in 1974 over one quarter of U.S. foreign aid went to such institutions.[77] The United States was not alone in making this move. From 1963 to 1973, developed countries as a whole doubled the percentage of foreign aid that they channeled through international bodies like the Bank.[78]

McNamara saw this trend as a welcome recognition that international organizations were ready to take the lead in providing foreign aid. He also correctly diagnosed it as an attempt by certain countries to reduce their aid budgets. Accordingly, he felt that it was vital that the Bank increase its assistance to fill the emerging financing gap at the same time that it encouraged wealthy countries to maintain their foreign aid levels. "At a time when the flow of capital aid is lessening, and the dangerous gap between the rich countries and the poor is growing, it is essential that the World Bank expand its lending activities to prevent the development effort from grinding to a halt," he told senior Bank officials in the summer of 1968.[79] "By taking a lead in development assistance," he continued, "we may encourage all those, rich and poor alike, who have begun to lose heart and slacken their pace."[80]

In order to handle the Bank's heavier workload, McNamara increased the size of the Bank's staff by expanding recruitment efforts and increasing salaries.[81] These moves yielded immediate results. In McNamara's first year, the Bank's staff grew from 767 to 961, and by 1976 the organization was employing over 2,000 professionals.[82] McNamara's hiring drive had long-lasting effects on the Bank. In addition to causing the organization to become larger and more bureaucratic, it made the Bank more international. In 1968, the vast majority of staff came from the United States and Western Europe.[83] McNamara wanted the Bank to be a global institution. Accordingly, he stepped up efforts to hire developing country nationals. As with his general recruitment efforts, this move was highly successful: in 1973, the organization employed people from 92 different countries.[84] Perhaps most importantly, McNamara's hiring drive entrenched economics as the Bank's main discipline. Reflecting its focus on infrastructure, in the Bank's early years its staff was dominated by engineers. McNamara, who studied economics in college, viewed economic analysis and policy advising as central to the Bank's work, however, tasks to which professionally trained economists were most suited. As a result, staff hired during his tenure were mostly economics graduates from American and European universities.[85]

In addition to recruiting more staff, McNamara improved the Bank's research program. His goal was to increase the effectiveness of the Bank's operations while burnishing the organization's reputation. McNamara's most important move in this regard was enlisting Hollis Chenery to become the Bank's chief economist. Chenery, a professor of economics at Harvard, had served as an official at USAID in the 1960s. He had achieved prominence for developing a model that attempted to quantify the amount of external assistance a country needed in order to sustain a given level of economic growth, and when he came to the Bank in 1970 he was considered one of world's foremost development economists.[86] Chenery sought to improve the Bank's research program in two ways. First, he divided the organization's research staff into three separate branches focusing on basic development topics, project-specific issues, and macroeconomic analyses of developing country economies. Second, he recruited economists directly from the world's top graduate programs. Taken together, these efforts enabled Chenery to construct a world-class development economics research program.[87] As one economist noted in 1979, "it is common knowledge that most of the best people in development are at the World Bank."[88]

It had become clear well before then that McNamara's efforts to turn the Bank into a more powerful organization had borne fruit. The expansion of the Bank's borrowing and lending portfolios demonstrated that the organization was moving from the margins to the center of the international development field. Yet McNamara focused on more than simply increasing the Bank's size. In his first years at the Bank, he also sought to alter the structure of power within the organization. Specifically, he attempted to consolidate authority in World Bank presidency by instituting quantitative planning systems and reducing the ability of member governments to supervise Bank management.

Control

When McNamara arrived at the Bank in April 1968, he was displeased to discover that the organization had no central accounting system in place.[89] The Bank did not make sophisticated projections about its future operations or maintain detailed records about its work. Moreover, the information that did exist was not standardized across departments.[90] McNamara complained to his aides that Bank data was so indecipherable that it resembled license plate numbers, a telling critique given that the situation that confronted him was akin to that which he encountered at the Ford Motor Company in the 1940s.

McNamara attempted to improve the Bank's accounting in a way similar to that which he implemented at Ford. During his first days as president, he ordered the Bank's senior managers to compile detailed reports on the organization's activities. McNamara specified both the content and form of this data. The information allowed him to populate charts detailing the Bank's historical borrowings in different markets, as well as its lending operations and disbursement rates broken down by country, sector, loan size, and maturity for each of the previous five years and aggregate five-year periods before that.[91]

According to John Blaxall, the staffer in charge of collecting information from the Bank's departments and transferring it to McNamara, the aging Whiz Kid used these "standard tables" to gain an understanding of the Bank as it presently existed and to determine how to lead the organization going forward. "What others saw as simply a sheet full of numbers," Blaxall remembers, McNamara "saw as data corresponding to categories he had himself thought about and specified."[92] To those less charitably inclined, including Bank staff who were encouraged by their supervisors to estimate figures when precise data was unavailable, this process also indicated McNamara's tendency to manipulate data by interpreting approximations as fact. "He was always after statistics he couldn't get," one former Bank staffer recalled. Some of it "was just make-believe . . . like body counts."[93]

Once McNamara had developed his first set of standard tables, he ordered the Bank's senior managers to draw up detailed plans for their departments for each of the coming five years.[94] McNamara had raised the possibility of long-term planning on his first day in office, and since the fateful April 4 President's Council meeting Bank staff had been busy compiling an expanded list of projects to meet this directive.[95] Belying the rationality McNamara sought to institute, staff assembled the reports in a haphazard fashion, in some cases using discarded project proposals.[96]

The lists that finally made their way to McNamara's office a few months later added up to a doubling of Bank lending over the coming five years, including large increases in lending to Africa and Latin America as well as for agriculture and education projects. These proposals formed the basis for the Bank's first five-year plan, which McNamara unveiled at the World Bank-IMF annual meetings in September 1968.

Although these proposals formed the basis for the Bank's expanded lending program, their greatest effect was felt inside the organization. By forcing staff to begin systematically detailing the Bank's activities, McNamara transformed the organization's basic approach. Whereas the Bank had tended to receive and process loan applications on a case-by-case basis, staff now found themselves formulating lending proposals on their own, devoid of significant input from borrowers and designed to meet predetermined lending targets.

In this way, McNamara's five-year plan inaugurated a period in which quantitative programming replaced the more qualitative, ad hoc style that had long characterized the Bank's lending operations.[97] "Up to that time, the Bank's approach to lending had been to wait until an opportunity arose," one former World Banker explained. "You wouldn't be pushing, because you were a banker. You would be waiting for your clients to come and say, 'I want to borrow money.' You certainly wouldn't have a huge plan for the country."[98]

These new planning systems also increased McNamara's control over the Bank. Most managers would have shared the information, if for no other reason than to increase transparency within the organization. But McNamara kept the data confidential.[99] He made only simplified versions of the standard tables available to the Bank's senior managers and mandated that staff not share information with government officials.[100]

Not surprisingly, many in the Bank bristled at McNamara's directives.[101] Some staff viewed development banking as a qualitative endeavor incapable of being reduced to McNamara's metrics. Bank staff also argued that setting lending targets would reduce the Bank's leverage insofar as it restricted the organization's ability to increase or decrease lending depending on the behavior of borrowing governments.[102] Resistance was so strong that some Bank managers continued to direct their departments to operate in the same manner as before.[103]

McNamara had encountered an entrenched bureaucracy seven years earlier, when his efforts to reform the Department of Defense met stiff opposition from the military brass. McNamara had responded by creating a Planning, Programming, and Budgeting System (PPBS), which subjected Pentagon operations to long range planning and analysis. PPBS allowed McNamara to increase his oversight of military spending—the true center of power within the Department—and tame the generals.[104] The results were so impressive that in 1965 Lyndon Johnson ordered all federal agencies to adopt PPBS-like systems.[105] At the Bank, McNamara created a Programming and Budgeting Department (P&B) to govern the allocation of resources within the organization. Because P&B reported directly to McNamara, this innovation further increased his control over the Bank.[106] Through such methods, McNamara overcame internal opposition to his proposals and, in the words of a former staffer, "forced the institution into a planning perspective over its own inhibitions."[107]

One of McNamara's most important initiatives was the creation in 1969 of the Country Program Paper (CPP), a document that appraised economic conditions in and prescribed lending programs for each of the Bank's developing country members.[108] Drafted by the Bank's regional departments and made to conform to the organization's lending targets, the CPP systematized the Bank's longstanding efforts to advise developing countries on economic policy matters and further entrenched quantitative programming into the Bank's operations.[109]

Because it was used as a basis for the Bank's lending decisions, the CPP was a prime example of the way McNamara's reforms of the Bank's internal procedures overlapped with his efforts to increase the organization's control over its member countries. McNamara's first move in this direction was to reduce the power of the Bank's Board of Executive Directors, the representatives of the organization's members who formally approved each one of the Bank's loans. Just one week into his tenure, McNamara directed the Bank's senior managers to lobby executive directors on issues before they came up for a vote.[110] McNamara also refused to allow executive directors to see reports from the Bank's staff and placed strict limits on discussion of loan decisions during Board meetings.[111]

McNamara justified these moves on both efficiency and equity grounds. He believed that the executive directors were largely incapable of understanding the complexity of the Bank's operations and that fully informing them would drain staff resources. McNamara also recognized that the directors represented their national interests. As he told the President's Council in 1972, "the Board could not be allowed to decide on country lending programs, since it would make such decisions on entirely political grounds."[112] Allowing the Board to be involved in decision-making could thus lead to interstate conflict and tarnish the Bank's apolitical image. McNamara's preference for centralized decision-making—while at the Pentagon he had stated "the more important the issue the fewer people should be involved"—also accounted for his desire to reduce Board power.[113]

McNamara used his authority to chair the Board's weekly meetings to reduce the time spent discussing specific loans. When combined with the tremendous expansion of the Bank's lending, this eliminated the ability of executive directors to have a meaningful say in Bank operations.[114] At the same time, McNamara continued to direct his aides to lobby executive directors, which enabled him to forge consensus behind the scenes.[115] He also discouraged executive directors from meeting in other venues, and he kept schedules of the Board's agenda secret until the last minute.[116] Executive directors occasionally protested these efforts. For instance, in 1972 the U.S.

representative to the Bank expressed "dissatisf[action] with the lack of discussion of the Bank lending program" among the Board.[117] However, the Board soon succumbed to McNamara. "The Board members' feelings," a former Bank staffer remembered, "were that they were steamrolled regularly by McNamara but that they were part of an increasingly important organization. In the end there was an accommodation, an adjustment to McNamara's style."[118]

In addition to reducing the power of the Board, McNamara sought to influence government officials directly. Besides hiring lobbyists to help secure passage of Bank funding bills in the U.S. Congress, he directed the Bank to begin lobbying the foreign offices of wealthy nations, in addition to their finance ministries and central banks.[119] He also tasked William Clark, the Bank's external relations chief, with improving the organization's public relations efforts.[120]

A tension lay at the heart of these efforts. McNamara prized the Bank's independence. Yet he also wanted the organization to expand. As such, he needed the financial support of developed countries. This tension would bedevil McNamara throughout his presidency. During his initial years, however, it led to one of the more salutary developments of his tenure, the creation of the Bank's operations evaluation department.

Prior to McNamara's arrival, the Bank did not systematically evaluate the effects of its operations.[121] Aware of this deficiency, McNamara listed the creation of an evaluation department on his initial ninety-eight point agenda.[122] McNamara failed to take any significant steps toward this end during his first year and a half in office, however.[123] Then, in December 1969, McNamara became aware that, in conjunction with the upcoming IDA III replenishment, Congress was considering having the General Accounting Office (GAO) investigate Bank operations.[124] McNamara saw this as a significant threat to the Bank's independence—a GAO audit would, he later said, "jeopardiz[e] the Bank's integrity"—and was, as such, worthy of a swift response.[125] He informed his senior aides that "immediate action" to improve the organization's own evaluation mechanisms was needed to blunt congressional inquiry, and, to this end, directed members of the President's Council to initiate a "pilot project" that would review completed Bank projects.[126] This mandate resulted in the creation of the Operations Evaluation Unit (OEU), which McNamara established in September 1970, just in time for him to boast to U.S. treasury secretary David Kennedy of the strides the Bank was making in evaluating its effectiveness.[127]

The OEU's initial work was limited. It employed only five full-time staff members and in its early years issued just two reports: an analysis of the Bank's twenty-year experience in Colombia and a summary of its efforts in the electric power field.[128] In the meantime, the GAO went ahead and published a report on the Bank.[129] While Burke Knapp, the Bank's longtime head of operations, found the report "comparatively harmless," McNamara remained "disturbed" by the notion that outsiders could gain information on the organization, and in order to blunt further inquiries called for more improvements in the Bank's evaluation mechanisms. As he told his senior aides in April 1972 "the increased interest on the part of governments was another reason for particular focus on Bank . . . supervision and operations evaluation."[130] With progress slow, a year later McNamara informed the President's Council that "more thought had to be given to how the Bank's evaluation activity should be organized in response to pressures from the outside," and shortly thereafter he issued a directive mandating that audits be conducted on all the Bank's loans.[131] In order to increase its impartiality, McNamara also decided to place the Bank's evaluation unit under the direction of a vice president with no operational responsibilities. On July 1, 1972, the Bank established an Operations Evaluation Department (OED) that reported directly to the Board.[132]

At the same time that he was seeking to curb outside interest in the Bank, McNamara positioned the organization to play a more active role in the affairs of its borrowers. After returning from his trip to Indonesia, McNamara informed the President's Council of his desire to establish Bank offices throughout the developing world. By 1970, the Bank had set up "resident missions" in Afghanistan, Ethiopia, Kenya, India, Indonesia, the Ivory Coast, Nigeria, and Pakistan.[133] The founding of these offices demonstrated the expansion of the Bank's lending program and exemplified the Bank's interest in dispensing policy advice as well as loans. As McNamara told Kofi Abrefa Busia, prime minister of Ghana, the Bank's resident missions were to engage in "constant dialogue" with host governments "in the area of economic planning and decision making."[134]

Similar concerns motivated the expansion of the Bank's "country mission" program.[135] McNamara systematized the Bank's longstanding practice of sending staff from the organization's headquarters to developing countries for short periods in order to collect information on the economy and make policy recommendations to government officials. To McNamara, a program of regular country missions would "provide the World Bank Group, other international institutions, government and intergovernmental agencies with a thorough knowledge and analytical assessment of the development problems and policies of individual member countries," as well as establish "a basis for discussions with the country concerned on its development policies and plans."[136]

In addition to expanding ties with developed and developing countries, McNamara brought the Bank into alliance with other international organizations. In his initial agenda, McNamara indicated his desire to "develop a plan to use the UN agencies . . . as separate arms of a unified development strategy," and during his first years as Bank president he built upon George Woods's efforts to forge ties with other international organizations.[137] In the early 1970s the Bank entered into partnerships with the World Health Organization (WHO) for population control and family planning programs, the International Labour Organization (ILO) for analysis of international employment issues, and the UN Industrial Development Organization (UNIDO) for the financing of industrial projects in developing countries.[138]

Not all these efforts went smoothly. A little over a month after taking office, McNamara dispatched Richard Demuth, director of the Bank's International Relations Department, to confer with officials at UNDP about the possibility of intensifying contacts between the two organizations. Demuth convinced UNDP Director Paul Hoffman to channel some of his organization's funds to the Bank's new resident mission in Indonesia. At the same time, however, Hoffman complained that the Bank was, through the resident mission as well as similar activities in other countries, trying to displace the UNDP from its traditional role in drafting investment plans for developing countries.[139] Hoffman was right to be concerned. As noted above, one of McNamara's initial moves as Bank president was to have the organization increase its country programming activities, which included the types of preinvestment studies conducted by the UNDP.[140] Although Hoffman argued that the Bank was infringing on UNDP territory, he was unable to do anything about it.[141] Instead, in 1970 the UNDP began seconding members of its staff to Bank missions.[142] Under pressure from other specialized agencies, the UNDP also dropped its plans to begin its own country mission program, declaring that it would henceforth "leave country performances to be judged by agencies such as the Bank."[143] While relations between the two organizations remained frayed over the years, the fact that the Bank's resources dwarfed those of the UNDP meant that the latter's complaints never amounted to much.[144] As one Zambian official put it at the time, "the rivalry between the UNDP and the Bank . . . isn't serious because the Bank's annual profits equal the entire UN budget."[145]

Reorganization

The Bank's ability to forge ties with and assume roles traditionally undertaken by other agencies demonstrated its growing power in the international development field. Partially because of McNamara's fundraising efforts, governments channeled an increasing share of their foreign aid through the Bank. By the end of McNamara's first five-year term as president, for instance, over 60 percent of all aid commitments made by international organizations to developing countries came from the Bank, up from 50 percent in 1968.[146] The financial dominance of the Bank forced bilateral and multilateral agencies to, in the words of an Ivory Coast official, "accept the Bank's leadership role" in development activities.[147] "Other international organizations are so insignificant that they couldn't compare with the Bank's operations," a Jamaican official noted.[148]

Significant problems accompanied the Bank's growth. The scale and pace of the organization's expansion strained an institution that had long operated in a conservative fashion. Longtime Bank staff struggled to adapt to the new workload, and within a few years the organization began to have trouble processing and supervising its loans. This resulted in a phenomenon known as "bunching," in which a large percentage of the Bank's loans were processed in haste at the end of a reporting period in order to meet lending targets. In the spring of 1970, McNamara noted that the Bank's staff was struggling to adjust to their "unprecedented operational load." That fall senior Bank staff expressed concern at the number of projects to be presented to the Board in the last quarter of the upcoming fiscal year. And the executive directors began to worry about their ability to monitor the organization's lending. By 1972, a significant share of the organization's projects were, in the words of a senior Bank official, "immature or 'non-starters,'" with 45 percent of projects proposed during the 1973 fiscal year having "low probability of materializing in that year, mainly for reasons of insufficient preparation and doubts about their justification."[149]

Not surprisingly, such issues negatively affected morale. Staff raised complaints that McNamara's "programming and budgeting exercises" had "place[d] undue emphasis on speed and performance in completing programs."[150] There were also worries about bureaucracy. In a rare meeting with mid-level staff in 1972, McNamara noted widespread dissatisfaction with "increased paperwork and large meetings."[151] "There is a morale problem," a longtime Bank staffer who had recently returned to the organization's headquarters from the field noted in 1970. "So many people are working under such pressure that the motivation which used to make us all work hard in good spirit (our sense of mission) has taken a big dip."[152] As one Bank official put it, the Bank had "reached a size and level of complexity at which it [could] no longer rely on the network of personal relationships among senior staff that enabled coordination to be achieved in the past."[153]

McNamara was conscious of these problems and gradually restructured the Bank in order to help cope with its increased workload. In the fall of 1968, he divided the Bank's Central Projects Department into specialized units dealing with agriculture, education, public utilities, and transportation, created departments for tourism, population, and special projects to oversee the organization's entry into these fields, and split the Africa and Asia Departments into departments for Western Africa, Eastern Africa, South Asia, and East Asia and the Pacific.[154]

These moves did not solve the problems that accompanied the Bank's growth. As a result, in 1972 McNamara hired the consulting firm McKinsey & Company to help him execute a Bank-wide reorganization.[155] The reorganization centered on replacing the Bank's longstanding division between Project and Area Departments with five regional departments, which would each contain their own project divisions.[156] McNamara carried out the 1972 reorganization with the speed and secrecy that had come to characterize his presidency. He kept the details of the reorganization confidential and, once he released them to staff, ordered that change take place over a single weekend.

The reorganization allowed McNamara to further his goal of getting the Bank to focus on country programming.[157] Whereas before 1972, the Projects Department established common standards across the Bank, following the reorganization project staff were placed under managers with a geographical focus. "The effect," the Bank's historians have explained, "was to increase the weight of countrywide lending criteria as against the specialized technical criteria of project staff. This change complemented the already established CPP system, and together they opened doors to the introduction of new lending considerations" tied more to countrywide conditions than those relating to specific projects.[158] McNamara justified the reorganization to the President's Council by claiming that it would enable "closer identification" between the Bank and its borrowers.[159]

Many Bank staff were unsure about the elevation of country programming. "There was a general aura that these program people were in a different world," remembers a former Bank staffer, since program-oriented staff members focused on entire countries and were "divorced from the more daily, pragmatic, on the ground" experiences of project staff.[160] World Bankers also expressed concerns about McNamara's personal control over the Bank, his obsession with quantifying development, and his intolerance of ambiguity. "McNamara didn't like anybody to admit that they didn't know absolutely everything that was going on," a former Bank staffer recalls.[161] "People almost trembled going in to see him," another remembers. "If you didn't have the answers, you could get decimated."[162]

These complaints were well founded. In his first years at the Bank, McNamara exacerbated tendencies that, though long present at the organization, would plague it over the coming years. While the Bank had long operated in an opaque manner, McNamara's centralization of power in his office not only failed to deter outside interest but, as we will see, also contributed to the organization's difficulty in retaining U.S. financial support. More importantly, McNamara's drive to increase the volume of Bank lending outstripped the organization's capacity to supervise its operations. Thus, just one year after the 1972 reorganization, members of the President's Council noted that the "continual pressure for more lending" had resulted in a "desperate scramble" to process loans.[163] Meanwhile, some observers began to worry that the organization had become more willing to "accept . . . questionable projects."[164]

All of this took its toll on staff. A Guyanese official noted that the "increased work load has imposed a strain on Bank people. Everyone works harder and longer hours."[165] Another observer noted that McNamara's imposition of quantitative lending targets and his willingness to promote favored junior staffers to senior positions "demoralized" many of the Bank's longtime workers.[166] "The Bank bureaucracy frightens me," an Indian official declared. "Younger, quantitative-managerial types are rising to important positions. People without experience with their bag of tricks from Harvard are looking for mathematical proofs of social projects."[167]

Nevertheless, to McNamara these issues were an inevitable, and not necessarily negative, byproduct of growth. Whether measured by the size of its lending portfolio, the breadth of its research, or the frequency with which it enlisted other organizations in its efforts, McNamara's active leadership pushed the Bank into a dominant position in the international development field. McNamara had turned the World Bank into a more powerful institution. Now the question became what to do with it.

CHAPTER 3

Developing Development

Today, the words "Our Dream Is a World Free of Poverty" are carved in stone in the lobby of the World Bank's headquarters in Washington, D.C. The phrase dates from the 1990s, when Bank management sought to develop a mission statement for the organization. The motto resonated with staff and continues to reflect the organization's self-conception. As one longtime World Banker has written, the "antipoverty mission is almost part of the water" at the Bank.[1]

It was not always this way. For much of the Bank's history, its primary focus was promoting economic growth, and it lending operations were almost exclusively limited to large infrastructure projects. Those at the Bank were not indifferent to the plight of the world's poor. But they viewed growth as a prerequisite for poverty reduction and felt that addressing living conditions within borrowing countries was beyond the organization's purview.

Robert McNamara changed this mentality. He believed that the Bank needed to expand its focus beyond promoting growth through infrastructure projects. He spoke openly about the importance of ensuring that Bank projects directly benefit the poor, and he pushed the organization into areas it had previously ignored, such as primary education and small farming. In the process, he elevated poverty reduction to the top of the Bank's agenda.

McNamara was interested in broadening the Bank's focus for a variety of reasons. His experience in Vietnam affirmed his belief in the connection between material want and political instability. His desire to leave a positive legacy attracted him to the antipoverty mission. His managerial mindset led him to view poverty reduction as an achievable objective. Frustration in the development community with growth-centric strategies further convinced him that the Bank needed to alter its approach.

McNamara waged his war on poverty on a number of fronts. He used his bully pulpit to speak about the plight of what he termed the "absolute poor."[2] He directed Bank staff to study the relationship between poverty and growth. And he had the organization fund projects aimed directly at the poor. Although this approach had its limits, in extending the Bank's focus from the conditions of developing countries to conditions within them, McNamara brought the Bank into contact with issues it had long avoided. In so doing, he positioned the organization to play a more active role in the affairs of developing countries.

Declaring War on Poverty

Before Robert McNamara's arrival, the World Bank subscribed to a relatively narrow definition of development. Although Bank staff and management were aware that development entailed more than building dams and highways, during its first decades the organization steered clear of making loans for health, education, housing, and other social sectors. In part, this was out of a concern that such projects would not produce measurable returns and might thereby raise questions about the Bank's creditworthiness. It was also a reflection of intellectual trends. Development economists in the 1950s and 1960s were concerned primarily with determining how to foster economic growth and tended to consider infrastructure investments as vital to this process. Pessimistic about developing countries' ability to generate income through exports, they saw foreign aid as necessary to enable governments to afford these internal improvements.[3]

Even when the Bank began to expand its focus in the 1960s, its desire to lend only for "directly productive" projects limited its work. For instance, its early agricultural loans were geared toward large-scale, commercial farmers, and its initial education loans went toward secondary and higher education, rather than primary schools. Such operations manifested the Bank's belief that poverty reduction was a consequence rather than a cause of growth. As McNamara's predecessor, George Woods, declared in 1967, the Bank had "one objective: the economic growth of the Bank's member countries."[4]

Robert McNamara came to the Bank with a broader understanding of development. In his 1966 "essence of security" speech he not only argued that poverty caused political instability but also spoke of development as something that meant more than economic growth. As McNamara put it then, "development means economic, social and political progress. It means a reasonable standard of living."[5] Not surprisingly, McNamara found the Bank's inattention to poverty unacceptable and, upon assuming the presidency, announced a shift in focus. During his inaugural address at the Bank and IMF annual meetings in September 1968, he argued that high rates of economic growth in developing countries were "cosmetics which conceal a far less cheerful picture [since] . . . much of the growth is concentrated in the industrial areas, while the peasant remains stuck in his immemorial poverty." Given "the connection between world poverty and unstable relations among nations," he promised that the Bank would increase its lending, channel more funds to the world's poorest countries, and identify and eliminate the "strangleholds on development" that had prevented the benefits of economic growth from reaching the poor."[6]

McNamara continued to sound these themes in his first years at the Bank. During a visit to South America, he announced that he was "concerned by the rigidity of social systems in which the mass of the people is poor, few are rich, and there is little chance for the many to move upward from poverty."[7] In 1969, he urged greater attention to problems of "structural unemployment" and "urban decay" in the developing world and declared that development should focus on "the advancement of the human condition."[8] In Ethiopia the following year, he stated that the primary goal of development should be to "create a fuller, happier, and more productive life for the people of the country."[9] As he put it in Cameroon shortly after that, "individual men and women are not only the ultimate cause of real development, but the ultimate objective as well."[10]

McNamara believed that scientific and technological advances had made eliminating world poverty a real possibility. Specifically, he saw the Green Revolution, the name given to a set of improvements in agricultural technologies that significantly boosted food production in parts of Asia and Latin America in the middle decades of the twentieth century, as an example of the ways seemingly intractable social and economic problems could be solved. "There is no cause for despair," he told Senegalese officials in 1969. "In Asia . . . I have seen the beginnings of an agricultural revolution which . . . could banish hunger from those lands in a few short years [and] . . . in my own country . . . I have witnessed the creation of a production machine which could abolish poverty from the earth by the year 2000."[11] McNamara also rejected arguments that foreign aid was money down the drain. "Can we during this decade act to assist . . . these two billion people to help them-selves to reduce the conditions of misery and deprivation which affect [their] lives?" he asked a U.S. television audience in 1971. "My answer is 'yes' we can." Throughout, he insisted that development was morally, economically, and strategically important. A "Marshall Plan for the world" was "not only possible but . . . necessary." Unless rich countries became more attuned to the problems of the developing world, "there will be great political instabil-ity and there will be lesser markets for our products."[12]

McNamara's personal sensibilities and background animated his interest in poverty reduction. As noted earlier, he exhibited missionary tendencies at a young age, telling a close friend that his life's goal was to "help the largest number."[13] He also came of age during the Great Depression. While he did not suffer directly, this experience made him aware of the devastating im-pacts of economic stagnation and mass unemployment. He also viewed Pres-ident Franklin Roosevelt's New Deal programs as an example of useful government intervention. As he later told filmmaker Errol Morris, "the so-ciety was on the verge of, I don't want to say 'revolution,' although had Pres-ident Roosevelt not done some of the things he did, it could have become far more violent."[14] And, while there is no evidence that McNamara's guilt about his role in Vietnam led him to make poverty a centerpiece of the Bank's work, the war did not disabuse him of his belief that underdevelopment posed a threat to political stability. After leaving the Bank, for instance, he wrote that "economic disparities among nations" was one of "the underlying causes of Third World conflict."[15]

Those around McNamara reinforced his interest in expanding the Bank's focus. His wife Margaret, a longtime advocate for domestic antipoverty pro-grams, helped draw his attention to the plight of the world's poor. While to-gether on a visit to Mali, she even convinced him to drop his opposition to Bank funding of health programs and initiate a plan to eradicate river blindness, which was affecting populations in West Africa.[16] McNamara also maintained ties with U.S.-based philanthropies, including by serving as a trustee of the Ford Foundation during his presidency. Members of these organizations encouraged him to put population control and poverty alleviation on the Bank's agenda.[17] In addition, McNamara often consulted the British author and foreign aid advocate Barbara Ward, whom he had met during his time in government. Ward urged McNamara to use the Bank to address global population growth, as well as education and rural develop-ment.[18]

Mahbub ul Haq, a Cambridge- and Yale-trained economist from Pakistan who would gain fame for spearheading the creation of the UN *Human Development Report* in 1990, was perhaps the most important influence on McNamara. As a senior advisor in the Bank's Economics Department and, later, as director of the Policy, Planning, and Program Review Department, ul Haq helped convince McNamara that development should focus on raising living standards and that that poverty alleviation could be a cause, rather than a consequence, of economic growth.[19] Ul Haq first came to McNamara's attention as a vocal critic of growth-centric development strategies. While an economist in the Pakistani government in the 1960s, he had seen how development approaches that prioritized industrialization failed to result in widespread improvements in living standards, even though they led to economic growth. As he put it, "a rising growth rate is no guarantee against worsening poverty."[20] Although initially hostile to ul Haq's critiques (ul Haq recalled that their initial encounters were "extremely unhappy ones [in which McNamara] suggested to me that this kind of belligerent questioning of growth, at a time that the World Bank was committed mostly to production projects, was totally uncalled for"), McNamara came to appreciate ul Haq's perspective, and by the early 1970s he was incorporating ul Haq's call to focus more attention on plight of the world's poor into his speeches.[21]

Dethroning Growth

Views like ul Haq's had become increasingly common by the time McNamara arrived at the Bank. In the late 1960s, statistics collected as part of the UN's Development Decade painted a mixed view of global development. Although many poor countries had grown impressively, the gap between developed and developing countries remained wide. Moreover, rates of poverty and inequality within many nations had not budged.[22] Such findings led some economists to question the very "meaning of development."[23] In 1970, David Morse, the head of the International Labour Organization, even called for the "dethronement of GNP" as the primary indicator of national development.[24] As British economist E. F. Schumacher, a leading critics of growth-centric development strategies, put it:

> Development of a country—very well! But does it not have to mean above all else the development of people? Industrialization—splendid!

But will the poor people be involved, and, if so, how many of them? Growth of the national income—excellent! But will it benefit the poor and enable them to develop? As we look back upon 'development' during the sixties—the "Development Decade"—we come to the disturbing conclusion that by and large, speaking very generally, development has gone ahead in many places but The People, the poor, the great majority, have been by passed and left out.[25]

Such critiques presented a significant challenge to the World Bank, which had long been one of the main institutional promoters of growth-centric development. McNamara recognized that the organization needed to shed its traditional image if it wanted to maintain its relevance. One of his main efforts in this regard was the organization of a study that would survey past development efforts and propose recommendations for the future. In the summer of 1968, McNamara convinced outgoing Canadian Prime Minister Lester Pearson to chair the report.[26] Although Pearson's team was to go about its work independently of the Bank, McNamara explained that the study's primary goal should be to convince skeptics that foreign aid remained a good investment. "I am facing the . . . problem of how to mobilize effective opinion in the 'North' behind an adequate development program," he told Pearson. "I believe you could make an enormous impact on opinion around the world and particularly in those key countries which need to be convinced of the urgency of the problem and the possibility of a solution."[27]

Given McNamara's charge, it was little surprise that Pearson's report, released less than a year later, was primarily a public relations piece designed to mitigate concerns about the effectiveness of foreign aid. While the report took up a number of important issues, such as the need for reductions in developed country import barriers, it downplayed evidence that development efforts had failed to reduce global poverty, arguing instead that that aid had an overwhelmingly positive impact. The report's most noteworthy conclusion was its call for wealthy nations to increase their levels of official development assistance to 0.7 percent of their national incomes by the end of the 1970s.[28] McNamara saw Pearson's study as a valuable lobbying tool and informed his aides that he was "anxious that the report reach the highest levels of government officials in the developed countries."[29]

Despite its limitations, Pearson's report provided a starting point for rethinking international development strategies. To this end, in February 1970 Barbara Ward brought McNamara together with development experts and officials for a conference at Columbia University to discuss the study's findings.[30] Participants critiqued the report for having failed to take account of the full dimensions of global development.[31] They also critiqued the 0.7 percent target as insufficient.[32] In addition to greater aid flows, participants highlighted the need for domestic and international policy changes. For instance, redressing economic disparities within poor nations required that governments adopt "income distribution [and] land and tax reforms." External debt forgiveness was also considered necessary to reduce inequality between rich and poor countries.[33]

McNamara relished the intellectual vitality of the conference. When the proceedings ended, he voiced his desire to tour the university. The organizers would have none of it. Columbia was only two years removed from one of the largest student uprisings in U.S. history, and the campus remained a hotbed of activism. Concerned about what would happen when one of the chief architects of the Vietnam War was seen strolling among the student body, they rushed McNamara into a taxi and sent him to the airport.[34]

If the former defense secretary remained a divisive figure in his home country, his willingness to speak about global poverty endeared him to many people working in development. While McNamara did not disclose his thoughts about the proposals raised at the Columbia conference, his remarks indicated his openness to rethinking traditional conceptions of development. "We must," he told the participants, "look to more than gross measures of economic growth. What we require are relevant development indicators that go beyond the measure of growth in total output and provide practical yardsticks of change in the other economic, social, and moral dimensions of the modernizing process."[35] He did not specify what these indicators were. Still, this was an unusual level of engagement for a World Bank president, and his willingness to acknowledge the need for reform was one of the reasons why some in the development field found his leadership during this time "phenomenal."[36]

Mobilizing the Bank

Speaking about poverty proved easier than getting the Bank to do something about it. McNamara struggled to reorient the organization's lending away from the large construction projects that had long dominated its portfolio. This was a result not only of the lack of a clear conception of what should displace infrastructure spending as the Bank's primary focus but also the product of internal resistance to expanding the organization's activities.

McNamara's attempt to make population control a Bank priority demonstrated these challenges. By the time McNamara arrived at the Bank, many observers had come to believe that the rapid growth of the world's population, estimated to have risen from 1.6 billion in 1900 to 3.7 billion in 1970, was a pressing economic, environmental, and political danger.[37] Over the previous years, nongovernmental organizations like the Population Council, the International Planned Parenthood Foundation (IPPF), and the Ford Foundation had spent millions of dollars on demographic research and population control efforts. The UN also called attention to the need to reduce birth rates in developing countries, and prominent thinkers argued that global population growth placed an unsustainable burden on the planet.[38] As Norman Borlaug, one of the fathers of the Green Revolution, put it, "the world's population problem is a monster, which unless tamed will one day wipe us from the earth's surface."[39]

McNamara shared these concerns, and he positioned the Bank to assist global population control efforts.[40] Soon after assuming the presidency, he directed staff to investigate ways the organization could support population control in the developing world and asked his chief economic advisor to research the likelihood that population growth would lead to famine in the coming years. He further ordered senior management to include population programs in the first five-year lending plan, investigated the possibility of creating specialized population research and project departments, and directed staff to "give full attention to the rate of population growth [and] the actions being taken to reduce excessive growth to acceptable levels" in country reports.[41]

McNamara also spoke publicly about global population growth. In his first address to the Bank and IMF annual meetings, he argued that the "rapid growth of population is one of the greatest barriers to the economic growth and social well-being of our member-states."[42] In Argentina, he argued that population growth represented a "dark side" that could undermine development throughout Latin America.[43] And in India, he warned that a "tidal wave of population growth" threatened to derail the subcontinent.[44] McNamara delivered his most extensive remarks on the issue at the University of Notre Dame in May 1969. He told the predominantly Catholic audience that global population growth would "diminish, if not destroy, much of [mankind's] future" and called on wealthy nations to "give every measure of support" to population control efforts in the developing world.[45]

McNamara's campaign bore some initial fruit. In 1969, the Bank established a special Population Programs Department and the following year approved its first population project, a $2 million loan to assist the government of Jamaica construct maternity hospitals that would supervise family planning efforts. Two years later, the Bank began working with the governments of Tunisia and Trinidad & Tobago on population control projects. And in 1972, it made loans for the construction of maternity clinics in Indonesia and India, the Bank's two most populous developing countries. The organization also conducted research on population growth and began to include sections on demographic trends in its country reports.[46]

Nevertheless, the Bank's population control efforts soon stagnated. Delays and cost increases plagued its population projects, and it made less than two dozen population loans over the following eight years, many of which were supplements to earlier loans.[47] McNamara grew frustrated. In 1974, he acknowledged that population projects were proceeding "very, very slowly."[48] The following year, he informed management that he was "uneasy about our population work," since "projects were not well formulated . . . often were not integrated into a country program; [and] . . . were not carried out effectively."[49]

The Bank's population lending failed for a number of reasons. For one, the population control movement ran out of steam during the 1970s as birth rates began to decline and evidence accumulated that initiatives were often ineffective and sometimes occasioned forced sterilizations. Developing country officials were also uninterested in the Bank's population loans. Latin American leaders rejected McNamara's calls to try to curb population growth with what an observer described as "florid indignation," and Bank staff found that their efforts in Africa "arouse[d] suspicion of white motives." In addition, population lending did not conform to the professional norms of the Bank's staff, which consisted mainly of economists and engineers. Perhaps more important, the fact that population loans tended to be inexpensive made them unattractive to staff who were under pressure to meet lending targets. Thus, Bank managers noted that they were "reluctant to schedule . . . projects like population in a time when rigid planning had become necessary." As McNamara later recalled, population "loans were small, and it took a tremendous amount of time to fashion the projects. So it was a burden rather than a plus" to staff.[50]

McNamara was aware from an early point that the Bank might struggle to develop a population control program. In the spring of 1969, a staffer in charge of formulating the first population loan to Jamaica told McNamara that he was having difficulty determining a "sizable project for Bank lending." The best the Bank could do, it seemed, was lend half a million dollars for construction of a maternity center in Kingston, a far cry from the multimillion dollar infrastructure projects the organization was used to funding. The staffer told McNamara that he could increase the loan amount if, in addition to funding the maternity center, the project also encompassed general health services. McNamara shot him down in language that was as calculating as it was cold. He was, he remarked, "reluctant to consider financing health care unless it was very strictly related to population control, because usually health facilities contributed to the decline of the death rate, and thereby to the population explosion."[51]

Indeed, for as much as he broadened the Bank's focus, McNamara could be remarkably indifferent to the plight of those in need. In 1969, he turned down a request from the UN High Commissioner for Refugees for help in erecting a water supply system for a Sudanese refugee camp because he did not consider it a proper "development project."[52] McNamara also declined calls to support community development initiatives because "the amounts of money" such projects would require were "relatively small."[53] And while Bank managers recommended lending for health projects as early as 1974, the organization did not begin to do so until the end of the decade.[54]

Instead, McNamara remained focused on increasing the volume of Bank lending. This reflected both his fixation with numerical targets and his conviction that a lack of capital was the main constraint on development, a view advocated by his recently recruited chief economist Hollis Chenery.[55] McNamara also spoke about the need for governments in developing countries to "reorient their development policies in order to attack directly the personal poverty of the most deprived 40 percent of their populations."[56] He had the organization expand its research to encompass issues like unemployment that previous presidents had considered peripheral to the organization's growth-centric agenda.[57] And he positioned the Bank to support scientific and technological solutions to development problems.[58] The most prominent of these initiatives were the Onchocerciasis Control Program, a network of governmental bodies, international agencies, and private companies established in 1972 to address river blindness in West Africa, and the Consultative Group on International Agricultural Research (CGIAR), in which the Bank coordinated funding for agricultural research among governments, international organizations, and private foundations.[59]

CGIAR reflected McNamara's awareness of the promise and perils of the Green Revolution. "Nothing has impressed me more than this successful agricultural revolution which is taking place," he told journalists in India in 1968. "I have seen farmers today whose harvest this year and last has doubled, tripled or quadrupled."[60] Like many observers, however, McNamara was aware that the majority of these gains had bypassed small farmers, a situation he found economically and politically problematic. As he told aides in 1969, "there was no doubt that the Green Revolution would predominantly increase the income of the rich peasants and thereby create additional social stress."[61]

McNamara's concern that the Green Revolution might turn red encouraged him to reform the Bank's rural development approach. Early in his tenure, he became convinced that the Bank not only needed to increase the overall amount that it lent for agriculture but also that more of these funds should be devoted to small farmers, as opposed to the large commercial farmers that had benefitted from previous Bank assistance.[62] To this effect, in 1971 he discussed with his aides the need for a rural development program focused on small farmers, and the following year the Bank established a rural development unit.[63] The centerpiece of the Bank's program was integrated rural development (IRD), which aimed to increase the productivity of small farmers through the provision of credit for the purchase of seed, farm machinery, and fertilizer, the construction of irrigation works to water crops and feeder roads to connect these farmers to national and international markets, and the establishment of training centers that would help educate participants in new agricultural methods. Such comprehensive interventions would, it was assumed, increase the productivity, incomes, and welfare of small farmers.[64]

The Bank also embarked on an ambitious urban development program in McNamara's early years.[65] By the late 1960s, the rapid growth of cities in developing countries had become a considerable source of concern.[66] This was due to the simple fact that many municipalities could not cope with the continuous influx of residents from the countryside. A 1972 Bank study, for instance, found that approximately one third of urban residents in developing nations lacked proper housing and utility services.[67] As with rural pov-

Figure 3. Visiting Senegal in 1969. Courtesy of the World Bank Group Archives.

erty, McNamara saw urban poverty as both an economic and political problem, warning that failure to ameliorate "unspeakably grim" conditions in third world cities would lead to "violence and civil upheaval."[68] To this effect, in 1970 he jettisoned the Bank's traditional aversion to lending for urban development projects by establishing an Urban Projects Division to determine how the Bank could help solve what he termed the "growing urban crisis" in the developing world.[69] The organization's urban development approach concentrated on "sites and services" projects in which the Bank funded the construction of basic housing and utility services. In 1972, the organization offered its first such project to the government of Senegal. The loan funded housing units, primary roads, water and power networks, sanitation facilities, primary and secondary schools, and health centers in Dakar and Thies.[70]

In addition to rural and urban development, McNamara sought to expand the Bank's support of education. The Bank had begun funding education projects in the 1960s, but its efforts were limited. Only four percent of

Bank education lending prior went toward primary education. Moreover, the
vast majority of education loans were for the construction of school build-
ings, rather than curriculum development or teacher salaries. Believing that
improvement of human capital was a necessary component of development,
McNamara ordered the Bank's senior managers to seek out ways to "substantially increase" education lending. As a result, the organization's education
portfolio grew from $187 million in the period between 1963 and 1968 to $761
million between 1969 and 1973. McNamara also changed the ways the Bank
supported education. At his direction, the organization increased its support
of primary education, funded teacher training and curriculum development,
researched the relationship between education and economic growth, and began to advise developing country officials on education policies.

Like his alteration of the Bank's structures and procedures, McNamara's
efforts to change the Bank's operational focus engendered internal resistance. Some staff felt that in trying to reform the Bank's approach Mc-
Namara was "slighting growth in order to pursue redistribution."[71] Others
saw poverty alleviation as a politically sensitive subject that developing countries should deal with on their own.[72] Organizational pressures also played a
role. According to one observer, staff were concerned that "time required to
design and supervise a project to ensure that it reaches the poor is excessive
in the context of the needs to meet deadlines, appraise traditional projects,
and meet quantitative lending targets." This mattered because of the widespread belief that "punctual, technically tight work" was critical for promotion.[73]

IRD projects were a particular source of tension. One former World
Banker remembers that IRD provoked "a lot of resistance" among the organization's agricultural hands.[74] Many complained that these projects were
"too complex and cumbersome" and that that they were "under pressure
from various managers and program staff to make rural development projects multisectoral or 'integrated'—even when they feel that a simple single
sector approach is more effective and preferable." Some saw quality being
sacrificed with the IRD approach and worried that "little weight was put on
making sure the projects were well implemented."[75] As one Bank staffer who
worked in East Africa during the early 1970s recalled:

Traditional old-hand project people thought IRD was basically
nonsense . . . much too utopian. They were often not very grounded
in the country politics, meaning people, because they were working

globally, would sort of fly into a country, meet with the President, accept his word, and then head out. And those projects, many of them, were not very successful . . . even though they had many more resources put into them.[76]

Bank staff also resisted McNamara's efforts to refine the way the organization measured its impact. For instance, in 1973 Bank management explored the possibility of creating a framework for estimating the "social rate-of-return" of Bank projects.[77] Yet Bank staff successfully opposed these efforts on the ground that it required them to "make up data, guess at parameters, and thus produce unprofessional analyses."[78] As the Bank's head of operations later recalled, management's attempts to introduce new evaluation metrics were "rudimentary" and "very imprecise" and, as a result, "nobody took it too seriously."[79]

Despite such setbacks, McNamara's efforts to expand the Bank's lending began to show results. In 1973, agriculture surpassed transportation as the

Table 1. IBRD/IDA Lending Commitments by Sector, 1968–1981 (percent of total, three-year average)

Sector	1968–70	1971–73	1976–78	1979–81
Directly poverty-oriented				
Rural development	3.2	7.6	16.5	15.3
Education (primary and non-formal)	0.2	0.8	1.4	1.6
Population, health, nutrition	0	0.7	0.6	0.3
Small-scale industry	0	0.2	1.7	1.7
Urbanization	0	1.3	2.6	3.4
Water supply and sewerage	1.6	4.7	4.6	6.7
Subtotal	5.0	15.3	27.4	29.5
Other				
Agriculture	16.1	13.3	15.8	13.4
Energy (power)	24.6	14.9	13.8	15.0
(oil, gas, coal)	0.3	0.9	0.9	3.5
Industry (including development finance companies)	15.7	16.4	16.5	13.5
All other	10.9	16.3	9.6	11.6
Total	100.0	100.0	100.0	100.0

Source: Task Force on the World Bank's Poverty Focus, *Focus on Poverty: A Report by a Task Force of the World Bank* (Washington, D.C.: World Bank, 1983), 6.

Bank's primary lending sector, and by the middle of the decade poverty-oriented projects constituted a quarter of the organization's lending.[80]

The Bank's New Approach

The reorientation of the Bank's lending was animated by the idea that, as McNamara put it in 1973, "growth is not equitably reaching the poor, and the poor are not significantly contributing to growth."[81] McNamara's solution to this problem was for developing countries to suspend their efforts to rapidly industrialize and, instead, capitalize on their unique resources. He felt, for instance, that the masses of poor people in developing countries could contribute to development by producing "precisely those labor-intensive goods which labor-scarce affluent countries need."[82]

In advancing these views, McNamara was influenced by his key advisors, especially Mahbub ul Haq, who impressed upon McNamara the need to incorporate, rather than bypass, the poor in development interventions. "He was convinced that growth was not trickling down," ul Haq later recalled of McNamara's thinking in the early 1970s, and "he wanted to know precisely how you could reach them." While it had a humanitarian component, McNamara's approach was not based on charity. Rather, in ul Haq's words, "the focus was on . . . increasing the productivity of the poor."[83]

Redistribution with Growth, a book published jointly by the Bank's Development Research Center and the University of Sussex's Institute of Development Studies in 1974, constituted the most comprehensive statement of the Bank's thinking at the time.[84] The study both reflected the belief in the need to pay greater attention to the poor and demonstrated that the Bank was only willing to go so far in advocating for fundamental changes.[85] "More than a decade of rapid growth in underdeveloped countries has been of little or no benefit to perhaps a third of their population," it began. "Although the average per capita income of the Third World has increased by 50 percent since 1960, this growth has been very unequally distributed among countries, regions within countries, and socio-economic groups."[86] Moreover, about half of the global population earned less than $75 per year.[87] In the authors' minds, these figures demonstrated the fallacy that developing countries needed to postpone addressing welfare and equity issues to accelerate their growth. "It is necessary to discard the conceptual separation between optimum growth and distribution policies," the study argued. "Distributional objectives [could not] be viewed independently of growth."[88] Despite these concerns, *Redistribution with Growth* proposed only modest reforms. Governments should not adopt more progressive tax systems because doing so would have "too high a cost in terms of foregone investment," and measures like land reform were impractical given the political resistance of wealthy landowners.[89] Instead, the authors argued that increasing human capital was the key to development. As a result, developing countries needed to make greater investments in education and public health.[90] "The transformation of poverty groups into more productive members of society," it concluded, "is likely to raise the incomes of all."[91]

If the Bank sought to forge a middle ground between the status quo and radical measures, it was also coming to view its role in a new light. Arguably the most important aspect of the Bank's approach under McNamara was the belief that lending for discreet projects was an inadequate means of promoting development. "Overall programs of 'policy packages' rather than a set of isolated projects," should be the basis for development efforts, the authors of *Redistribution with Growth* argued.[92] "What we need—and what we must design," McNamara reiterated in one of his speeches, "is a comprehensive strategy that will constitute an overall plan into which particular policies and individual projects can be fitted as logical, integral parts."[93] As he explained, because development would only come about through a "reorientation of the attitudes and life styles of hundreds of millions of people," the Bank's "central test" was to formulate "a sound development plan" for developing countries.[94] One Bank staffer recalled the logic of the Bank's move toward more comprehensive interventions. "As McNamara saw a need to engage in rural development, with poverty, with urban development, the organization came to recognize that everything connects to everything else."[95]

McNamara's expansion of the Bank's agenda was an important moment in the history of development. In the decades prior to McNamara's presidency, poverty was widely considered an implicit development goal, and development was largely synonymous with accelerating economic growth. Poverty alleviation remained the domain of nongovernmental organizations, while governments and international organizations focused on promoting industrialization. Yet in getting the Bank to focus on things like rural and urban development, and through his speeches on the need to improve conditions for the global poor, McNamara helped place poverty onto the development agenda.[96] By the mid-1970s, concerns with poverty became widespread at the national and international levels. For instance, in 1973, the U.S. government

Figure 4. Addressing the opening session of the 1973 World Bank-IMF annual meetings in Nairobi, Kenya. In his speech, McNamara called on the international community to attack "absolute poverty." Courtesy of the World Bank Group Archives.

reformed its foreign aid program so as to better meet the needs of poor people in developing countries. A few years later, the International Labour Organization was calling on governments and aid agencies to shift their development goals toward meeting people's basic needs.[97] By 1975, Bank officials noted that the poverty focus had begun to "penetrate" development discourse around the world.[98]

Despite its influence, the Bank's approach suffered from a number of flaws. Bank publications, research and operational documents, and McNamara's public and private statements provided a highly tautological explanation for global poverty. The poor were poor because, in the words of one observer, they "lacked jobs [or] . . . were unproductive."[99] While the Bank paid homage to the importance of economic reforms, it devoted scant attention to issues of policy implementation. The farthest the Bank tended to go in this direction was to call for increased political will on the part of developing country officials in making their nation's economic policies more progressive. And, though the organization at times was critical of borrowing governments, such concerns did not systematically influence lending decisions.[100] The Bank's avoidance of politics extended to the international level. For example, while McNamara emphasized the need for industrialized nations to lower their import barriers to assist developing country exporters, he argued that wealthy nations could make their greatest contribution to global development by increasing their foreign aid flows, preferably channeling this assistance through the Bank.

Finally, the Bank's interest in reducing global poverty never displaced its concern with promoting growth.[101] "Policies aimed at diminishing income inequalities through direct redistribution of wealth will not be sufficient," McNamara said in 1975. "No degree of egalitarianism alone will solve the root problem of poverty."[102] As he later put it, "there was no way one could address poverty in the developing world by redistribution" alone. Instead, "increasing output in the society" required "invest[ing] where you get the highest rate of return . . . the poor."[103] Viewing poverty reduction as a question of the productivity of the poor meant that its efforts targeted individuals who had enough resources to make productive use of external assistance, people who by definition were not the poorest.[104] IRD, for instance, targeted farmers who owned small plots of land, rather than tenants.

McNamara also upheld the Bank's macroeconomic orthodoxy by stressing the importance of limiting inflation, reducing budget deficits, and liberalizing trade. To take a few examples, in 1970 he praised Colombian president Carlos Lleras Restrepo's "efforts to restrain inflationary pressures" as well as his broader concern for "financial stabilization."[105] He privately urged Costa Rican president José Figueres Ferrer to improve the country's fiscal position.[106] And he informed Central African Republic President Jean-Bédel Bokassa that reducing the country's import barriers was a condition for Bank assistance.[107] As McNamara explained to an interviewer, in order to grow developing countries needed to "increase their private savings [and] . . . expand their trade."[108]

Although McNamara continued to advance a vision of development that focused on growth and stability, the poverty focus marked a departure from the Bank's past insofar as it increased the organization's willingness to intervene in the domestic affairs of developing countries. McNamara's effort to expand the Bank's agenda brought the organization into contact with issues that it had previously considered domestic and, as such, outside its control.

As one observer noted at the time, the Bank had begun to embark systematically on "efforts to influence the general development policies of the countries which borrow from it on issues much more politically delicate, much
more traditionally domestic, than issues related to growth in the gross national product on which the Bank Group has in the past attempted to exert
leverage or influence."[109] McNamara himself admitted as much when he
noted in 1975 that "we are trying to help the developing nations remake their
societies."[110]

To this effect, McNamara felt that the Bank's major contribution would
be to promote policy reform in developing countries, rather than to provide
finance for particular development projects. This change did not go unop-
posed. In the early 1970s, developing country officials voiced their concerns
about the Bank's "serious interference in governmental affairs."[111] There was
a danger, noted one Tanzanian official, that the organization was coming to
view itself as "a world planning authority supplanting national effort."[112] No
less a figure than Eugene Black, the Bank's third president, who had made
project lending the primary focus of the organization, warned McNamara
that his focus on "constructing global development strategies" was taking the
Bank beyond the limits envisioned by its founders.[113] Despite such concerns,
McNamara pressed on. As the Director of the Bank's International Relations
Department boasted in 1973, "the Bank can do practically anything it wants to
do in pursuit of its objectives. The important issues to discuss are not
whether the Bank can do this or that but whether it should and how."[114]

The Ghosts of Vietnam

It is not surprising that McNamara, a former Kennedy and Johnson official,
brought to the World Bank the modernizing spirit that had characterized the
U.S. foreign aid program of the 1960s. Nor was his transition from the military to the development field unusual given the ways techniques developed
to promote national security, such as systems analysis, frequently found civilian applications in the 1970s.[115] Because of his unique history, however, Mc-
Namara benefited from this transition more than most. The Bank presidency
not only provided him with a convenient excuse for maintaining his silence
on Vietnam, but it also allowed him to maintain a significant degree of
influence on the world stage. In addition, the Bank allowed McNamara to at
least partially rehabilitate his reputation. After a 1975 appearance on the

television program *Bill Moyer's Journal*, for instance, viewers wrote Mc-Namara praising him for his "charisma" in explaining the dimensions of global development.[116] McNamara's efforts at the Bank even won over some critics of the Vietnam War. "There are some of us out there who would like to know how a man so associated with the foreign policy of the Johnson administration could lead the World Bank toward its present policy," a man from South Carolina told McNamara. "We have come a long way since 1968."[117] As one of McNamara's former aides explained, "I do not believe the assertion that McNamara was at the World Bank in some kind of repentance mode. I think he had these core instincts. Nevertheless, I do think people came to have a different view of him as a result of his passionate commitment to development."[118]

Even so, McNamara the World Banker continued to be involved in Vietnam. While at the Bank, he conferred with Henry Kissinger, Richard Nixon's influential national security adviser, on U.S. policy in Southeast Asia. McNamara encouraged Kissinger to withdraw U.S. forces from Vietnam, but he also let Kissinger know that he supported the administration's secret plan to bomb Cambodia.[119] In response to a request from the U.S. Department of State, McNamara also had the Bank provide assistance for a UN-sponsored program for development of the Mekong Delta.[120] The Bank provided technical assistance to the government of South Vietnam and hosted South Vietnamese officials at its headquarters.[121] In 1973, McNamara dispatched a "reconnaissance mission" to the country to locate suitable projects for Bank funding.[122] And following a request from South Vietnamese president Nguyen Van Thieu, he convened a meeting of industrialized nations in Paris to discuss establishing an aid group for South Vietnam.[123] McNamara argued that "unless aid in the amount, kind, and quality appropriate to the circumstances of Indochina is forthcoming in the next year or two, the prospects of lasting peace and stability toward which the governments of Indochina and others have been striving will be largely endangered."[124]

Indeed, for all the change that he wrought at the Bank, McNamara could not escape his past. At the World Bank he was as much a symbol of the establishment as he had been at the Department of Defense, and demonstrators frequently confronted him over his past and current work. Two years after crowds in Calcutta forced him to flee the city, authorities had to erect barricades to keep protesters from storming the 1970 IMF-World Bank annual meetings in Copenhagen. The following year, the *New York Times* published the Pentagon Papers, a confidential history of U.S. involvement in Vietnam that McNamara had commissioned in 1967. The Pentagon Papers

revealed the depths of official deception during the escalation of the war, re-
viving memories of McNamara's dishonesty just as he was starting to make
his mark at the Bank. The 1972 release of *The Best and the Brightest*, David
Halberstam's scathing critique of the war's mismanagement, further fueled
the fire. Within the Bank, the book became "required reading," and staff
began to wonder whether they could trust their boss.[125] In the fall of that
year, a man tried to throw McNamara overboard a ferry that was taking
him to his vacation home on Martha's Vineyard.[126]

Nevertheless, those who continued to see McNamara as a symbol of the
Vietnam War missed the broader impact that he was having as president of the
World Bank. Under McNamara, the organization helped to bring a number
of countries into the Western orbit. With McNamara's encouragement,
Romania joined the Bank in 1972, and over the coming five years its government received nearly half a billion dollars in Bank assistance.[127] The Bank
was also an important source of aid for Yugoslavia as it solidified its "market
socialist" model in the 1970s.[128] Under McNamara, the organization forged
ties with the government of Egypt as the country embarked on capitalist reforms, and as noted earlier it helped Indonesia integrate into the international economy.

As was true of his time at the Ford Motor Company and the Department
of Defense, Robert McNamara was both a symbol and agent of historical
change at the Bank. After streamlining assembly lines as the U.S. consolidated its industrial might in the 1950s and overseeing the war in Vietnam as
U.S. military power crested in the 1960s, he now found himself riding the
wave of globalization at the Bank, capitalizing on the emergence of new
countries, markets, and ideas. Nevertheless, global forces would soon over-
take both him and his organization.

CHAPTER 4

Global Shocks

On September 24, 1973, Robert McNamara delivered the World Bank president's annual address to the Bank and IMF Boards of Governors. Speaking to government officials and press assembled in the auditorium of the new Kenyatta Conference Center in Nairobi, Kenya, he recounted the Bank's tremendous expansion over the previous five years. During his first term as president, he noted, the Bank had met or exceeded all the goals he had set for the organization when he arrived. These included doubling the Bank's lending, channeling a greater share of its funds to the world's poorest countries, and increasing its support of education and agriculture.

These accomplishments notwithstanding, McNamara announced that the Bank still had important work to do. Although the economies of many developing countries were growing at an impressive rate, conditions for the poorest people were not improving as rapidly as he hoped. Calling on wealthy nations to increase their foreign aid commitments, McNamara implored his listeners to think about "a condition of life so degraded by disease, illiteracy, malnutrition, and squalor as to deny its victims basic human necessities." Unlike the "relative poverty" found in many developed countries, such "absolute poverty" affected "hundreds of millions" of people in the developing world. "One-third to one-half of the two billion human beings in those nations suffer from hunger or malnutrition," he noted. "Twenty to twenty-five percent of their children die before their fifth birthdays . . . the life expectancy of the average person is twenty years less than in the affluent world . . . and eight hundred million of them are illiterate."[1]

McNamara declared that eliminating absolute poverty was both a "moral obligation" and necessary for the "expansion of trade, the strengthening of international stability, and the reduction of social tensions." In order to address these issues, he announced that the Bank would continue to expand. It would double its lending over the next five years, conduct more research on the causes of and solutions to poverty, support "policies and projects which will begin to attack the problems of absolute poverty," and adopt "socially oriented measure[s] of economic performance" in its operations.[2]

McNamara's speech was not supposed to be the main event in Nairobi. A few days earlier, government officials, bankers, and journalists from around the world had gathered in the Kenyan capital for the first IMF-World Bank annual meetings held in Africa. Preparations for the conference had been intense. Because of the large number of visitors, hotels were overbooked, and some tourists had to rent space in hastily erected tent cities on their way to and from the country's wildlife parks.[3] Observers expected the demise of the Bretton Woods monetary system to dominate the proceedings.[4] Accordingly, attention focused on the IMF, which played a central role in such issues, rather than the World Bank.

Yet McNamara's address turned out to be the seminal moment of the conference. While the discussions over international monetary policy stalled, McNamara's speech left a lasting impression. Representatives from developing countries applauded the former defense secretary's call for increased foreign aid.[5] The press praised his "eloquent reminder" of world poverty.[6] And development specialists saw the speech as evidence that the Bank had assumed a leadership role in the field.[7] Decades later, scholars would describe the Nairobi address as a "landmark" that provided momentum for global antipoverty efforts.[8] Some have even credited McNamara's speech with introducing the concept of absolute poverty.[9]

McNamara's words were important. Following the speech, poverty alleviation became a central objective at the Bank and the broader development community. Nevertheless, his war on world poverty would soon face its greatest challenge. Less than two weeks after the Nairobi meetings concluded, Egypt and Syria launched a surprise attack on Israel seeking to reclaim territory that they had lost in the Six Day War. Shortly thereafter, Arab members of the Organization of Petroleum Exporting Countries (OPEC) placed an embargo on oil exports to the United States in response to the Nixon administration's decision to aid Israel. Although the fighting ended in late October, OPEC continued to deploy the "oil weapon" over the coming months. In November, OPEC cut oil production 25 percent below September levels. The following month, it doubled the price of crude. By January 1974, world oil prices were four times higher than they had been at the beginning of October 1973.

McNamara was far away from these events when they began to gather steam. A lifelong mountaineer, he spent much of November 1973 on vacation in Nepal, catching his breath after a decade that had seen him rise to the heights of power as John F. Kennedy's secretary of defense, fall to personal and professional lows as the architect of the Vietnam War, and then resurrect himself in unexpected ways as president of the World Bank. McNamara did not have much time for reflection. Upon returning to Bank headquarters in early December, he became aware that OPEC's actions posed a direct threat to the economies of oil-importing developing countries. When OPEC announced further price hikes later that month, he and others in the Bank panicked. "After the quadrupling of world oil prices," read a memorandum that McNamara found on his desk the morning of January 1, 1974, "things will never be the same again. We cannot expect a return to normality."[10]

Those words proved prophetic. In addition to the oil crisis, over the coming years a host of external events, including reduced support from the U.S. government and increasingly vocal critiques of mainstream development approaches, influenced the Bank. Although in many ways the organization proceeded down the path that McNamara had laid for it—it continued to expand, it further refined its procedures, and it devoted more of its resources to poverty-oriented lending and research—the upheavals of the 1970s ensured that things were never the same for the Bank or its president.

The Oil Crisis

The 1973–74 oil crisis came after years of increasingly tense negotiations between oil-rich countries and Western petroleum companies operating in those nations over oil pricing. In 1960, Iran, Iraq, Kuwait, Saudi Arabia, and Venezuela organized themselves into OPEC with the purpose of advancing their interests as oil-producing countries vis-à-vis the handful of foreign-owned energy companies that had dominated the industry since the 1940s. Until the oil crisis, these "Seven Sisters"—the Anglo-Persian Oil Company, Gulf Oil, Texaco, Royal Dutch Shell, Standard Oil of New Jersey, Standard Oil of California, and the Standard Oil Company of New York—enjoyed wide latitude in determining oil production and setting prices. By the early 1970s, however, OPEC, whose membership grew to fourteen in 1973, had declared that countries had a right to exercise absolute sovereignty over their natural resources.[11] When hostilities between Israel and Arab countries renewed in 1973, Arab members of OPEC asserted this right by increasing the posted price of crude and placing an embargo on oil exports to the U.S. and other countries that were supporting Israel.[12]

The oil crisis was one of the most significant events in contemporary history. By wresting control of this vital commodity OPEC challenged U.S. hegemony in the Mideast and beyond, inspired developing country leaders around the globe to demand changes to the international political economy, and created rifts among Western nations, some of which disagreed with the U.S. decision to aid Israel. The oil crisis also sent shockwaves through the world economy. It exacerbated economic difficulties facing many Western countries, placed a tremendous burden on oil-importing developing nations, and generated windfalls for many oil-producing countries.

McNamara and other Bank officials recognized that the oil crisis would have dire consequences for most developing countries. In addition to seeing higher energy bills, slower growth in developed countries promised to reduce demand for developing country exports and further depress foreign aid levels. Early in the crisis, the Bank's staff estimated that the foreign exchange required by oil-importing developing countries to fund their energy imports would increase fivefold by the end of the decade.[13] Agricultural sectors, which had become the Bank's main priority, would be particularly hard hit. As a report prepared by the Bank and the UN Food and Agriculture Organization (FAO) noted, "the critical impact of the energy crisis [would be] immediately felt on the generation of power for irrigation [the] . . . accentuated the rise in fertilizer costs" and "severe" increases in the price of pesticides and herbicides.[14] One Bank official put it more bluntly. "The Green Revolution would receive a serious blow from the increase in oil prices."[15]

Bank staff issued even grimmer predictions after OPEC announced another price hike at the end of December 1973, estimating that the current account deficits of oil-importing developing countries would jump by 67 percent in the coming year. Whereas foreign aid and private borrowing had covered previous shortfalls, staff now worried that "no immediate solutions seem in sight to cope with this additional deficit." For low-income developing countries like Pakistan, Bangladesh, Sri Lanka, and Kenya, the effects would be devastating. In the case of India, staff estimated that the cost of oil imports would increase from $400 million in 1973 to $1.35 billion in 1974. Middle-income countries such as Ghana, Korea, Morocco, the Philippines, and Thailand would not fare much better. Since these countries were in "no position to incur new debt by borrowing at conventional terms to pay their oil bill," it appeared that "a drastic reduction in their living standards, unemployment, and social unrest" would ensue. Even relatively well-off developing countries like Argentina, Brazil, Turkey, and Uruguay would suffer. Although these nations could meet some of their financing needs through borrowing, doing so would increase their debt burdens and negatively affect growth.[16]

Recognizing that the consequences of the oil crisis were even more dramatic than he initially feared, McNamara moved quickly to position the Bank to meet the financial needs of oil-importing developing countries.[17] Rather than speak out against the price increase, he sought to convince OPEC members to increase their foreign aid. In January, he requested personal meetings with the Finance Ministers of Iran, Kuwait, and Saudi Arabia and dispatched Munir Benjenk, the head of the Bank's Middle East and North Africa Department, to the region to "collect intelligence about the intention of oil-producing nations regarding aid" to oil-importing developing countries.[18] McNamara was "disturbed by the apparent lack of concern [among OPEC members] for the problem facing developing countries" and wanted to impress upon them the developmental impact of their actions.[19] McNamara also tried to get OPEC members to partner with the Bank in helping oil importers finance their energy bills. Rather than calling for reduced prices, McNamara offered OPEC members "an unqualified guarantee of assistance" if they agreed to channel some of their profits to the Bank, which would relend these funds to oil-importing developing countries.[20] McNamara also pledged that the Bank would help OPEC "identify and prepare development or sector projects" in these countries for OPEC financing and manage a "special soft-loan fund on behalf of OPEC."[21]

McNamara's outreach to the oil rich nations of the Middle East was not simply a result of the oil crisis. Rather, he had courted these countries since his first days at the Bank. In the ninety-eight point agenda that he drafted for himself in 1968, he wrote that he planned to devote "particular emphasis to Kuwait, Saudi Arabia, and Libya" in his fundraising efforts, and during his initial years as president he stepped up the organization's borrowings in the region.[22] Beginning in 1968, the Bank raised $20 to $30 million annually from the Saudi Arabian Monetary Agency (SAMA), and between 1968 and 1973 the organization sold over $400 million of its bonds in Kuwait and Libya.[23] McNamara's interest in OPEC had even led him to predict a spike in oil prices months before the oil crisis. Returning from a trip to the Middle

East in February 1973, he told his aides that "there was an emerging oil monopoly on the part of the producing nations [and] . . . eventually the consumers in the West would have to pay."[24] Like a good banker, McNamara was aware that this presented an opportunity. Since there was "a lack of planning on the part of producer nations on how to use the enormous future revenues from oil," he felt that it was imperative that the Bank "continue to borrow in the area in the future."[25] As he put it a few months later, the oil-rich countries of the Middle East constituted "the largest . . . pool of medium—and long-term investable capital in the history of the world."[26]

In the wake of the crisis, McNamara reiterated his desire to tap OPEC surpluses by advocating for increasing assistance to oil-importing developing countries, telling a meeting of development officials that they should round up "Arab funds for aid."[27] Failing to provide this assistance would ensure that the war on absolute poverty would be over before it began. As the Bank's 1974 *Annual Report* explained, "without a major effort by the international community 800 million people around the world can expect almost no improvement in their conditions of life for the rest of the decade."[28]

Despite such pleas, wealthy countries were unwilling to help. Reporting on a visit to Europe, a Bank staffer observed that "the substantial increases in oil prices are expected to have a profound [negative] effect on the willingness of the European populace and its leaders to make major efforts toward increased development aid."[29] The same story was playing out in the United States, where the Nixon administration felt that helping to offset the cost of oil imports would signal acceptance of OPEC's actions. Perhaps most concerning was the fact that no assistance was forthcoming from OPEC, either. "Oil-producing countries still displayed a lack of understanding for the magnitude of the problem," Benjenk told other members of the President's Council upon his return from the Middle East. Governments in the region believed that the Bank was "exaggerating the problem" and officials had "given little thought to aid programs."[30] "The climate regarding aid had deteriorated," a Bank senior manager concluded.[31]

The only place the Bank could look for help, it seemed, was across the street. At the same time that Bank officials were growing concerned about the international community's lack of a response to the oil crisis, the IMF began exploring ways that it could help countries cope. To this effect, in early 1974 IMF managing director Johannes Whitteveen initiated plans to have his organization provide concessional loans to oil-importing countries. Shortly thereafter, senior Bank and IMF officials agreed to "exchange information . . . and remain in close contact" as their respective responses took shape.[32]

Some good news arrived in February, when Jahangir Amuzegar, the Iranian representative to the Bank and IMF, informed Bank management that Iran was thinking about establishing an organization that would provide assistance to oil-importing developing countries on favorable terms. During his visit to Iran, Benjenk had apparently managed to convince Iranian authorities that the country should help poor countries finance their oil imports. According to Benjenk, Iranian Prime Minister Amir-Abbas Hoveida had been "surprised at the magnitude of the needs of the developing countries" and had asked him to put the Bank's concerns in writing so that he could show them to the Shah.[33]

The Bank's senior managers had reservations about the proposal. "There was no need for a new institution," Burke Knapp, the Bank's vice president of operations, told Amuzegar. Instead, "the new funds could be handled under existing procedures." Nevertheless, the Iranians insisted on the need for their own organization—oil producers must, Amuzegar responded, "have some say in the disposition of the funds they provided"—and a week later McNamara and Whitteveen were in Tehran to help hammer out the plans.[34] During the meetings, McNamara and Whitteveen convinced the Shah to contribute $1 billion for a new concessional lending organization whose day-to-day operations would be jointly managed by the Bank and the IMF. The Shah also agreed to lend $700 million to the IMF and $200 million to the World Bank for their efforts to help oil-importing developing countries cope with the increased price of oil.[35]

"The scheme which had been proposed by the Shah was unusual," McNamara confided to Bank and IMF officials during a break in the meetings, "even irrational," and demonstrated the Shah's desire to bolster his image in the developing world. But since he "saw no chance of getting more concessionary funds from developed countries," he felt that he had to support the Shah's plan.[36] To press gathered in Tehran, McNamara described the proposal "as imaginative a proposal and important a proposal as was the Marshall Plan."[37]

Other oil producers soon followed suit. In March, the head of SAMA assured McNamara that Saudi Arabia would "tak[e] care of the Bank's future financing needs." Meanwhile, Libyan leaders informed Bank officials that they were ready to invest "substantial amounts" in the organization. And

Algerian President Houari Boumediène even gave McNamara a "tentative commitment" to lend to the Bank—a significant event considering that the government of Algeria had previously criticized the Bank as a neocolonial institution.[38]

Within months, the Bank ramped up its OPEC borrowings, raising $200 million from Iran, $101 million from Libya, $76 million from the United Arab Emirates, $85 million from Kuwait, and $23 million from Venezuela in 1974 alone. The Bank's operations in Iran, Venezuela, and the UAE con-stituted its first long-term borrowings in those nations.[39] All totaled, the Bank raised over half a billion dollars from oil-exporting countries in the year following the oil crisis, about 31 percent of its total borrowings during the period and more than double the amount raised from those countries in the previous year.[40] In 1974, the Bank raised $240 million and $30 million from the governments of Nigeria and Oman, and in December of that year it borrowed $750 million in Saudi Arabia, which at the time constituted the single largest bond placement in the Bank's history.[41] All totaled, in the year and a half after the oil crisis almost 80 percent of the Bank's borrowings came from OPEC members.[42]

McNamara's World Bank was not the only beneficiary of oil money. In the wake of the crisis, OPEC members also expanded their bilateral assis-tance programs. Mainly, though, they invested their surpluses in Western capital markets. By one estimate, more than 80 percent of the current ac-count surpluses of oil exporting countries went to developed countries and offshore markets.[43] By comparison, from 1974 to 1981 OPEC members con-tributed 1.4 percent of their current account surplus to the Bank, which was not their preferred multilateral lending vehicle.[44] OPEC members provided more assistance to the OPEC Fund for International Development (OFID), created in 1976, and the International Fund for Agricultural Development (IFAD), established the following year, than they did to the Bank.[45]

A few reasons account for the Bank's relative lack of success in raising funds from OPEC. The primary one was financial. Bank bonds were less at-tractive than other investments. In negotiations with Saudi officials, for instance, Bank staff struggled to explain why, as a development bank, the organization offered lower interest rates than private borrowers; indeed, the Bank was only able to secure its $750 million issue in Saudi Arabia by borrowing at a relatively high rate.[46] The Bank was also hamstrung by a per-ception that the major countries controlled it and, through the institution, advanced their foreign policy interests. That the Bank's vice president of finance at the time was a former British colonial officer did not alleviate such concerns.[47] Finally, OPEC leaders appear to have grown tired of the Bank's fundraising pleas. As one staff member put it to McNamara, officials in the region did "not appreciate advice on how to invest their money."[48]

Compounding these difficulties was the fact that OPEC's surpluses turned out to be lower than expected. Over time, increased oil prices reduced demand for oil, and OPEC's profits did not continue to increase quite so rapidly in the years after the crisis.[49] Thus, in March 1975, McNamara noted that he had encountered a "depressed mood" on a recent trip to the Middle East, where current account surpluses had been cut in half from the previous year.[50] This, compounded with the organization's difficulty raising funds in the region, meant that by the mid-1970s the Middle East had become almost an afterthought in terms of Bank fundraising.[51]

At the same time, the Bank continued to have difficulty convincing developed countries to increase their foreign aid budgets. Reporting on a trip to Japan and Europe in the summer of 1974, Bank vice president of finance Siem Aldewereld informed McNamara that domestic concerns, not the plight of oil-importing developing countries, predominated. Japanese authorities were "worried about the lack of growth of their economy and inflation," and European officials were focused on "the stability of the banking system."[52] Indeed, despite the financial needs of oil-importing developing countries, official development assistance from developed countries actually decreased in 1975 and 1976.[53]

The U.S.-Bank Rift

In addition to its fundraising struggles, the Bank's relationship with the U.S. government deteriorated. This rift was significant given that the two had always enjoyed close relations. Since the Bank's founding, the United States had provided critical financial and political support, and the Bank, in promoting market-based development, had advanced U.S. foreign policy interests. Although McNamara's Bank continued to work toward this goal, Congress's desire to exert more control over U.S. foreign policy, growing discontent among the American public with foreign aid, and the predilections of the Nixon and Ford administrations produced a number of conflicts.

Tension between the Bank and the U.S. government was not on the horizon at the beginning of McNamara's presidency. Rather, McNamara's early efforts to increase the Bank's reach dovetailed with the Nixon administration's foreign aid goals. Reflecting mounting budgetary pressures, in 1969 Nixon announced that the U.S. government would seek to reduce its relative contribution to international development efforts. This entailed a greater emphasis on stimulating private investment in developing countries as well as encouraging other governments to increase their foreign aid outlays, including by channeling more funds through international organizations like the World Bank.[54]

Yet Nixon's desire to internationalize foreign aid generated a backlash in Congress.[55] Concerned about the executive branch's dominance of U.S. foreign policy, in the early 1970s members of Congress sought to increase their oversight of the World Bank and other international development organizations. The Foreign Operations Subcommittee of the House Appropriations Committee, chaired by conservative Democrat Otto Passman, was central to this effort. Passman, a prominent critic of foreign aid who once boasted that his "only pleasure in life is to kick the shit out of the foreign aid program of the United States," had voted against every foreign aid bill since the Truman Doctrine loans to Greece and Turkey in 1947. In 1955 he assumed the chairmanship of the Foreign Operations Subcommittee and, in this role, regularly secured deep cuts in executive branch foreign aid funding requests.[56] In the early 1970s, Passman turned his attention to international organizations. In the spring of 1971, the Foreign Operations Subcommittee rejected a Nixon administration request for appropriations for the World Bank and the Inter-American Development Bank (IBD), which led to the first time in history that Congress failed to fulfill an executive request to allocate funds to a multilateral development bank (MDB) in which the United States was a member.[57]

While Passman tried to starve the Bank, others sought to control its behavior. In the late 1960s and early 1970s, the U.S. government grew concerned about the expropriation of American property by foreign governments.[58] The Nixon administration employed a variety of means, including using its influence in the World Bank, to prevent expropriations. In 1969, Nixon requested that McNamara try to dissuade Peruvian president Juan Velasco Alvarado from nationalizing U.S.-owned oil companies operating in Peru.[59] Two years later, Nixon convinced McNamara to strengthen Bank rules against lending to governments that had expropriated foreign property without adequate compensation.[60] Although they also sought to discourage expropriations, however, many members of Congress opposed the administration's efforts to deal with expropriations in an informal manner. Accordingly, Henry Gonzalez, a Democratic representative from Texas, led a campaign to extend prohibitions on issuing bilateral aid to expropriating governments by requiring that U.S. representatives to the MDBs vote against loans to such governments.[61] The Gonzalez Amendment to the Foreign Assistance Act, which was signed into law in 1972, demonstrated Congress's interest in maintaining its oversight of the U.S. foreign aid program as it became more multilateral.

Congress was particularly interested in supervising the World Bank. In 1973, the U.S. General Accounting Office issued a report that criticized the Bank over its lack of transparency. Because the Bank did not make information about its operations publicly available, the report concluded that Congress could not be sure that U.S. contributions to the organization were being used "efficiently and effectively."[62] As a result, U.S. resistance to the Bank increased. Over the coming years, legislators attempted to place numerous restrictions on appropriations bills mandating how the Bank could use U.S. funds. The scrutiny that accompanied Bank funding legislation caused delays in U.S. contributions to the Bank, and by the middle of the decade the United States was consistently behind on its payments to the organization.[63]

Initially, it seemed that the Bank would be able to rely on the support of the Nixon administration to overcome congressional opposition. The Bank's management had long enjoyed favorable relations with the executive branch, and Nixon's vow to increase the percentage of U.S. foreign assistance that was channeled through multilateral institutions aligned with McNamara's expansionary plans for the Bank. Even though McNamara had served in Democratic administrations, Nixon also appeared to value his perspective. For instance, in 1969 they met to discuss Japan's plans to increase international development assistance.[64] As one Bank staffer who worked with McNamara recalled, the Nixon administration was "favorably disposed" to the Bank and McNamara had "a lot of credibility" as its president.[65]

Nevertheless, U.S. officials soon came to feel that they were losing control of the Bank as it grew in size and as McNamara consolidated his power over it. Signs of trouble emerged after Bangladeshi demands for independence from Pakistan erupted into a regional war in the spring of 1971. Pakistan was an important U.S. ally, and the Nixon administration pressured McNamara to cut off lending to India, which had come to the aid of Bangladesh.[66] At the time, India was the Bank's largest borrower, and McNamara, eager to assert the Bank's autonomy, rebuffed the administration.[67] Nixon's

feelings toward the Bank were further inflamed that summer when the
United States failed to convince McNamara to withdraw loans to Guyana
and Bolivia because of expropriation disputes in those countries. The United
States subsequently voted "no" when the loans came up for a vote, marking
the first time in the organization's history that the U.S. government formally
opposed a loan that had been recommended by management.[68]

Frustrated by its inability to control the Bank, the Nixon administration
gave only "belated and grudging support" to McNamara during initial discussions over his appointment to a second term as Bank president in 1972.[69]
Although the United States eventually supported McNamara's reappoint-
ment, relations between the Nixon administration and the Bank remained
poor. In a direct rebuke of McNamara's expansionary plans, in the spring of
1973 the U.S. representative to the Bank called for capping the organization's
operating budget, and later that year it was revealed that Nixon had placed
McNamara on one of his "enemies lists."[70]

Deliberations over the fourth replenishment of IDA (IDA IV) in 1973
and 1974 brought tensions between the World Bank and the United States to
a boil. It was clear from an early point that IDA IV would be trouble. In 1971,
U.S. treasury secretary John Connally informed McNamara that the Nixon
administration would seek to reduce the U.S. contribution to IDA.[71] The following year, the administration signaled its reluctance to expand U.S. multilateral aid commitments by reducing U.S. funding of the IDB and the Asian
Development Bank (ADB).[72]

Negotiations for IDA IV began in December 1972 with McNamara seeking $4.5 billion in new commitments, a doubling, in nominal terms, of the
previous IDA replenishment.[73] At a meeting in London the following March,
donor countries agreed to contribute 60 percent toward this goal on the condition that the United States provide the remaining 40 percent. U.S. representatives countered by offering to contribute 30 percent. McNamara proposed a
compromise: the United States would contribute 33 percent but would be
allowed to stretch its contributions over five years instead of three.[74]

While other countries were willing to accept this deal, negotiations with
the Nixon administration stalled, and by the time of the Bank-IMF annual
meetings in Nairobi that fall the fate of IDA remained uncertain. In a private meeting with U.S. treasury secretary George Shultz, McNamara laid
out the stakes of the impasse. Other countries were waiting on the U.S. to
solidify its commitment before they contributed their own funds, McNamara

noted. Because no country was willing to step forward, IDA would soon run out of money. This would not only hurt developing countries—many of which were struggling to cope with the fallout from the oil crisis—but also raise questions about the West's commitment to development. McNamara was so frustrated he threatened to resign if the Nixon administration failed to come around. There was no way, he told Schultz, that he would "continue as president of a bankrupt organization."[75]

Events in Nairobi put McNamara's concerns to rest. After McNamara delivered his opening address calling for an attack on absolute poverty, U.S. negotiators agreed to their share of the IDA IV replenishment. But U.S. support came with a number of conditions, including demands that the United States be allowed to stretch out its contribution to IDA IV over four years, that the Bank establish more sophisticated procedures for evaluating the impact of its projects, that IDA's future growth be curtailed, and that the Bank lend to South Vietnam.[76]

The contribution still required Congressional approval. Discontent over the Nixon administration's prosecution of the Vietnam War had led to significant deterioration in congressional support for foreign aid, however.[77] In 1971, the Senate rejected a bill authorizing the U.S. foreign aid program, and two years later Congress amended the Foreign Assistance Act to require that the foreign aid program jettison short-term security concerns in favor of meeting basic needs of people in developing countries.[78] Congress voted down the IDA IV appropriation bill in January 1974. Although McNamara had arranged to keep IDA afloat, the defeat came as a surprise, and over the coming weeks he scrambled to convince other donor countries to release their contributions in advance of the United States. Meanwhile, the Nixon administration lobbied Congress to secure passage of the bill.[79] After much handwringing, Congress eventually approved the U.S. contribution in July.

Tensions between the Bank and the U.S. government continued to deteriorate over the coming years. McNamara's efforts to formulate an international response to the oil crisis ran counter to the Nixon administration's cultivation of a system in which OPEC countries invested their surpluses in Western banks and government securities.[80] Administration officials also considered the Bank's failure to condemn OPEC a direct rebuke of their efforts to force a reduction in prices and worked behind the scenes to derail the Iranian plan to establish a Bank-IMF managed concessional lending agency.[81] And in 1975, the Senate's Permanent Subcommittee on Investigations alleged that in failing to condemn OPEC's actions the Bank was working toward "the establishment of a permanent floor price for crude oil at such a high level [so as] . . . to benefit primarily the OPEC countries."[82]

William Simon, U.S. treasury secretary from 1974 to 1977, was the Bank's most powerful critic. Simon believed that free market capitalism was the surest route to economic growth and viewed the Bank as an overgrown bureaucracy that, in lending to socialist governments, hindered, rather than promoted, development. In a speech to the Bank and IMF annual meetings in Manila in 1976, he argued that when it came to development there was "no substitute for a vigorous private sector mobilizing the resources and energies of the people."[83] In articulating this vision, Simon reflected conservative critics of foreign aid who argued that official development assistance prevented poor countries from addressing fundamental economic problems.[84] McNamara, who while sharing a positive view of the private sector believed that governments could play a positive role in development, complained to his aides that Simon "operated from the basic belief that private enterprise could solve the problems of the [developing world] and that the Bank should be judged on conventional terms as applied to commercial banks."[85]

Simon was particularly critical of McNamara's effort to formulate an aid-based response to the oil crisis. He saw as hypocritical McNamara's efforts to raise funds from OPEC at the same time that he warned about the developmental impact of oil price increases. He also opposed the Bank's policy of borrowing from and lending to oil-producers in relatively equal amounts, a practice known as "offset borrowing." Simon viewed such arrangements as antithetical to U.S. interests because they rewarded oil-producers and denied the United States a source of foreign exchange. "When an OPEC country lends funds to the Bank, it is in fact only a transfer from holdings of treasury bills to holding of Bank bonds and does not burden that country's foreign reserve holdings," a treasury official informed a Bank staffer in 1974. "On the other hand, it gets an additional loan from the Bank."[86]

Simon frustrated some of McNamara's major plans for the Bank. Because of U.S. pressure, McNamara put the brakes on his plan to double the Bank's lending, which he had announced in his Nairobi speech.[87] The Bank's Articles mandated that the organization not have outstanding loans that exceeded the amount of its subscribed capital. Doubling the Bank's lending thus required increasing the Bank's capital base. McNamara began discussing with some of the organization's members increasing the Bank's capital in 1974, but he soon ran into resistance. At a Board meeting that March, the

U.S. Executive Director questioned whether "a marked expansion of the Bank's program was really necessary," and shortly thereafter Nixon officials informed McNamara of their opposition to his proposed second five-year lending plan because it would require an increase in the Bank's subscribed capital.[88] This was enough to scuttle McNamara's plans. Whereas he initially sought a general capital increase of $40 billion, double the Bank's existing level, after two years of frustrated negotiations he had to settle for an increase of just $8.5 billion.[89]

The United States also prevented McNamara from changing the terms of Bank assistance. Frustrated that the United States had "held down" the Bank and IMF in securing financial agreements with Iran and other oil exporters in the months after the oil crisis, McNamara began looking for other ways to increase the Bank's ability to provide financial assistance to oil-importing developing countries.[90] In late 1974, he floated a proposal that the Bank begin issuing debt instruments to middle-income developing countries on terms that were more favorable than IBRD loans but less concessionary than IDA credits.[91] Negotiations over the establishment of this Intermediate Financing Facility, or "third window," commenced in January 1975, and that summer the Bank's Board of Governors authorized McNamara to proceed toward a goal of making $1 billion in third window loans the following year.[92] Nevertheless, the proposal failed to go far. While the Bank initially sought to mobilize $225 million in donations from its members to subsidize interest payments on $1 billion third window loans, just $154 million was committed.[93]

Unlike Simon, Henry Kissinger, who served as national security advisor and secretary of state under Nixon and as secretary of state under Ford, considered the Bank a useful instrument of U.S. foreign policy. Kissinger was particularly interested in using the Bank to undermine proposals for a New International Economic Order (NIEO), a set of demands issued in 1974 by the Group of 77 developing countries for global economic reform. For years, intellectuals such as Argentine economist Raúl Prebisch had argued that developing countries needed to demand changes to the international economic order. With the oil crisis fresh on everyone's mind, in May 1974 the UN General Assembly adopted a resolution for the "Establishment of a New International Economic Order" (NIEO). Among other demands, the resolution called for a moratorium on developing country debt payments, easing developed country import restrictions, and the creation of an international fund to stabilize commodity prices.[94] At root, the NIEO was intended to encourage the distribution of resources to the global South.[95]

At first, McNamara was interested in the proposals. A few days after passage of the resolution, he met with UN secretary general Kurt Waldheim to discuss how the Bank could help mobilize increased foreign aid and stabilize commodity prices.[96] But McNamara's support ended there. He considered the demands too political for the Bank and informed his aides that he questioned "the appropriateness of the Bank openly taking policy positions on most items."[97] McNamara also saw the NIEO as a threat to the Bank's work. For instance, developing country proposals to create permanent machinery to restructure sovereign debt would render irrelevant the informal "Paris Club" meetings of government creditors that the Bank managed. As a result, McNamara maintained the Bank's distance from the NIEO. He refused to address developing country demands in public statements, and he had the organization avoid fora that focused on the proposals.

Kissinger tried to bring the Bank into the fray. He sought to counter the NIEO's demands for structural change by indicating that the U.S. government was prepared to increase its multilateral aid commitments.[98] He supported McNamara's goal of increasing the Bank's capital and in 1975 proposed the creation of an "international resources bank," to be managed by the World Bank, that would facilitate investment in minerals, oil, and natural gas projects.[99]

Kissinger's interest in using the Bank to blunt developing country demands for an NIEO ran up against Simon's attempt to reign in McNamara and touched off a struggle within the Ford administration over U.S. policy toward the Bank. In addition to the capital increase over which Simon prevailed, the two clashed over Bank lending to Nigeria, an OPEC member. Whereas the Treasury Department had opposed Bank lending to Nigeria since the outbreak of the oil crisis, Kissinger viewed Nigeria as an important U.S. ally and encouraged Simon to call off his campaign to terminate Bank lending to the country.[100] Kissinger informed Simon that "more detriment than gain" would result from a cutoff, given that this would jeopardize relations with "the largest, most powerful black African nation." Instead, Kissinger argued that it was in the U.S.'s best "interests to assist the Nigerians in constructing a policy framework for development which is generally Western-oriented with a large role for market forces," something toward which "the World Bank can play a major role."[101] Kissinger also claimed that by lending to Nigeria the Bank could undermine the NIEO. "Nigeria is expected to play a key role" in negotiations over the NIEO, Kissinger informed Simon, and "we will need moderate friends in the developing country group." As if this were not enough, Kissinger pointed out that the United States could not uni-laterally control the Bank. "Other major donors have given us virtually no support in our earlier efforts to persuade the Bank to stop lending to OPEC countries," he wrote, and, if the Treasury Department continued to oppose Bank loans to Nigeria, the United States "would be fighting alone a battle we are going to lose."[102]

There were, in other words, limits to how far the United States could push the Bank. As Kissinger predicted, the organization continued to lend to Ni-geria over the coming years. Moreover, for all William Simon's problems with McNamara, he never thought the United States should withdraw from the Bank, as some conservatives had begun advocating. In fact, Simon agreed with the Bank's president on the need to expand the International Finance Corporation (IFC), the organization's private sector investment arm.[103] Still, the U.S. government's opposition to many of McNamara's efforts, particu-larly his desire for a large increase in the Bank's capital, demonstrated the extent to which the U.S.-Bank relationship had deteriorated and portended more serious problems in the years ahead.

Development's Discontents

Increased U.S. scrutiny of the Bank reflected broader dissatisfaction with mainstream development efforts. During the 1970s, intellectuals and activ-ists from across the political spectrum challenged the concept and practice of development, as well as the operations of the Bank itself.

Despite the fact that mainstream development theorists argued that the state should play a strong role in guiding the development process, their emphasis on the positive role of private capital and prioritization of growth over equity had long left them open to attacks from the left. In the 1950s, critics began to take particular issue with the notion that economic ties between rich and poor nations were mutually beneficial. Significant in this regard was work done by economists Raúl Prebisch and Hans Singer, who examined historical patterns of world trade and concluded that com-modity producers suffered from declining terms of trade (the relative prices of a country's exports to imports) compared to producers of fin-ished goods.[104] The implication of this observation was that trade with in-dustrialized nations hindered rather than assisted the economic growth of poor countries.

This "structuralist" thesis overlapped with a more radical critique of the international political economy known as dependency theory. Beginning in the late 1950s, thinkers such as Paul Baran, Celso Furtado, Samir Amin, and Andre Gunder Frank expanded on Marxist critiques of capitalism and imperialism by arguing that the West had grown wealthy by actively suppressing the nations of the developing world.[105] As Frank explained in 1966, "contemporary underdevelopment is in large part the historical product of past and continuing economic and other relations between the satellite underdeveloped and the new developed metropolitan countries. . . . When the metropolis expands to incorporate previously isolated regimes into the worldwide system, the previous development and industrialization of these regions is choked off or channeled into directions which are not self-perpetuating or promising."[106]

Inspired by dependency theorists, in the 1970s critics took issue with the World Bank's lending and advising activities.[107] Early in the decade, British researcher Teresa Hayter published a book chastising the organization for pressuring developing countries to liberalize their economies.[108] Others argued that, despite the Bank's new focus on small farmers, large landowners continued to receive most of the benefits of the organization's agricultural loans.[109] Still others saw the Bank's antipoverty campaign as a rhetorical maneuver designed to undermine support for more radical development approaches.[110] Aart van de Laar, a Bank staffer turned critic, encapsulated many of these views when he explained that, given that organization's dependence on private funding, "it would be wrong . . . to expect too much from the envisaged distributional slant of Bank policy."[111]

Observers also highlighted the negative environmental impacts of development projects. In the late 1960s researchers drew attention to the ways large-scale development projects, such as hydroelectric dams, disrupted local ecosystems. Concerns were also raised about the Green Revolution's environmental impact.[112] As one critic wrote in 1973, "many awful things can happen when science and technology are turned loose on the orders of planning officials in Washington."[113] Such concerns gave rise to the idea that global development was unsustainable. Important in this regard was the 1972 publication of *The Limits to Growth*, a compilation of computer projections that purported to show that the earth could not sustain continued economic expansion.[114] As a result of such views, some analysts argued that international development efforts needed to be scaled down. A year after the publication of *Limits to Growth*, British economist E. F. Schumacher released

Small Is Beautiful: A Study of Economics as if People Mattered. Schumacher argued that natural resources limited the potential for continued economic growth and, as a result, development efforts should focus on sustainability. To this end, he advocated for decentralized, labor-intensive, and environmentally friendly methods of production, so-called "intermediate or appropriate technologies."[115] People affected by Bank-financed development projects also pushed for change on environmental and social grounds. For instance, in 1974, local communities in the Cordillera region of the Philippines, worried that a Bank-financed dam would displace hundreds of families in the area, prevented construction from getting underway, which forced the Bank to cancel the project two years later.[116]

Such resistance highlighted the overlap between environmental critiques of development and those focused on the need to ensure that aid did not serve as a tool of repression. In the 1970s, members of the emerging human rights movement described foreign aid as problematic insofar as it often propped up abusive regimes. In addition to facing challenges over the ecological impacts of its projects, the Bank was criticized for providing funds to authoritarian governments. Bank support for the government of Augusto Pinochet in Chile drew particular condemnation. By the middle of the decade, the organization's Public Affairs Department reported it had been inundated with complaints about Bank lending to Chile.[117] McNamara himself noted that "he had "hardly visited a country where there was not an article in the local newspapers about Chile and the World Bank."[118]

Gender-based challenges also emerged during the time. Before the decade, development theorists paid scant attention to the specific contribution that women could make to development. To the degree that they considered gender issues, they generally held that development would equalize relations between the sexes, including by allowing more women to enter the formal workforce.[119] This changed in the 1970s. Second-wave feminists in Western nations started to draw attention to the status of women in the developing world, while people in developing countries stepped up their efforts to place development issues onto the agendas of international bodies such as the UN Commission on the Status of Women (CSW).[120] Development experts also began to focus more attention on gendered aspects of development.

A key moment came in 1970 with the publication of *Woman's Role in Economic Development* by Dutch agricultural economist Ester Boserup. Boserup argued that the introduction of modern market relations disrupted economic systems in which women played a more central role and documented the barriers women in developing countries faced in gaining formal employment. To Boserup, this situation not only increased gender inequality but also slowed developing countries' growth.[121] Over the coming years, scholars researched the informal labor markets in which women participated, issues of sexual discrimination in developing countries, and the impact of technological change on gender relations, among other topics.[122] Meanwhile, government officials heeded calls to place women's issues on the development agenda. In 1973, the U.S. Congress amended the Foreign Assistance Act to mandate that more of the county's aid go toward projects specifically designed to improve the status of women (although the same Act limited the amount of funds that could go toward family planning services).[123] And the International Women's Conference in Mexico City in 1975 held special seminars on the importance of integrating women in development projects.[124]

The ideological development that would have the most lasting impact on the Bank and the broader development community took place in the field of economics. During the 1970s, a growing number of economists argued that only market forces were capable of producing the conditions needed for sustained growth and poverty reduction in developing countries.[125] The father of this "counterrevolution" in development economics was P. T. Bauer, who, beginning in the 1950s, challenged development theorists' optimistic views of government intervention. Instead of productively guiding the development process, Bauer argued that the state fostered corruption and inefficiency. As he put it in 1959, development required "a redirection of the activities of government away from policies restricting the energies and opportunities of its subjects and away from acts of emulation of the pattern of the Soviet world."[126] Bauer further argued that foreign aid exacerbated these problems. In his view, aid-financed projects were more likely to be unproductive since they were not subject to competition, drew scarce resources away from more productive endeavors, and enabled borrowing governments to avoid making necessary policy changes.[127]

Bauer remained a solitary figure for most of the 1950s and 1960s. Nevertheless, the economic dislocations of the 1970s brought new adherents to his side. Mirroring the broader rejection of Keynesian approaches, a growing number of economists argued that state-led development strategies, which included government ownership of industry and efforts to restrict imports to protect domestic industry, were hindering growth. One of the earliest and most vocal proponents of this view was Harry Johnson, a Canadian professor of economics at the University of Chicago.[128] Johnson considered multinational corporations potentially useful "development agent[s]" that could provide capital and expertise to poor countries. As such, he called for greater levels of foreign investment.[129] In the 1970s, Bela Balassa, a Hungarian economist and consultant to the World Bank during the McNamara years, provided empirical data demonstrating the adverse impacts of trade restrictions on economic growth.[130] Anne Krueger, an economist at the University of Minnesota who would become the Bank's chief economist in the early 1980s, also drew attention to the inefficiencies of import restrictions.[131] At the same time, Oxford economist Ian Little, a pioneer in the movement to develop a framework for appraising the social impact of development projects, called for developing nations to turn away from strategies designed to protect domestic industry.[132] Even Yale economist Arthur Okun, who had chaired President Johnson's Council of Economic Advisers, reflected a growing distrust of the government's ability to reduce poverty and inequality when he argued that such efforts could impede growth.[133]

Such critiques found many adherents, including U.S. treasury secretary William Simon. Although Simon was largely unable to force the Bank to change course, his opposition reflected the erosion in the Bank's relationship with the U.S. government as well as mounting discontent with prevailing development approaches. This discontent, in turn, formed part of a larger change in the Bank's world. Increased oil prices presented a dire challenge for many developing countries. The decline in U.S. support for the Bank raised questions about the West's commitment to foreign aid. And the consensus that "development" was something that could, or should, be attained eroded.

The Bank, which had undergone a profound transformation in McNamara's first years, was caught off guard by the challenges of the 1970s. Eventually, however, it regrouped and, under McNamara's direction, adapted to its new economic, political, and intellectual environments. In so doing, it emerged a fundamentally different organization than the one that it had been at the start of the decade.

CHAPTER 5

Navigating Turbulence

The economic, political, and intellectual upheavals of the 1970s presented significant challenges to Robert McNamara's ambitious vision for the World Bank. In forcing a rise in world oil prices, OPEC's actions in 1973 and 1974 highlighted the financial vulnerabilities of many of the world's poorest countries and threw a wrench into McNamara's plans to reduce global poverty. Although some nations were able to ease the strain by borrowing, the growing willingness of private banks to lend to developing countries rendered the Bank's funds less attractive to many governments. On another front, demands for a New International Economic Order (NIEO) demonstrated that the Bank remained unpopular throughout the global South. Meanwhile, Western support for foreign aid diminished as a result of budgetary pressures and dissatisfaction with the results of aid efforts. By the mid-1970s, the Bank found itself adrift. While it had become a larger and more active institution, global events outpaced its capacity to respond.

It was in this context that Bank officials convened in February 1978 to discuss how they could increase the organization's relevance. Shahid Husain, vice president of the Bank's East Asia and the Pacific Department, began the meeting by noting that the NIEO had raised fundamental questions about the Bank's role in the international system. "The broad consensus" in which the organization had operated over the last three decades, he said, "was becoming more elusive because of . . . the sharpening confrontation between North and South." While developing countries considered the Bank "an intellectual leader," they thought that it was "vulnerab[e] to outside pressures," particularly from the U.S. government. McNamara noted that the Bank was in a quandary. "In pressing for increased capital flows and in its trade policy statements, the Bank had a pronounced pro-South policy position." Nevertheless, developing countries "mistrust[ed] and misunderst[ood]" the organization. "The problem," as William Clark, the Bank's public relations chief, framed it, "was that the South felt that the Bank was associated with the North and the North felt that the Bank was associated with the South."[1]

Bank officials agreed that the best way to deal with this problem was to have the organization reach out to officials in developing countries in order to demonstrate that the Bank was advancing their interests. To Burke Knapp, the organization's longtime head of operations, Southern demands were partially the result of the Bank having "not done enough to educate the makers of political choices" in the global South. Ernest Stern, who would soon take over from Knapp as the Bank's second most powerful official, took it a step farther. "The Bank's publications program was too much research-weighted," he complained, "designed to inform the world of the Bank's intellectual leadership rather than to appeal to policy makers." Husain concurred. Addressing widespread distrust "required a far broader dialogue with policymakers." Accordingly, the Bank should "adopt a more aggressive approach of educating" officials in developing countries. McNamara agreed. The Bank must, he concluded, "develop closer relations" with leaders in those nations, since only by "mak[ing] the Bank's wealth of information and expertise available to policymakers" could the organization ensure that its advice was heeded.[2]

The meeting reflected an important but subtle change within the Bank. In response to the challenges of the 1970s, McNamara had the organization place greater emphasis on its counseling and knowledge generation functions. When the rise of private lending in the wake of the oil crisis threatened to make Bank lending less important, McNamara directed the organization to provide advice for Western banks looking to invest in the developing world. In response to developing country demands for the NIEO, he had the Bank intensify its policy advising efforts. And to address critics of foreign aid, he had the organization play a more active role in propagating its views about development. While the Bank had relied on its nonfinancial functions in the past, by the late 1970s these roles had become as central to its work as its project financing.

From Bank to Consultant

The financial needs of oil-importing developing countries were the primary concern of both McNamara and the Bank for much of the 1970s. As we have seen, soon after the 1973–74 oil crisis, it became apparent that these countries would have trouble obtaining foreign exchange to afford oil imports and, as a result, their economic growth would slow. As a 1975 Bank study put it, "the external capital required to sustain modest growth targets is beyond the capacity of present financial institutions."[3] Inflation, itself partially a result of the oil crisis, exacerbated the situation. Although IBRD lending commitments increased 15 percent in nominal terms between the Bank's 1975 and 1976 fiscal years, in real terms this constituted an increase of just 9 percent, while the inflation-adjusted value of IDA commitments actually declined by 1 percent during this time.[4] Both IBRD and IDA lending declined slightly the following year, as well.[5] Preventing developing countries from slipping into recession, not eliminating world poverty, would become the Bank's main priority.

While the oil crisis presented a challenge to the Bank, it was an unprecedented opportunity for others. In the mid-1970s, many oil-exporting countries, unable to absorb their profits domestically, deposited large portions of their surpluses in Western banks. Increasingly interested in expanding their foreign operations, banks re-lent these "petrodollars" to developing nations, particularly in Latin America. As a result, private borrowing by developing countries grew significantly. The external debts of developing countries increased sixfold between 1972 and 1981, and by the early 1980s "the nine largest U.S. banks had committed the equivalent of 250 percent of their capital to loans to developing countries."[6]

Initially, McNamara was concerned about petrodollar recycling. In January 1974, he told the President's Council that while it was "likely . . . that the Eurodollar market would be flooded by dollars resulting from oil revenues and that creditworthy countries would be able to borrow in that market in the short term, if developing countries do so repayments will be very burdensome."[7] The Bank's primary objective, he said, should be to ensure that developing countries "receive as much aid as possible on favorable terms."[8] As he put it to U.S. officials a few years later, private lending "cannot be a substitute for Official Development Assistance from public sources [since] . . . creditworthiness limits the amount of capital that can be supplied by commercial banks . . . for the poorest nations."[9]

Nevertheless, as the limits on the Bank's ability to meet the financial needs of oil-importing developing countries became evident, McNamara began to embrace petrodollar recycling. If the Bank could not obtain intermediate OPEC surpluses itself, the organization could at least help steer private

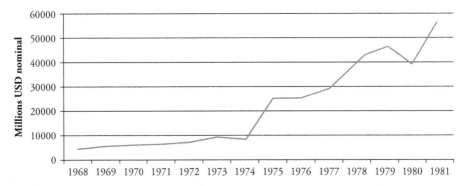

Figure 5. Private capital flows to developing countries, 1968–1981.
Source: Organization for Economic Cooperation and Development, Query Wizard for International Development Statistics.

funds to countries that needed them. In the summer of 1974, he asked Bank staff to determine how a "recycling mechanism of the banking system" could meet the requirements of oil-importing developing countries, and shortly thereafter he declared that one of the Bank's main goals should be to assist in the "orderly recycling of oil revenues."[10]

Given the lack of official responses to the oil crisis, McNamara's support for petrodollar recycling made sense. However, this development presented a significant challenge to the Bank. As private banks lent more funds to developing countries, the Bank's importance as a source of capital diminished. In 1970, private lenders committed about twice as much money to developing countries as the Bank. By the end of the decade, they were lending more than five times as much.[11] To Burke Knapp, the Bank's longtime head of operations, the implications for the Bank were "alarming"[12]

As a result, the Bank's nonfinancial functions began to assume greater importance.[13] To maintain relevance in developing countries, McNamara had the organization devote more attention to "technical assistance" efforts, which focused on helping officials form investment programs and oversee development projects. McNamara had expanded the Bank's work in this area before the onset of petrodollar recycling.[14] As early as 1972, the Bank recognized that its "financial resources are less significant than the position it holds on the international development scene and its still rising capability for helping each individual member confront its own dilemmas in light of experience acquired by others."[15] Following the oil crisis, the Bank began to devote even more attention to technical assistance, particularly for countries that no longer relied on its capital.[16] For instance, the Bank provided the Iranian government, which became a net lender to the Bank after the oil crisis, assistance for "institution-building" and "administrative and financial improvement" projects.[17] It entered into an agreement with Saudi Arabia to train officials in project analysis and to help the government draft a national employment policy.[18] And shortly thereafter, the Bank initiated administrative training programs in Kuwait, Algeria and Libya.[19] The Bank's technical assistance operations were not limited to OPEC members. In 1974, it issued its first stand-alone IBRD loans for preinvestment studies to Chile, Colombia, and Oman, and the following year it established a Project Preparation Facility (PPF) to coordinate its burgeoning technical assistance activities.[20] Many Bank projects also came to include distinct advisory services during this time.[21]

At the same time, McNamara forged ties with private financial institutions. The Bank had long sought to magnify its impact by financing projects with other lenders, and by the early 1970s the organization was making around thirty cofinanced loans per year.[22] As with its technical assistance efforts, the Bank stepped up this activity in the mid-1970s. In 1975, it announced that it was initiating "a specific program that has, as its aim, the participation of the private sector in its operations," and over the next five years the organization financed projects with 148 private banks. By the end of the decade, the Bank was describing private cofinancing as a "regular feature" of its work.[23]

Cofinancing exemplified the Bank's unique role in financial globalization. During the 1970s, the Bank served a "matchmaker" that both helped Western banks expand their foreign operations and assisted developing countries in expanding their private borrowings.[24] The organization described its role as helping developing countries determine "the identity of those commercial banks that may be interested" in lending.[25] For private financial institutions, the Bank filled a critical role in locating investment opportunities and assessing a country's creditworthiness.[26] McNamara even allowed banks access to the organization's country and project reports as a means to facilitate cofinancing.[27]And private banks, in the words of Bank staff, "seemed to look at the World Bank's presence [in developing countries] as a sign of confidence."[28] As one Brazilian journalist noted, "the World Bank's lending helps us greatly to raise money from other sources [since it] . . . increases international confidence in our economy."[29]

Table 2. World Bank Co-Financing Operations, 1973–1980 (millions USD nominal)

			Sources of co-financing							
	Projects with co-financing		Official		Export credit		Private		World Bank contribution		Total project cost
Year	No.	Value	No.	Value	No.	Value	No.	Value	Bank	IDA	
1973	37	496.2	30	313.0	10	183.2	0	0.0	478.9	308.0	2813.1
1974	48	1463.0	44	788.8	11	589.5	2	84.7	1092.6	184.3	5446.0
1975	53	1940.3	48	923.3	10	962.0	1	55.0	1033.6	346.1	8817.4
1976	73	2255.1	61	1079.7	16	902.9	5	272.5	1583.3	403.1	9620.3
1977	81	2289.1	72	1547.9	9	191.3	9	549.9	1866.2	698.0	9916.5
1978	87	2426.4	77	1757.2	15	539.3	7	129.9	1827.5	798.8	11730.0
1979	109	3149.4	88	1976.3	16	659.2	13	513.9	2993.3	1146.2	14004.8
1980	93	6516.3	68	2458.6	23	2282.3	21	1775.4	3129.9	1605.2	21535.5

Source: World Bank, *Review of World Bank Co-Financing*, 17.

By the late 1970s, most observers had concluded that the Bank's primary importance lay not in its lending but, instead, in its consultative functions. For instance, Yugoslavian authorities informed senior Bank officials that the Bank's "advice was more valued to them than the Bank's money," and in 1978 the Bank's West German director argued that the "value of the Bank's contribution in the developing countries is not so much a function of the individual project" but of the "nonfinancial role of the Bank, reflected in giving policy advice, helping to implement sound development strategies, and setting up viable institutions."[30]

Although most of McNamara's attention focused on carving out a role for the Bank in the aftermath of the oil crisis, he was also concerned with developing country calls for the NIEO. In 1976, for instance, he told his aides that he was alarmed that "no one anywhere seemed to have formulated a positive program for the North/South dialogue."[31] Part of his concern stemmed from the fact that developing countries criticized the Bank for ignoring their demands. There was a "hostile UN reaction (mainly from the G77) to the [Bank's] basic needs approach," William Clark, the Bank's head of public relations, told McNamara in January 1978. Many developing country leaders had come to see the Bank's focus on poverty alleviation as "a cop-out."[32] As McNamara put it, a consensus was building among developing countries that the World Bank "was the rich countries' substitute for the NIEO."[33]

As with his response to petrodollar recycling, McNamara addressed this situation by relying upon the Bank's nonfinancial functions. In order to overcome the "continuing impasse" in the NIEO, in 1977 he proposed that West German Chancellor Willy Brandt head an international commission to propose cooperative solutions to the North-South debate.[34] "There was no question that the intellectual foundation for handling the North/South problems was lacking," he told Bank management when describing the proposal.[35] The Brandt Report would help solve this by "creat[ing] a better understanding of the major development issues, in order to portray more clearly both to policymakers and to the general public the interaction of developed and developing economies, and the joint efforts needed to deal with economic development problems."[36] Meanwhile, the Bank initiated work on a series of annual reports that would, in McNamara's words, "build an integrated framework [for] development strategies."[37] As he told the Bank's Board, these reports would provide an "intellectual foundation for exploring particular development strategies at the general or sectoral level," create a "framework for the Bank's own strategy," and "facilitat[e] the dialogue on development strategy which we pursue with member government[s]."[38] This initiative resulted in the 1978 creation of the *World Development Report*, which over time became the Bank's flagship publication.[39] At the same time, Bank officials also sought to expand the organization's "policy and planning dialogue with countries" as a means to both channel Southern demands in less radical directions and maintain the Bank's relevance.[40]

Dealing with the United States

Although the Bank was able to utilize its nonfinancial resources to adapt to new economic and intellectual conditions, it struggled to maintain a constructive relationship with the U.S. government. As Congressional support for foreign aid waned in the mid-1970s, some U.S. officials saw McNamara's failure to respond to U.S. directives, such as the Nixon administration's call to cut off lending to India during the South Asia crisis, as evidence that the World Bank was operating against U.S. interests. These views were misguided. During the McNamara years, Bank loans tended to flow to U.S. allies, as well as former colonies of the organization's European members.[41] Moreover, the Bank continued to advance the expansion of capitalism in the developing world.[42] And even when the Bank acted independently, it often bolstered U.S. foreign policy efforts. The Bank's termination of lending to Chile in the early 1970s provides a prominent example of this dynamic.

When Chileans elected Salvador Allende president in September 1970, the Bank had three loans to the country "in the pipeline" (approved by the Board and waiting to be disbursed): loans of $1.5 million and $7 million for education projects and $10.8 million for road construction. Although Allende, a member of Chile's Socialist Party, had promised to increase the country's autonomy from Washington, McNamara did not view his election as a reason to hold up these loans. On November 16, two weeks after Allende was inaugurated, he told the head of the Bank's Latin American department to "proceed with the project work in Chile and not use the recent change in government as a reason to delay projects in the pipeline."[43]

The Nixon administration, by contrast, viewed Allende as a significant threat to U.S. interests in the region and tried to destabilize him by, in Nixon words, "mak[ing] the [Chilean] economy scream."[44] Part of this effort included cutting off Bank lending to Chile. In a set of strategy papers sent to Henry Kissinger in December, an Ad Hoc Interagency Working Group on Chile indicated that the United States was preparing to use its influence in the World Bank to isolate Allende. Specifically, the proposal called for the U.S. director of the Bank to raise "questions concerning areas where Chilean performance and policies may be most vulnerable with respect to future IBRD financing."[45]

Meanwhile, Allende began making good on many of his promises. He nationalized foreign-owned copper and banking companies, accelerated land reforms, and expanded public education and health programs. The speed with which these measures were undertaken disrupted the economy, however, and in 1971 the government sought to reschedule its external debt.[46] The Bank subsequently reassessed its position toward Allende. Citing concerns about the country's creditworthiness, management refused to bring a proposed $21 million agricultural loan to Chile to the Board for a vote.[47] McNamara justified this move by claiming that "in the absence of fundamental economic stability it is simply impossible for Bank funds to be used productively for the benefit of the Chilean people and with the reasonable probability of repayment."[48]

Although the extent of U.S. influence in securing this decision remains unclear, available evidence suggests that the Bank was primarily concerned about the possibility of Chile defaulting on its outstanding loans to the organization.[49] At the same time that Bank officials stopped preparation of new loans to Chile, they refused to negotiate with Chilean authorities over the country's repayment of debt to the Bank.[50] In opposing such a move, Bank officials argued that the organization's need to maintain its creditworthiness outweighed all other concerns. "There is no question that the adverse effects of rescheduling debt service payments due to the Bank would be pronounced," Burke Knapp, the organization's vice president of operations, informed McNamara. "If, contrary to our views, member governments should take the position that the [Bank] should participate in reschedulings, it would be essential for us to discuss with them what measures they would be prepared to take to restore the damage to the Bank's financial position and to its ability to borrow in the capital markets which would result from such action."[51]

Over the coming months Bank managers sought to convince Chilean officials to scale back their reforms. These efforts culminated in April 1972 when McNamara, who had travelled to Santiago to attend the third meeting of the United Nations Conference on Trade and Development, expressed to Allende his concerns about Chile's economic prospects, which Bank staff had come to consider "gloom[y]."[52]

Relations between the Bank and Chile continued to deteriorate. Because no new loans were forthcoming, in 1972 Chile stopped servicing its debts to the Bank.[53] Fearful of the damage that a default would do to the organization's credit rating, Bank management rethought its earlier opposition to rescheduling Chile's debt. In the summer of 1973 McNamara agreed to write off a large part of Chile's obligations and, in return for a promise that Chile would resume payments on the remainder of its debt to the Bank, made preparations to issue two new loans to the country.[54] These moves came despite U.S. objections. As McNamara told his aides that July, the United States had "been against this . . . new form of cooperation with Chile . . . and was lobbying for support to oppose it."[55] In other words, by threatening to default on its debt to the Bank, the Allende government had effectively played off the Bank's desire for institutional survival. Thus, while Bank officials described the settlement as having come "at some cost to the Bank," they felt that Allende's actions left them no choice but to go forward with the new loans.[56] Before the proposal had a chance to go to the Board for approval, Allende was deposed in a U.S.-backed coup. Bank officials dropped the rescheduling plan and resumed lending to Chile, now under the dictatorship of Augusto Pinochet.[57]

In addition to demonstrating the ways internal factors rather than out-side pressures tended to inform Bank decision-making, the Chilean case highlighted the limits of the organization's development approach. In Allende's Chile, the Bank missed an opportunity to work a government that was committed to reducing poverty. As Mahbub ul Haq explained in an internal Bank memorandum in 1976:

> We failed to support the basic objectives of the Allende regime, either in our reports or publicly. If we had done that, we could have been freer to make the legitimate point that "economic" costs of these objectives were unnecessarily high and could be reduced by proper economic management. We could have gone further and shown what set of economic policies would have been consistent with these objectives. Instead we mumbled about exchange rates, fiscal balance and price distortions without ever trying to establish a link between our theology and Allende's concerns.[58]

The Bank's withdrawal of support from Allende did little to stem American opposition to the organization. At first, the 1976 elections seemed to bring welcome news in terms of the Bank-U.S. relationship. Otto Passman, the Bank's main congressional critic, lost his seat in the House of Representatives, and Jimmy Carter, who had called for increasing U.S. foreign assistance levels on the campaign trail, defeated Gerald Ford for the presidency. McNamara looked forward to a new era in Bank-U.S. relations. One former Bank staffer remembers the former Kennedy and Johnson official boasting that, with a Democratic administration in the White House, he would be able to get what he wanted "by clicking his fingers."[59]

But McNamara underestimated the depth of congressional hostility to foreign aid, generally, and to the Bank, specifically. After Passman, the chairmanship of the House Foreign Operations Subcommittee passed to Maryland Democrat Clarence Long. Although more liberal than his predecessor, Long was also a foreign aid critic who used his position to secure regular reductions in U.S. multilateral aid commitments[60] Long and other congressional critics were not only concerned that aid was ineffective but also that too much of it was going toward administrative overhead, including salaries for Bank staff. In 1977, Congress called on President Carter to withhold funds from the Bank if management denied the U.S. director access to information on employee compensation.[61]

Figure 6. At the 1972 meetings of the United Nations Conference on Trade and
Development in Santiago, Chile. In public, McNamara called on governments to
improve conditions for the "bottom 40 percent" in the developing world. In private,
he pressured Chilean President Salvador Allende to scale back his socialist reforms.
Courtesy of the World Bank Group Archives.

McNamara's objections that the Bank's operating budget came from
the interest payments on its loans—meaning that the citizens of developing
countries, not U.S. taxpayers, paid the Bank's staff—fell on deaf ears.[62] In
1978, he vetoed a salary increase for Bank staff.[63] Not surprisingly, this upset
many in the Bank. Morale following the decision was "very bad," a Bank official told McNamara; some staff even felt that members of Congress might
have had a "personal vendetta" against McNamara because of his role in the
Vietnam War.[64]

Indeed, by the late 1970s many in the Bank had come to believe that Congress was "determined to dominate or destroy" the organization.[65] Congressional refusals to fill the Carter administration's funding requests for the
Bank and other multilateral development banks demonstrated an unprecedented depth of opposition to foreign aid, and there was "a general bewilder-

ment" within the Bank about whether the U.S. government supported the organization.[66]

Some of the confusion was because U.S. opposition to the Bank often concerned issues that many considered unimportant, such as demands from members of Congress that the Bank refrain from funding projects that would compete with American producers.[67] At times, however, U.S. resistance to the Bank centered on subjects that raised fundamental questions about international development, as when Congress tried to prevent the organization from lending to governments that denied their citizens human rights.

McNamara and the Bank would have been able to ignore the emergence of the human rights movement had some American officials not sought to make human rights a part of U.S. foreign policy. Instead, as part of the congressional revolt that followed the Watergate scandal and the winding down of the Vietnam War, the left wing of the Democratic Party sought to reassert a commitment to a more humane foreign policy by adopting the language of human rights. At the direction of Minnesota congressman Donald Fraser, in 1973 the House Subcommittee on International Organizations and Movements began to highlight human rights issues, and following the Chilean coup he and others began to argue that the U.S. government needed to incorporate human rights concerns into U.S. foreign policy.[68]

Part of this effort centered on linking foreign aid to human rights. Concerned that U.S. dollars were being used to prop up abusive regimes in the developing world, in 1974 Congress mandated that no aid funds be given to governments that violated human rights.[69] The following year, Congress sought to prevent multilateral institutions that received U.S. funding from aiding abusive regimes.[70] In 1977, Congress slashed appropriations for the IDB because of its lending to the military dictatorship in Argentina. And that fall the U.S. House of Representatives rejected a Bank funding bill on the grounds that the organization was lending to governments that denied their people basic human rights.[71]

McNamara strongly opposed these efforts. Over the previous years, the Bank had lent to a range of abusive governments, and he was concerned that conditioning U.S. funding of the Bank on human rights grounds might jeopardize the organization's independence and growth. Human rights presented "a very difficult problem," he informed his aides, "since no clear guidelines of a program or political action had been worked out by the United States to support its strong philosophical position."[72] In order to overcome U.S. opposition,

McNamara argued that the Bank needed to insist that its mandate limited it to addressing "economic rights . . . such as ability to live [and] improvements in life expectancy" rather than "civil rights," such as freedom of the press and the right to a fair trial.[73] "The most basic of human rights is the right to minimal levels of nutrition, health, and education," he told the press in 1978. "With respect to those human rights, there is no institution in the world that is more sensitive to them, or doing more to advance them, than this institution."[74]

McNamara did not have to worry for long. When members of Congress attempted to insert a clause in an appropriations bill mandating that the U.S. representative to the Bank vote against loans to abusive governments, lobbying by the Carter administration, which was sympathetic to human rights concerns but opposed blanket bans, resulted in a watering down of the restrictive language.[75] During this time, the Bank's other members also indicated their opposition to tying Bank lending to human rights.[76] Thus, while the Carter administration ended up instructing the U.S. director to the Bank to oppose loans on human rights grounds, this rarely failed to prevent the Board from approving them.

Other U.S. efforts to influence the Bank's behavior were similarly unsuccessful.[77] For example, despite the fact that the U.S. director, under orders from Congress, voted against every loan to India between 1974 and 1977 because the country had not signed the 1968 Nuclear Non-Proliferation Treaty, the Board approved all loans to India on which it voted during these years.[78] In some respects, such efforts reduced U.S. power in the Bank. As one contemporary observer explained, "because it was known that the United States had to vote against those credits [nobody] really listens to what the U.S. representative says."[79]

U.S. power also declined due to its reduced role in funding the Bank. As we have seen, McNamara sought to diversify the Bank's borrowings. As a result, American holdings of Bank bonds fell from 42 percent in 1969 to 17 percent in 1981.[80] Contributions from the U.S. government to the Bank also declined in the McNamara era. Whereas the United States provided 32 percent of the Bank's capital subscriptions in 1968, in 1981 this figure stood at 23 percent, which reduced U.S. voting power on the Board.[81] Meanwhile, McNamara solidified his personal control in the Bank. In 1977, he received unanimous backing for a nearly unprecedented third term as president. As U.S. treasury secretary Michael Blumenthal wrote in a memorandum to President Carter recommending that he reappoint McNamara, "the

Table 3. U.S. Voting Table: "No" Votes and Abstentions on World Bank Loans, 1945–1980

Date	Country	Project	Millions USD (nominal)	Reason
7/75	Honduras	Port facilities	3.0	Cost effectiveness
12/75	Algeria	Cement factory	46.0	Cost effectiveness
3/76	Afghanistan	Agriculture	10.0 (IDA)	Cost effectiveness
3/76	Benin	Roads	9.0 (IDA)	Cost effectiveness
3/76	Cameroon	Roads	15.0 (IDA)	Cost effectiveness
6/79	Ecuador	Private industry	50.5 (IFC)	Cost effectiveness
12/74	Nigeria	Agriculture	21.0	No need for funds
12/74	Nigeria	Agriculture	21.0	No need for funds
12/74	Nigeria	Agriculture	19.0	No need for funds
12/74	Nigeria	Agriculture	29.0	No need for funds
12/74	Nigeria	Agriculture	17.5	No need for funds
3/72	India	Oil tankers	83.0 (IDA)	Inappropriate use of funds
4/72	Tunisia	Electric power	12.0	Protecting U.S. producers
6/73	Zambia	Tobacco	11.5	Protecting U.S. producers
9/76	Tanzania	Tobacco	8.0 (IDA)	Protecting U.S. producers
11/77	Swaziland	Sugar	8.4 (IFC)	Protecting U.S. producers
2/78	Malaysia	Palm oil	26.0	Protecting U.S. producers
6/71	Guyana	Sea dikes	5.4	Expropriations
6/72	Iraq	Education	12.9	Expropriations
1/73	Iraq	Irrigation	40.0	Expropriations
5/73	Syria	Water supply	15.0 (IDA)	Expropriations
11/73	Peru	Education	24.0	Expropriations
12/76	Congo	Education	8.0	Expropriations
12/77	Laos	Agriculture	8.2 (IDA)	Forestall congressional earmarking
8/78	Vietnam	Irrigation	60.0 (IDA)	Forestall congressional earmarking
1974–77	India	26 IDA credits	—	Nuclear nonproliferation
1977–79	Afghanistan	3 IDA credits	—	Human rights
1977–79	Argentina	12 IBRD, IDA, IFC	—	Human rights
1977–80	Benin	2 IDA credits	—	Human rights
1977–80	Chile	2 IBRD loans	—	Human rights
1977–79	El Salvador	1 IBRD loan	—	Human rights
1977–79	Ethiopia	3 IDA credits	—	Human rights
1977–80	Guatemala	1 IBRD loans	—	Human rights
1977–80	Korea	1 IFC loan	—	Human rights
1977–79	Laos	3 IDA credits	—	Human rights
1977–80	Paraguay	3 IBRD loans	—	Human rights
1977–80	Philippines	4 IBRD, IFC	—	Human rights
1977–80	Uruguay	7 IBRD, IFC	—	Human rights
1977–80	Vietnam	1 IDA credit	—	Human rights
1977–80	Yemen	7 IDA credits	—	Human rights

Sources: Lars Schoultz, "Politics, Economics, and U.S. Participation in Multilateral Development Banks," *International Organization* 36, 3 (Summer 1982): 549–50; Brian Crowe, "MDB Loans to Selected Countries since January 1977," October 7, 1980, RG 56, Office of the Deputy Assistant Secretary for Developing Nations, Office of International Development Banks, Subject Files, 1980–1981, Box 5, U.S. National Archives and Records Administration.

negative factor of McNamara's association with the Vietnam War has been largely neutralized in these last ten years through his vigorous activities on behalf of poor people in the developing countries."[82]

Nevertheless, McNamara's desire to further increase Bank lending obliged him to continue to seek U.S. support. Aware that he could not take U.S. funding for granted, he spent considerable time defending the Bank from criticism, expanding its public relations efforts, and lobbying U.S. officials.[83] As one of his associates remarked at the time, McNamara was "unnaturally hemmed in by his fear of losing U.S. support and with it the necessary replenishments of capital."[84]

It would be over World Bank involvement in Vietnam, of all places, that this became clear. In 1976, the Vietnamese government requested development assistance from the Bank. McNamara thereafter dispatched staff to scout out lending prospects, and in 1978 the organization made its first loan to the country.[85] Other Americans could not put the ghosts of Vietnam behind them as easily as McNamara. In 1979, Republican congressmen Bill Young of Florida succeeded in attaching an amendment to a Bank funding bill which prohibited the organization from continuing to lend to Vietnam and other communist countries.[86] Young's amendment represented a significant problem for the Bank. IDA's charter prevented it from accepting conditional contributions, which meant that the Bank would have to reject the funds.[87] To McNamara, the situation demonstrated that "the Bank might in the near future face a serious tradeoff between independence and growth."[88] McNamara sought to prevent the amendment from being included in the final appropriations bill by privately assuring members of Congress that the Bank would not make any new loans to Vietnam.[89] He would justify the cutoff by arguing that the Vietnamese government was not following a "rational development policy."[90] With McNamara's promise in hand, Young withdrew his amendment and Congress approved a clean IDA funding bill.[91] Vietnam did not receive another Bank loan until 1993.

Responding to Critics

If McNamara's actions contributed to a growing sense that the Bank was a tool of U.S. foreign policy, the various critiques of development that emerged in the 1970s had little impact on the organization. In rare cases, the Bank sought to suppress its most vocal opponents. In one instance, Bank officials tried to force Teresa Hayter's publisher to remove sections of her critical study on the Bank's efforts to influence borrower policies.[92] More regularly, McNamara sought to pacify critics by highlighting the organization's antipoverty lending.[93]

McNamara also paid lip service to the environmental aspects of development. In 1970, he announced that the Bank would seek to ensure that environmental criteria factored into its lending decisions. Shortly thereafter, he recruited an environmental adviser to oversee this work. The following year, he directed staff to consider environmental impacts when preparing and appraising projects.[94] McNamara also spoke about the importance of environmentally friendly development strategies. In 1972, he bemoaned the "monstrous assault on the quality of life" that resulted from uncontrolled industrialization, called for more research on the environmental consequences of development projects, and urged wealthy nations to help poor countries adopt policies that would "yield a combination of high economic gain with low environmental risk." McNamara insisted that reducing poverty, which he labeled "the most dangerous pollutant," could be achieved without sacrificing the environment.[95]

Yet—perhaps because McNamara was unwilling to acknowledge such tradeoffs—the Bank neglected to incorporate environmental concerns into its work. Local efforts to scuttle Bank projects on environmental grounds, such as the campaign against the Chico Dam project, were rarely successful. More commonly, environmentalists took issue with the organization for failing to conduct "adequate impact assessments" of its projects, a fair critique given that McNamara's commitment to the environment was more rhetorical than substantive.[96] Under his watch, the environmental department was significantly under-resourced. Moreover, his conception of environmental issues was limited. For instance, the first task that he gave the Bank's environmental advisor was to respond to complaints that an energy project in Tanzania might spoil the view at a nearby game park.[97] On an organization-wide level, Bank staff lacked the requisite expertise to assess the environmental impacts of projects and were given little time to learn about such issues.[98] And even when they flagged a problem, pressure to lend tended to override environmental concerns. In one case, when a junior staff member obtained photographic evidence showing that a Bank-financed land settlement project in Malaysia had failed to meet an environmental requirement, his supervisor ordered him to drop the issue because "the loan is disbursing well."[99]

Similar dynamics characterized the Bank's response to gender-based critiques of development. The organization initially addressed such issues in 1975, when it participated in the First World Conference on the Status of Women in Mexico City.[100] Following the conference, McNamara created a Women in Development Office to address the gender implications of the Bank's work and hired Gloria Scott, a Jamaican economist, as its head. Over the coming years, Scott was instrumental in placing women in development issues onto the Bank's agenda.[101] According to one former Bank staffer, she "helped to sensitize the Bank staff" to gender concerns, particularly the importance of ensuring that projects did not bypass women.[102]

Despite these efforts, the Bank took minimal steps to incorporate gender concerns into its work during the McNamara years. Most gender-related research focused on reducing birth rates, which led critics to note the organization's "reluctance to value gender equity as a goal in itself."[103] Like the Bank's new environmental unit, Scott's office lacked sufficient resources to ensure that gender factored into lending decisions. The Women in Development Office also lacked the power to hold up projects that might bypass or negatively affect women.[104]

The Bank's response to conservative critiques of development orthodoxy was an exception to its tendency to sidestep its detractors. Although for much of the decade Bank policy and research documents reflected an emphasis on the importance of both the public and private sectors, by the late 1970s the Bank had begun to more openly advocate for economic liberalization.[105] This shift was especially pronounced in the Bank's trade policy recommendations. Whereas in the early 1970s the Bank sometimes encouraged government protection of domestic manufacturers, country reports in the late 1970s emphasized the need to eliminate all forms of protectionism. Thus, a 1979 Bank study noted that, while staff had long taken "benevolent attitudes toward import-substitution policies . . . they were now advocating vigorously for fairly neutral incentive systems combined with reasonably liberalized trade regimes."[106]

Accelerated Development in Sub-Saharan Africa: An Agenda for Action, a Bank study commissioned at the request of African finance ministers in the fall of 1979, exemplified this shift.[107] Nicknamed the Berg Report after its chief author, Bank economist Elliot Berg, it described the economic crisis then facing nations on the continent. In many countries, growth was decelerating, balance of payment deficits increasing, and agricultural sectors stagnating.[108] The Berg Report identified long and short-term causes of these problems, from the legacy of colonialism to declines in global commodity prices, but it found that the most important factors were "domestic policy inadequacies," such as overvalued exchange rates, protectionist trade policies, and bloated public sectors. In order to address Africa's economic problems, the Berg Report thus called for various policy changes, including the privatization of state-owned enterprises and the lifting of price controls. The Report also advocated an increased role for external actors in facilitating these policy changes.[109] Specifically, it argued that organizations like the Bank could, through policy advice and financial incentives, help African countries create a "suitable policy framework" for growth.[110] Although the Bank had sounded many of these themes before, many inside the organization found the wholesale rejection of state-led development strategies "revolutionary."[111] Whereas the Bank had long been willing to sanction a significant role for the public sector in the development process, it now viewed government intervention as detrimental.[112]

The Bank's ideological shift reflected the revival of neoclassical approaches in the economics profession during the 1970s and benefitted from the advocacy of individuals in the organization. During the 1970s, a handful of economists who held negative views on the role of the state in development gained prominence in the Bank. Foremost among these was the Hungarian-born economist Bela Balassa, who as a consultant to the Bank refined his scholarship on the negative effects of protectionism on growth.[113] Deepak Lal, an Indian-born economist, also advocated a greater role for the private sector in development while at the Bank in the late 1970s.[114]

Such views resonated because they provided a ready explanation for the development failures of the 1970s. By the end of the decade, many in the Bank had concluded that prevailing development approaches, including the organization's much-heralded antipoverty projects, had not achieved their intended results. There was also broader discontent with specific countries' growth strategies. For instance, in the late 1970s, McNamara reassessed his previous optimism about Tanzanian President Julius Nyerere's socialist economic policies when confronted with data showing that the country's economy was in shambles.[115] Bank staff and management also began to attribute failure of the organization's projects to borrowers' economic policies. "We had problem after problem after problem," a World Banker who worked in East Africa remembers. "A lot of them were governance issues, and what we came to appreciate is that nothing can work in an adverse policy and political environment."[116]

The Bank's embrace of a more conservative development vision, like its growing emphasis on its advising functions, marked a critical moment in the organization's history. Although the Bank had long stressed the importance of the private sector, and while it had often utilized its nonfinancial functions, the challenges of the 1970s forced the Bank to change its basic approach. If the quintessential Bank activity of the 1950s and 1960s was funding large infrastructure projects, by the late 1970s the organization's policy advising and knowledge generation functions had become central to its work.

CHAPTER 6

Fighting Poverty

The scale and pace of change within the World Bank during Robert Mc-Namara's presidency begs the question: how successful was the organization in promoting development? The scope of the organization's operations, not to mention the inherent difficulty in evaluating the effectiveness of development interventions, makes it impossible to answer this question completely.[1] In McNamara's thirteen years as president, the Bank made over 2,500 loans for projects ranging from the construction of dams to the development of tourist industries. The organization also undertook many nonlending activities, from managing international research centers to coordinating consortia of aid donors. The dearth of contemporary analyses of Bank operations, as well as the inaccessibility of much of the organization's reporting on its activities, makes reaching conclusions about the Bank's record even more difficult.[2]

Nevertheless, available evidence indicates that the Bank's record during the McNamara years was poor. The organization failed to achieve basic objectives in its three main areas: lending for specific projects, advising developing countries on policy matters, and attending to global economic affairs. With respect to the first function, Bank-financed projects were beset by delays and cost overruns, and anticipated rates of return largely failed to materialize. More problematically, during this period the Bank funded a number of coercive interventions, including projects that involved forcibly removing people from their homes. In its role as a policy advisor, the Bank struggled to influence many borrowing governments, particularly those that became less dependent on its capital as the 1970s progressed. The Bank's efforts to help manage the global economy also left much to be desired, as the organization proved unwilling and unable to redress mounting imbalances in the global financial system as a debt crisis became imminent in the late 1970s.

Of course, not all these problems were entirely, or even primarily, the Bank's fault. Many projects failed because borrowing governments did not implement them properly. Moreover, it would be strange if failure did not accompany the Bank's entry into new types of lending. Nor was McNamara directly implicated in all of the Bank's work. He did not supervise projects and could not singlehandedly prevent governments from borrowing beyond their means. Besides, many of these issues—including the funding of projects that had destructive human and environmental consequences—existed both before and after McNamara's presidency. Yet it would be wrong to let McNamara entirely off the hook. The strategic and organizational changes he initiated contributed to many of these failures. Specifically, in prioritizing the Bank's institutional growth, he diverted attention from ensuring that the quality of the organization's lending remained high and that borrowing governments had the capacity to absorb more loans.

Project Lending

As we have seen, the Bank's financing operations expanded both quantitatively and qualitatively under McNamara. The organization lent more money to more countries and for more types of projects than ever before.

Rural development was the centerpiece of the Bank's expanded lending program. McNamara considered smallholder agriculture a key to reducing poverty in the developing world. In his 1973 Nairobi address, he declared that there was "no viable alternative to increasing the productivity of small-scale agriculture if any significant advance is to be made in solving the problems of absolute poverty" and argued that "without rapid progress in smallholder agriculture throughout the developing world there is little hope of achieving long-term stable economic growth."[3] McNamara also feared that failure to share the gains from the Green Revolution would lead to violence.[4] To address these problems, he oversaw a tremendous expansion of the Bank's rural development program. Whereas before his arrival the organization limited its agricultural lending to constructing irrigation works and providing modern equipment to commercial farmers, under McNamara the Bank began to fund the installation of small wells, livestock development, and countrywide rural development programs.

Central to the Bank's rural development efforts were integrated rural development (IRD) projects, which sought to deliver "packages" of inputs to groups of small farmers in developing countries. The Bank extended credit to purchase modern seed, fertilizer, and equipment, constructed feeder roads to connect participating farms to market, established schools and clinics, and provided agricultural training,[5] believing that such comprehensive interventions would greatly increase the productivity and incomes of target groups. The Bank expected one IRD project for cotton farmers in Brazil, for instance, to double yields within six years, while those in Colombia and the Philippines could raise the annual incomes of participating farmers by as much as 400 percent.[6]

Nevertheless, the Bank's rural development projects encountered a host of problems. The organization's PIDER project in Mexico, one of the largest Bank projects in the McNamara era, illustrated many of these issues. In 1972, Mexican president Luis Echeverría established the Programa de Inversiones para el Desarrollo Rural (Program for Rural Development Investments, PIDER) to coordinate the country's rural development efforts and deliver services to small farmers in some of the poorest parts of the country.[7] The following year, the government of Mexico sought Bank funding to assist with these efforts. As a condition for its support, Bank officials had Mexican authorities modify the program to place more emphasis on investments in agricultural production, rather than the provision of social services.[8] Having secured this agreement, in 1975 the Bank made the first of three loans to the Mexican government. The organization's initial $110 million was intended to cover roughly 40 percent of the expenses in 30 of the 45 targeted regions, with most of the funds going toward credit, irrigation, livestock development, fruit production and soil and water conservation. The loan would also provide for the construction of feeder roads, farmer training, and an extension of electricity to participating locales.[9] The Bank expected that as a result of its efforts, the annual incomes of 750,000 people would double over eight years, unemployment would decrease, and, though not the main focus, literacy and health would improve.[10]

Difficulties immediately beset PIDER. Local agencies focused on delivering social services struggled to meet the Bank's requirement that investments be geared toward increasing agricultural production. In addition, Bank and Mexican officials failed to implement delivery and oversight mechanisms to guarantee that farm inputs reached intended beneficiaries.[11] As a result, an analyst who surveyed the project in the late 1970s found that a "large majority" of the targeted population had "received relatively few benefits."[12] Fewer than half the irrigation units functioned properly, and in some places 95 percent of targeted families failed to benefit from the project.[13]

Similar issues plagued the Bank's other rural development projects. A few months before the Bank made its initial commitment to PIDER, it lent $50 million to the Mexican government to fund the construction of "small irrigation works, support services for rainfed agriculture, marketing facilities, feeder roads, potable water, sewerage, electricity, primary schools, health facilities and community centers" in the Papaloapan River valley in the eastern part of the country.[14] One of the Bank's first IRD projects, the Papaloapan project was intended "to expand food production, raise incomes and improve the quality of life of about one million people" in the region.[15] As with PIDER, problems plagued the project. Bank evaluation reports noted that "insufficient budgetary allocations, limited capacity within the [local executing agency and] . . . lack and poor performance of contractors in the remote project area" prevented the project from producing expected results.[16] Half the original components had to be dropped, construction was completed three years behind schedule, and the Bank ended up canceling 48 percent of the loan. The organization concluded in a subsequent evaluation that "the integrated approach proved impossible on such a large project area."[17]

In Mexico and elsewhere, the Bank's difficulty supervising rural development projects led to corruption and the diversion of resources away from intended beneficiaries. In Bangladesh, a large landowner was able to convince local authorities to construct a Bank-financed well on his land, rather than in the village where it was supposed to be located. The company in charge of supplying parts for the project also inflated the prices that it charged the Bank.[18] The organization's Upper Region Agricultural Development Project in Ghana also saw a significant deflection of benefits. The project's objectives demonstrate the ambition of the Bank's rural development approach. The Bank intended its $21 million loan, agreed to in 1976 and supplemented with funds from the governments of Ghana, the UK, and the Netherlands, to provide for, among other things, establishment of 90 service centers to provide credit, training, seeds, and fertilizers to small farmers, construction and improvement of 120 small dams and 100 existing dams, construction of 700 village wells, and creation of an adult literacy program.[19] Yet rhetoric outpaced reality. The local agency charged with overseeing the project proved unprepared for this task, and two years after ground was broken, few of the support centers were up and running, with much of the material smuggled out of the country.[20]

Because they had to work through governments, Bank officials felt help-less, meekly noting that the situation was "quite depressing and discourag-ing."[21] However, an independent researcher who studied the project found that its main flaw was that the intended beneficiaries had no voice in the process.[22] Many small farmers did not know how to obtain the benefits, and as a result better-informed large landowners were able to shape the project to suit their interests. One smallholder managed to get this message across to a Ghanaian official who toured targeted areas in the summer of 1979. "A few years back," he said, "there was word that the World Bank was going to come and help poor farmers in this region."

> We were all happy and thought that at last somebody had heard our cries because as you know we have suffered for too long in this part of the country. . . . However, it has been some time now and we have not heard about them again. It appears, however, that in fact the World Bank people did come to Bolgatanga because we have been seeing many cars and white people and we are told it is World Bank people. This is what is worrying me because we have not received any help from them and in fact these days things are getting very hard for us poor people.[23]

The Bank also proved unable and unwilling to recognize the importance to its work of ethnic divisions in developing countries. The organization's Mutara Agricultural Development Project in Rwanda provides one example. Begun in 1974, the Bank intended the project to improve the lives of approx-imately 10,000 poor farmers in the highland regions in the northern part of the country by resettling them on government-supervised farms, "paysan-nants," where they would receive small plots of land, modern agricultural technologies, and training.[24] An audit conducted just a few years after the Bank disbursed the loan, however, found that the funds were put to a much different use. Local officials spent most of the money on construction of the implementing agency's headquarters. They canceled social services and irrigation components. And many of the land titles ended up in the hands of wealthy individuals who lived in other parts of the country.[25] To René Lemarchand, a consultant hired by the Bank in 1978 to appraise a follow-up loan, the reason was clear. The Hutu-dominated government had no interest in helping the mostly Tutsi farmers who were supposed to benefit from the project; instead, Bank resources helped the Hutus consolidate power.[26] Yet rather than reassess its role, the Bank censored Lemarchand's report and in 1979 sunk another $8.8 million into the project.[27] Not surprisingly, the project continued to fail. Bank evaluation reports later concluded "many pastoralists from the region had left for Uganda out of fear of the project and the intentions behind it."[28]

Indeed, the Bank's rural development projects sometimes forced peasants off their land. An independent investigation of the organization's work in Nigeria, for instance, concluded that the Bank failed to make adequate preparations for the thousands of people whose lands were flooded as the result of the construction of two dams. Even farmers who were able to maintain their holdings fared poorly. Unable to afford the inputs intended to help them increase production, many had to sell their land at reduced prices.[29] Likewise, a project to improve the productivity of small farmers in the São Francisco River valley in Brazil resulted in the relocation of many to smaller plots. In one instance the Bank gave so little thought to helping Filipino villagers displaced by new irrigation works that a staffer involved in the project admitted that "a whole municipality was going under water" as a result of the organization's negligence.[30]

Even more troubling were the Bank's land clearing and population relocation schemes. Between 1968 and 1978, the organization made seven loans totaling over $160 million to the Federal Land Development Authority (FELDA) in Malaysia for projects to move peasants to palm oil and rubber farms in recently cleared tropical rainforest in the central and southern parts of the country. On the surface, these initiatives appeared highly successful. Because most of the land previously lay fallow, agricultural productivity in the region had nowhere to go but up. Thus, the Bank later boasted that "FELDA is undoubtedly one of the most important and efficient settlement agencies in the world."[31] But the economic benefits of these projects came at a high price. According to American environmental writer Bruce Rich, the projects "ignored all provision for pollution control" and ended up eliminating about 6.5 percent of Malaysia's rainforest.[32] The Bank's Northwest Region Development Program (Polonoroeste) project in Brazil, prepared near the end of McNamara's tenure, also led to severe environmental damage. Begun in 1981, the project provided for construction of highways and roads in the region to serve its goal of attracting settlers for cultivation of coffee, cocoa, and other export crops. The scheme ended up causing more problems than it solved. Migrants overwhelmed the implementing agency, large parts of the forest burned, and thousands of indigenous people were displaced.[33]

The Indonesian transmigration project was one of the most harmful interventions in the McNamara era. In 1976, the Bank made the first of a series of loans to assist the Suharto regime's relocation of half a million families from Java to some of the country's less populated outer islands. Officials justified the project as a way both to relieve overcrowding on the country's main island and to increase productivity in less populated areas.[34] But the Bank should have been aware of the disastrous consequences this project would entail. Even before the organization made its loan, the Indonesian government had been forcibly removing native populations on the islands to make way for Javanese settlers. The Bank ignored concerns about the coercive nature of the project and made the loan, which like many projects was later found to have suffered from poorly run implementing agencies and lack of environmental monitoring.[35] McNamara's support for the project in the face of its many problems eventually became a source of "bitterness" for some members of the Bank's staff.[36]

If the Bank's population relocation schemes demonstrated the extent of the organization's hubris under McNamara, more common problems related to its inability to ensure that projects were carried out properly. As much as the Bank grew under McNamara, over 90 percent of staff resided in Washington, meaning that borrowing governments implemented most parts of each project. Since the Bank's rural development initiatives usually included numerous components, they involved a number of local agencies with little history of working together, and this led to complaints that countries lacked the administrative capacity to implement projects.[37] One Bank staffer told a journalist in 1977 that theories about development "broke down" when put into practice. "We've over-committed," another remarked. "It's more difficult than we thought."[38]

Even some of the Bank's seemingly straightforward interventions ran into obstacles. As noted above, a central component of the rural development program was providing small farmers with instruction in modern agricultural techniques. Many of these efforts took the form of a "training and visit" system (T&V), developed in the early 1970s by Bank staffer Daniel Benor. T&V involved instruction of farmers by experts from Bank-supported national agricultural research institutions. Every two weeks field agents from central agencies would travel to villages to train a handful of "contact farmers," who would then disseminate this knowledge to others in the area.[39]

India, which borrowed $200 million from the Bank for T&V projects be-
tween 1977 and 1982, was the largest recipient of T&V funds. Despite this
substantial commitment, however, observers noted that T&V was a total
failure. Few people showed up to the training sessions, and those who did
were not aware that they were supposed to pass their knowledge on to others.
Indian officials ended up devoting more resources to constructing their
headquarters than supporting staff, and the quality of instruction was poor.[40]
Indian critics came to refer to T&V as "talk and vanish."[41]

Like many Bank interventions, T&V projects were self-perpetuating, as
officials viewed the "failure" of farmers to participate as a reason to enlarge
the program. Thus, while the Bank intended T&V projects to be an inexpensive means of training small farmers, they ended up costing significant
money, much of which was paid by developing countries. As one observer at
the time noted, "the introduction of T&V has committed the Indian taxpayer to considerably enhanced recurrent expenditure on agricultural extension once the World Bank disappears from the scene."[42] While much of the
blame rested with Indian officials who were more interested in securing
benefits for themselves than the intended beneficiaries, the Bank was also at
fault. In order to maintain an appearance that the projects were a success,
the organization suppressed critiques of the program. The Bank "preached
T&V like a religion," one researcher found. "No questioning of the concept
was permitted."[43]

Problems also plagued the Bank's agricultural extension efforts in Peru.
In 1980, the organization initiated a T&V project in the northeast of the
country to help rehabilitate local agriculture, which had suffered from ne-
glect at the hands of the country's military government. Soon after the program started, however, staff in Peru began to express frustration at their
"inability to carry out the training method effectively," a problem they attributed to "serious financial constraints, lack of relevant training, and poor
conditions of service."[44] To one observer, this led to "marginalization" of
peasants in the region. Unable to adapt their focus to meet the needs of small
farmers, T&V staff provided the bulk of their assistance to large farmers.[45]
Indeed, the Bank itself later admitted that its agricultural extension efforts
in Peru and elsewhere suffered from a "top-downward approach to farmers'
needs, meaning that [small] farmers have been left out of the decision-
making process."[46]

Although it would take some time for the full extent of the Bank's rural
development failures to come into focus, it was clear by the end of the 1970s

that the organization's antipoverty projects had generally failed to meet their goals. In 1978, the Bank reviewed nine of its initial "new style" rural development projects (defined as those in which over 50 percent of the intended beneficiaries were low-income groups) and found that three were "total failures" that had to be canceled before implementation, while in four others the majority of benefits had accrued to relatively well-off farmers.[47] McNamara himself admitted to the Bank's Board that "agricultural and rural development projects often did increase the skewedness of income distribution and that he did not know what to do about it."[48]

The Bank's rural initiatives were not a total failure. A number of projects led to significant productivity gains. According to one analyst, the organization's first IRD effort in Paraguay "resulted in production value-added of approximately 150 percent in real terms over the project life."[49] Some regions served by PIDER saw spectacular achievements as well. In the state of Guanajuato, for instance, a researcher concluded that "maize production on newly irrigated plots increased by 245 percent, bean production by 660 percent, and chile production by 1,850 percent."[50] The Bank estimated that a few of its rural development projects in Africa had raised agricultural production sevenfold, while a project for the development of Indian dairy farming was found to have increased the quantity of milk brought to market by almost 250 percent in the span of a few years.[51]

Yet these cases appear to have been exceptional. In 1989, the organization reviewed eighty-two agricultural projects approved between 1975 and 1982 and rated almost 45 percent as having achieved an "unsatisfactory" economic rate of return.[52] In over 40 percent of the irrigation projects that were analyzed, production "declined after the investment phase was completed," while in a significant number of cases the physical components of the project had proven "less durable than expected."[53] Although the Bank experienced particular difficulty in sub-Saharan Africa, where it estimated that "21 of 36 area development projects failed between 1974 and 1986," problems were found elsewhere as well.[54] In Latin America and the Caribbean, for instance, 89 percent of rural development projects implemented between 1973 and 1977 "had disbursement shortfalls of 10 percent or more."[55] And 30 percent of the Bank's agricultural and rural development projects implemented between 1980 and 1985, many of which were prepared during the latter stages of McNamara's tenure, either failed to come to fruition or achieved rates of return below 10 percent, compared with 17–25 percent of projects in other sectors.[56]

Bank officials attributed these failures to developing countries themselves. They blamed the low success of its initial IRD projects in Nigeria, for
instance, on government policies like agricultural price controls that dis-
criminated against the rural sector.[57] The Bank offered similar justifications
for the failure of its rural development efforts in Tanzania, ignoring its role
in supporting the failed collectivized farms, "ujamaa villages," by faulting
the government for paying insufficient attention to the role of private incentives in agricultural production.[58]

Yet the Bank was also to blame. Leaving aside the organization's support
for coercive initiatives such as the Indonesian transmigration program,
under McNamara the Bank regularly overestimated the capacity of local
agencies to implement what were often incredibly complex projects.[59] In addition, as with T&V in India and the Mutara project in Rwanda, the Bank
refused to correct course when presented with evidence of poor results.
Finally, the organization failed to use its power to try to overcome the problems that hamstrung its projects. This was particularly true with land reform.
The Bank now acknowledges that unequal tenure systems hindered many of
its rural development initiatives.[60] Yet under McNamara, the Bank repeatedly abandoned its commitments to encouraging its borrowers to adopt land
reforms and continued to direct funds to large commercial agriculture.[61] For
instance, at the same time that Bank management and staff expressed frustration at the slow pace of land reform and other distributional efforts in
Brazil, the organization was directing the bulk of its agriculture lending to
livestock development projects that benefited large landowners.[62]

In addition to rural development, McNamara expanded the Bank's urban
development program. Sites and services (SS) projects were the focus of many
of these efforts. Like IRD, SS were comprehensive interventions. The projects offered poor city dwellers the opportunity to purchase or rent housing
in residential developments that included basic utility and social services.
Bank staff also expected the construction of these developments to generate
short-term employment.[63] The Bank expected its SS to be a cost-effective alternative to the heavily subsidized public housing units that many developing
countries had struggled to maintain over the previous years.[64] As a Bank policy paper put it, these projects would "limit the burden on public authorities,"
thus ensuring that they were "replicable on a wide scale."[65]

SS initially appeared to be a success. An early evaluation conducted by
two Bank researchers of four of the organization's initial SS projects found
that they led to increased production of low-cost housing, affordability for

low-income groups, and the generation of "substantial amounts of employment and income" from rents, taxes, and construction.[66] Housing units in
one of the Bank's initial projects in Zambia, for instance, "cost less than one-
fifth as much as the least expensive government-subsidized housing," while
those in El Salvador averaged "less than half as much as the cheapest conventional house."[67]

A closer look at the Bank's record during the McNamara era reveals a
more complex picture. As with rural development, in a number of cases the
organization's urban initiatives exacerbated inequality in targeted regions.
Independent researchers investigating the Bank's 1977 SS project in Madras,
for instance, found that by increasing the value of land in the area, it priced
many poor families out of their homes.[68] The Bank's initial SS project in
Dar es Salaam suffered a similar fate. Staff estimated that the project would
benefit 160,000 low-income residents of the city through the provision of
10,600 newly serviced plots, improvements of existing squatter settlements,
the construction of community facilities, and the establishment of a housing bank that would provide credit to help low-income groups purchase or
rent the units. Despite assurances to the contrary, the housing bank ended
up providing loans to only those individuals who could guarantee that they
would repay, meaning that the project ended up excluding most people in the
area.[69] A Bank evaluation conducted in 1984 found that fewer than half the
units the government reported as being completed were actually finished
and occupied.[70]

Problems also beleaguered the Bank's efforts in Indonesia, the largest recipient of urban development loans during the McNamara era. An independent analyst hired by the Bank to appraise its Kampung Improvement
Program in Jakarta in 1978 found that the project's "top down" nature limited its effectiveness. The decision-making process bypassed intended beneficiaries, and most people were uninterested in maintaining what they viewed
as "an imposed package."[71] Moreover, the program also raised the price of
land and property taxes in the area, forcing many residents to leave for settlements on the outskirts of the city.[72]

Similar issues characterized some of the Bank's urban development
efforts in the Philippines. In 1976, the organization made a loan to the government for an SS and slum-upgrading project in Manila's Tondo district.
The project's proposal provides a sense of the large number of components
in SS projects. Among other things, the loan was to fund water supply, sew-
age, and road repair, establishment of a line of credit for housing materials,

the creation of educational facilities, community centers, and a health center, the provision of mixed commercial/residential sites, a new vocational and skills training program, the construction of traffic signals, and equipment for traffic police.[73]

The reality was much different. According to one report, 4,500 squatter families were removed from their homes to make room for the development, and just 30 percent of the people in the area were able to afford the new units.[74] This occurred after the Marcos regime had already evicted 60,000 squatters from another part of Manila to "beautify" the city for the 1976 Bank-IMF annual meetings.[75]

Even where SS did produce positive results, the projects tended to require large subsidies from local governments. Bank researchers who surveyed the organization's initial SS projects concluded that their relative success had come at great cost. Without subsidized interest rates on home loans, for instance, many poor city dwellers would have been unable to afford to stay in the new developments.[76] Thus, while the projects had provided shelter and services to many, "the goal of large-scale replicability that is so much the object of the sites and services paradigm" went unmet.[77] These high costs meant that local governments also struggled to maintain existing developments.[78]

Although rural and urban development projects were the main parts of the Bank's poverty-oriented lending program, they constituted a fraction of the organization's lending during McNamara's presidency, as indicated below.

How successful, then, were the Bank's projects as a whole during this period? Available evidence paints a depressing picture. An analysis by Bank researchers of 1,015 projects carried out over the organization's history found that the gap between staff estimates of economic rates of return versus rates at the time the project was actually completed grew significantly under McNamara. The researchers hypothesized that this was primarily because staff appraisal reports overestimated future gains, but the data also show that even when adjusting for this, rates of return on Bank projects remained below their historical average.[79] Although the fact that the Bank expanded its lending to riskier areas may explain some of the decline, circumstantial evidence shows that McNamara's drive to expand lending entailed reduction in loan quality. Projects were frequently delayed and went over budget.[80] And, in the mid- to late 1970s, Bank staff began to complain about management's emphasis on quantity rather than quality. "The pressures to carry out lend-

Table 4. Distribution of IBRD and IDA Commitments by Sector, 1968–1981

Sector	Percentage of total
Agriculture and rural development	28.3
Development finance companies	8.6
Education	4.7
Energy	16.8
Industry	7.1
Nonproject	5.3
Population, health, and nutrition	0.7
Small-scale enterprises	1.3
Telecommunications	2.5
Transportation	16.3
Urbanization	2.6
Water supply and sewerage	5.2
Technical assistance and tourism	0.5
Total	100

Source: IBRD/IDA, *Annual Report*, 1981, 12–13.

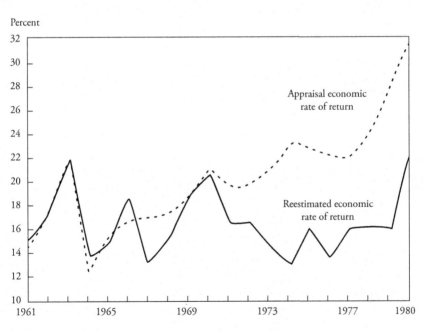

Figure 7. Appraised and reestimated rates of economic return for selected Bank projects, 1961–1980. Source: Gerhard Pohl and Dubravko Mihaljek, "Project Evaluation and Uncertainty in Practice: A Statistical Analysis of Rate-of-Return Divergences of 1,015 World Bank Projects," *World Bank Economic Review* 6, 2 (May 1992): 274.

ing programs, and to bring projects to the Board on schedule, have an undue influence on staff decisions," a 1977 internal Bank report noted. "In
effect, the scales are weighted in favor of doing things on time, even when
quality considerations should prevail."[81] As one Bank official later explained,
"the main object was to go out and make loans. And many of the projects
just folded."[82]

Policy Advising

Since its beginning, the Bank supplemented its lending operations by seeking to influence the economic policies of its borrowers, usually under the
rationale that a sound policy environment was vital to the success of its
projects. The organization helped draft national development plans and
brought government officials to its headquarters for training.[83] Occasionally,
the Bank also included conditions in its loans specifying reforms the borrower was to adopt upon receiving funds. For example, Bank loans for
hydroelectric projects typically contained clauses stating the manner in
which the local implementing agency was to determine electrical rates, although the organization tended to leave macroeconomic policy advising to
the IMF.[84]

As we have seen, McNamara was determined to increase the Bank's ability to influence the behavior of its borrowers. During his first years in office,
he increased the regularity and comprehensiveness of the Bank's missions
to developing countries, opened Bank offices in some borrowing countries,
and conducted his own dialogues with developing country leaders. He soon
found that the Bank's power as a policy adviser was limited. Increasingly
able to tap other funding sources, many developing countries ignored the
Bank's advice. Compounding these difficulties was McNamara's determination to increase Bank lending. Because developing countries knew that the
organization was driven to meet lending targets, threats to cut off funding,
which historically had been an important source of leverage for the Bank, rang
hollow.

The limits of the Bank's influence were evident in Brazil, the site of Mc-
Namara's most intensive effort to encourage poverty-oriented economic reforms. Brazil, one of the Bank's largest borrowers, was a classic example of
the problems of growth-centric development strategies. The economy had
grown impressively in the postwar decades, yet significant poverty and in-

equality remained. As such, McNamara was pleased when, soon after he took over the Bank, members of the military government running the country expressed their desire to improve conditions for Brazil's poor by, among other things, devoting more resources to the impoverished northeast part of the country.[85]

The slow progress of these efforts frustrated McNamara, however, and in 1970 he told a Brazilian official that he was "disturbed by the fact that Brazil was not doing very much for better income distribution or for employment."[86] Unhappy with the criticism, the government rejected Bank proposals to establish an office in the country.[87] Bank managers encouraged Mc-Namara to cut off lending to Brazil, but he wavered on the grounds that this would do little good. The country is "so big," he stated. "They are going to tell us to go to hell."[88]

Relations between Brazil and the Bank remained strained for the rest of the decade. In his speech to UNCTAD in 1972, McNamara pointed to Brazil's poverty as an example of the ways growth had not reduced inequality or poverty in developing countries, which prompted a sharp rebuke from Brazilian Finance Minister Antônio Delfim Neto.[89] The government's repression, in turn, disturbed some Bank officials. In a 1973 memorandum to McNamara, Hollis Chenery, the organization's chief economist, argued that the "brunt of our influence in Brazil at the present time should be directed at social justice."[90] McNamara did not directly address Chenery's concern. Instead, a few days later he directed the head of the Bank's Latin America Department to increase funding of poverty-oriented projects in the country.[91]

The Brazilian government, perhaps aware that the Bank would be unwilling to stop lending, informed Bank staff that it "welcomed" the organization's antipoverty loans.[92] Despite this rhetoric, the government was reluctant to work with the Bank on these projects, and by 1975 McNamara had had enough. In response to an internal Bank report that "the Brazilian government's commitment to large-scale programs for improving small farm productivity [is] lacking," he told the Bank's head of operations that, "if the Brazilian government had no program for increasing the productivity and the level of income of large numbers of its poor," the Bank should not make new loans to the country.[93]

But by that point the Bank was so overextended in Brazil that it could not stop lending. Should the Bank cut off Brazil, the country would start paying more money back to the Bank in the form of repayments on old loans than it was receiving from the organization. The possibility that a negative net transfer would jeopardize McNamara's calls for rich countries to increase their funding of the Bank convinced McNamara to continue lending to Brazil.[94] McNamara stopped criticizing the government, and in the early 1980s Bank officials admitted that the organization had "little policy impact" in Brazil.[95]

In Brazil and elsewhere, governments became less willing to listen to the Bank not just because they knew that lending cutoffs were unlikely but also because they were increasingly able to tap alternative sources of capital. This was particularly true in oil-exporting developing countries. For example, although the Bank's initial dealings with Iraq were cordial thanks to McNamara's insistence that the country receive loans over the objections of the Nixon administration, which was upset at lingering disputes from the nationalization of the Iraq Petroleum Company, the relationship turned hostile within a few years. The Iraqi government took issue with certain conditions to the Bank's assistance, such as a requirement on rate pricing in a telecommunications project, and the country stopped borrowing from the Bank in 1973.[96] Similar issues emerged in Iran. While Bank lending to Iran surged in McNamara's first years, Iranian authorities frequently complained about the advice that came with these funds. The Shah was especially upset that Bank loans for education were allocated to secondary and vocational schools rather than universities, and he bristled at what he perceived as the organization's critique of the government's agricultural policies.[97] In a meeting with McNamara in 1973, he voiced his objections to what he considered were "evidences of Bank leverage to force policy changes in Iran." McNamara reassured him that the Bank's only objective was "to assist him in the dramatic revolution which he [had] underway."[98] Nevertheless, tensions remained high. Although McNamara officially supported the Shah's plan to establish a concessional lending agency to help oil-importing developing countries cope with the price increase brought about by the first oil crisis, he was never sold on the proposal. For its part, the government of Iran essentially cut off ties with the Bank once the plan fell through. Iran refused to contribute to the third window that McNamara created to augment the Bank's lending in response to the oil crisis, and in 1976 Iran terminated the Bank's technical assistance operations in the country.[99]

The Bank struggled to influence policy in many non-oil exporting developing countries, as well. Efforts to reform the Malaysian transportation sector were fraught with problems, and throughout the 1970s the Bank struggled to convince Colombian authorities to reform the country's tax system and reduce import restrictions.[100] The Bank tried to get Guatemala's rightwing government to increase social spending, but the government's aversion to such measures as well as its access to capital from the U.S. government and commercial banks undercut these efforts.[101] And, though McNamara was pleased by Indian prime minister Indira Gandhi's efforts to "effectively address its population problem," which included forced sterilizations, and was largely uncritical of her suspension of the Indian Constitution in 1977, the organization was frustrated by the country's reluctance to adopt Bank-prescribed agricultural pricing reforms—a problem that was partially attributable to its desire to lend.[102] As one Bank official explained at the time, since "lending levels are sacrosanct targets . . . we may have locked ourselves in a position that impedes leverage."[103]

The Bank had more success in Indonesia. As noted earlier, McNamara came to the Bank determined to accelerate the country's reintegration into the organization. He had the Bank establish an office in Jakarta and met with Suharto soon after assuming the Bank presidency. McNamara was particularly keen on having the Bank advise Indonesian officials on economic policy matters. For instance, in 1968 he told his aides that the Bank's "technical assistance," not its funding, was the most important service it could offer the country.[104] The Bank's early efforts focused on helping the government settle its debts with external creditors. Later, the Bank had limited success in encouraging officials to adopt policies aimed at expanding food production for both domestic consumption and export, reducing the power of state-owned enterprises, and tackling corruption.[105] Bank staff was also involved in helping to draft Suharto's third five-year development plan in the late 1970s.[106]

Although the specific advice the Bank dispensed varied by country, its basic approach remained focused on promoting stability, growth, and international economic integration.[107] It thus encouraged governments to remove barriers to foreign investment, relax trade restrictions, adopt anti-inflationary monetary policies, and reduce public expenditures.

The Bank's relationship with the government of the Philippines during the 1970s illustrates the basic thrust of the organization's policy advice.[108] Like many developing countries, the Philippines maintained high levels of protectionism to foster domestic industry. Ferdinand Marcos, elected president of the country in 1966, was eager to attract foreign capital to the Philippines, however, and in his first years proposed legislation that offered multinational companies various incentives to invest in the country.[109] The

Bank supported these moves and was thus disappointed when local indus-
trialists and leftists were able to defeat some of the measures.[110] When Marcos
declared martial law in 1972, the Bank threw its support behind the president, viewing the suspension of democracy as vital to the Philippines' economic prospects and increasing its lending to the country.[111] The Bank also
encouraged Marcos to pursue a development strategy centered on increasing the country's export of labor-intensive manufactured goods, such as
textiles.[112] Marcos adopted some of these measures, and exports began to
rise. Nevertheless, Bank officials expressed frustration at the fact that some
protectionist measures remained in place. Thus, in 1977 an internal Bank
report argued that "tariff reform is becoming increasingly urgent since high
effective protection rates appear to be sheltering various inefficient industries."[113] The absence of such reform led organization officials two years later
to argue for a total "restructuring of the economy itself."[114] In other words,
despite the fact that the government had adopted many recommended measures, Bank officials remained frustrated by the pace of reform. As we will
see, the belief that organization needed to do more to promote comprehensive
policy change in the Philippines and elsewhere contributed to McNamara's
decision to begin making loans that were conditioned on borrowing governments adopting Bank-prescribed reforms.

Global Management

The Bank's project lending and policy advising efforts took place amidst the
backdrop of a dramatic increase in the indebtedness of developing countries.
At the beginning of the 1970s, the total external debt of the world's developing countries was about $69 billion, which constituted approximately
10 percent of their combined incomes. By 1980, these figures stood at $494
billion and 20 percent. Populous middle-income countries like Brazil, whose
external debt skyrocketed from $6 billion in 1970 to $72 billion in 1980, and
Mexico, which despite being an oil producer saw its obligations grow from
$7 billion to $57 billion during this time, were the largest debtors. Much of
this debt came in the form of variable interest rate loans from private creditors. Low-income developing countries, whose debt was held mainly by official lenders like the Bank, joined the party as well. Kenya, for example, saw
its external debt jump from $478 million in 1970 to over $3 billion by the end
of the decade.[115] Although some were worried about these developments,

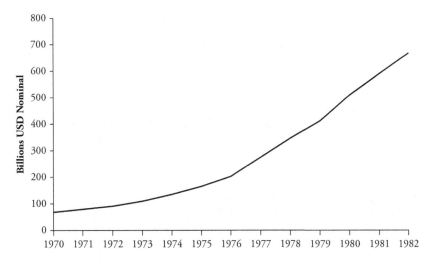

Figure 8. External debt of developing countries, 1970–1982. Source: World Bank, International Debt Statistics.

most did not fully understand the consequences. Developing countries needed to finance their oil imports somehow, and high levels of inflation and low interest rates made it relatively inexpensive to borrow. Meanwhile, private creditors were largely unconcerned about lending to sovereigns. Although developing countries' debts had risen significantly in the 1960s, sovereign defaults were rare. As Citigroup chair Walter Wriston famously quipped, "countries don't go out of business."[116]

McNamara demonstrated concern about sovereign debt issues at the beginning of his presidency. In discussions with aides in 1969, he noted that projections indicated that there would be "serious debt servicing and creditworthiness problems for the future" in many developing countries. He viewed this as indicative of an "increased need for funds of the developing countries on soft terms."[117] As McNamara explained to the finance minister of Malawi in 1970, "the emergence of major international indebtedness problems in recent years has shown that, without the full awareness of the governments concerned, private debt has built up in a number of cases to magnitudes which have presented governments with serious problems for the management of their balance of payments."[118]

McNamara viewed debt not as an obstacle to be overcome but, rather, as something that needed to be managed. Specifically, he felt that the lack of information about the debt servicing capacities of developing countries—at the time no international organization systematically collected this information—distorted the market. With lenders unable to assess sovereign creditworthiness, usually measured as the ratio of a country's interest and principle repayments to its export earnings, they might make unwise investment decisions. Poor information would also lead borrowing governments to over or under extend themselves.

As such, in McNamara's first years he attempted to improve the way the Bank collected and disseminated information about the creditworthiness of its borrowers. Early in his tenure he complained that "the debt service problems of individual debtor countries had still not been adequately examined within the Bank" and shortly thereafter directed staff to create an "early warning system on external indebtedness."[119] This resulted in the creation in 1970 of the *World Debt Tables*, an annual report that published detailed information on developing countries' external debts.[120] McNamara also sought to increase the Bank's own lending to help countries manage their debt repayments. To this effect, McNamara was more interested in maintaining the Bank's ability to help countries roll over their debts than in reducing those debts themselves. In the early 1970s, he repeatedly rebuffed calls from developing countries to reschedule their obligations to the Bank by claiming that the organization's "difficult position as a capital market borrower" precluded it from doing so. The Bank "did not have the flexibility of a commercial bank nor did it have the taxing capacity of a government," he explained, and rescheduling Bank loans would have "potentially destructive effects" on the organization's creditworthiness.[121]

The Bank's ambivalence toward sovereign debt issues remained even as the external debts of developing countries began to explode in the wake of the 1973–74 oil crisis. McNamara was aware that commercial loans often carried terms less favorable than those provided by public creditors like the Bank. Yet he thought that high levels of inflation made servicing this debt manageable. He and other Bank officials also worried about the effects that would ensue if the organization were to raise red flags. For instance, while the Bank began warning the Mexican government about the country's growing debt-service ratio in the mid-1970s—in 1975 McNamara told Mexican officials the country "might encounter serious debt management problems" in the near future—the Bank greatly expanded lending to the country during the period in part because it wanted to avoid informing other lenders about the precariousness of Mexico's position.[122] "The Bank profile in Mexico should not be lowered precipitately," an internal report explained. "Probably the most important [reason is] . . . the impact on Mexico's creditworthiness of a sharp withdrawal by the Bank; Mexico had stretched its credit in the world's capital markets to a point where any explicit loss of confidence on the part of an agency like the World Bank would have disastrous consequences on the country's creditworthiness."[123]

McNamara spelled out his thinking on debt issues in his 1976 address to the Bank-IMF annual meetings. He acknowledged that developing country debt had risen significantly over the previous years but insisted that such "increases are not large when adjusted for inflation, and they appear still smaller when account is taken of the growth in exports." As a result, McNamara predicted that "even in 1980, the debt service burden of these nations, in relation to their exports, is likely to be about the same as in 1973."[124] Rather than debt relief, more lending was needed to encourage "productive investment."[125]

But the Bank's analyses of developing country debt, which some in the financial community looked to when making investment decisions, were flawed, relying on overly optimistic growth projections to argue that external debts of developing countries were manageable.[126] As one Bank official noted in 1977, Bank reports sought to paint a "reassuring picture of the debt situation" that would serve as "a useful antidote to the loose talk about a debt crisis."[127]

The Bank thus downplayed concerns about the possibility of a debt crisis. While some Bank officials acknowledged that a growing number of developing countries were having difficulty servicing their debts, they dismissed such problems as "the concern of the financial community." McNamara agreed. "What was required," he told Bank management in 1977, was not a reduction of lending but "continued rollover and expansion."[128] McNamara reiterated these points at that year's Bank-IMF annual meetings. After declaring that "the private capital markets [had] responded well to the emergency needs of the developing countries for credit in the wake of the oil crisis," he argued that the belief that "this dramatic growth in external borrowing—particularly the borrowing from commercial banks—is unsustainable, and that if it is allowed to continue there will eventually be a generalized debt crisis," were misplaced. "Such a crisis was not inevitable," he insisted. "The debt problem is indeed manageable."[129]

Nevertheless, concerns about the stability of the international financial system began to mount. By 1978, Bank officials were warning about significant "riskiness in [the Bank's] loan portfolio," and many countries began asking the Bank to reschedule their obligations to the organization.[130] Members of the Bank's Board worried about "the heavy dependence of middle income countries on commercial credit . . . since a sharp reduction in the availability of financing could trigger the kind of debt crisis that all wanted to avoid."[131] And Ernest Stern, the Bank's Vice President of Operations, noted that the organization's country analyses had regularly overestimated developing country creditworthiness.[132]

World events drove home the precariousness of the situation. The destabilization caused by the Shah of Iran's downfall in January 1979 touched off a second round of oil price increases. That fall, U.S. Federal Reserve chair Paul Volcker began to raise U.S. interest rates in order to rein in inflation in the country. These developments had a devastating impact on the economies of developing countries. Oil-importing countries were suddenly forced to devote more of their resources to energy, and the real value of the dollar-denominated, variable-interest rate loans that many of these countries had taken out over the previous years skyrocketed.[133]

By the end of 1979, concerns emerged in the Bank about a wave of sovereign defaults. An October memorandum drew attention to the likelihood that, if private banks failed to increase their lending to developing countries, those nations would face the possibility of default.[134] In November, McNamara confided to his aides that he was "uneasy about delinquent repayments by Bank borrowers."[135] And the following month, staff reported concerns about the ability of developing countries to continue servicing their external debts.[136]

McNamara made every effort to keep these projections from becoming public. In an interview with the *Times of London* in 1980, he argued that the situation remained manageable. "Never underestimate the complexity and sophistication of the international financial system, its ability to cope. The system as a whole hasn't yet reached its limit."[137] McNamara also scrubbed the 1980 *World Development Report* clean of findings that might trigger concerns about global financial stability. Whereas the draft version predicted that real interest rates would stabilize at around 3 percent in the near future, enough to provoke significant debt service problems in many countries, McNamara insisted that the final report list this figure as 1 percent.[138]

Nevertheless, concerns within the Bank continued to grow. In January 1981, Bank Treasurer Eugene Rotberg reported that, unlike in 1974, commercial banks who were absorbing OPEC funds did not appear willing to expand their lending to developing countries. McNamara responded that "the

Bank ought to raise red flags now."[139] However—as he had done ten years earlier when presented with evidence of impending disaster in Vietnam—McNamara refused to make his concerns known. The 1981 *World Development Report* insisted that the organization "expects the borrowing needs of the middle income countries to be met largely by the commercial banking system."[140]

McNamara was wrong, as private banks curtailed their sovereign lending in the early 1980s. Unable to rollover its debts, in 1982 the government of Mexico declared that it was defaulting on its external debt. A number of other developing countries soon followed suit. With private banks overextended abroad, the inability of developing nations to service their loans precipitated a global debt crisis that, at the time, posed the greatest threat to the stability of the world economy since the Great Depression.[141]

Accounts of the origins of international debt crisis of the 1980s tend to downplay the Bank's role. The tale is usually explained as a classic case of boom and bust, with private bankers and developing country officials sharing blame.[142] When observers have assessed the Bank's record, criticism is usually muted. As one observer wrote, "it would be unfair to fault the Bank for failing to foresee the debt crisis. Few predicted the gravity of the global recession of the early 1980s or foresaw soaring interest rates and the sudden retreat of the commercial banks."[143]

But it was more than a coincidence that the conditions that led to the debt crisis coincided with McNamara's presidency of the Bank. Although the organization was not alone in failing to predict the crisis, it shares some of the blame. This is not just because of the poor performance of its own portfolio but also because it regularly overstated the creditworthiness of developing countries and, in so doing, sent incorrect signals to a market that often relied on its forecasts. Throughout his tenure, McNamara remained focused on increasing the Bank's lending and, when he realized that many countries would have trouble servicing their debts, decided to keep this knowledge secret lest it precipitate a crisis of confidence. In other words, under McNamara the Bank was unwilling and unable to recognize a bubble and take action. Although such shortsightedness is common in financial history, it bears striking similarities to his refusal to speak out or change course when, as U.S. defense secretary a decade earlier, he realized that the war in Vietnam was unwinnable.

CHAPTER 7

The Birth of Structural Adjustment

In a speech to the United Nations Conference on Trade and Development in Manila on May 10, 1979, Robert McNamara announced that the World Bank would consider making loans to assist developing countries to undertake "needed structural adjustments for export promotion."[1] The statement came toward the end of a long speech on the role of trade in development and did not make a significant impression at the time. Nevertheless, McNamara's words marked an important development. The onset of structural adjustment lending (SAL), in which the Bank provided loans to developing countries on the condition that they adopt certain policy reforms, was a seminal moment in the organization's history. From 1980, when the Bank made its first structural adjustment loans to the governments of Bolivia, Kenya, the Philippines, Senegal, and Turkey, SAL became an increasingly prominent activity. The following year, the Bank issued six more structural adjustment loans. The next year, it made eleven. In 1989, that number increased to fifty-two. Indeed, although no longer termed "structural adjustment," policy-conditioned lending continues to occupy a central place at the Bank, which before 1980 almost exclusively funded discreet development projects.[2]

SAL emerged for a variety of reasons. Foremost among these were problems in the Bank's project-based lending approach. Because project loans required that staff identify and appraise specific development projects before the Bank disbursed money, they tended to be a relatively slow means of channeling capital to developing countries. This became an issue in the late 1970s as developing countries' balance of payments deficits worsened and as repayments on outstanding Bank loans threatened to exceed disbursals. The Bank's inability to induce policy change in developing countries also frustrated the organization's management. The need to find a way to transfer capital to developing countries more rapidly, combined with the desire to make developing countries heed the Bank's policy recommendations, convinced McNamara to propose SAL.

SAL brought the organization into the IMF's territory, further blurring the line between the two institutions. Because the conditions tied to adjustment loans covered issues like exchange rate policy and levels of government spending, SAL also led the Bank to become more involved in the internal affairs of developing countries.

Aware that the Bank's Articles of Agreement allowed nonproject lending only in exceptional circumstances, McNamara portrayed structural adjustment as a temporary solution to a short-term problem. In private, however, he acknowledged that adjustment lending would become an enduring part of the Bank's work. This development was unsurprising. SAL marked the apotheosis of the Bank's approach under McNamara. It formalized the organization's shift from a focus on project financing to policy advising and gave operational significance to the emerging consensus that developing countries needed to reduce the level of government intervention in their economies if they wanted to grow. Like McNamara's earlier moves to elevate poverty alleviation on the Bank's agenda, SAL was predicated on a belief in the utility and necessity of comprehensive intervention in the affairs of developing countries. But, as with his war on world poverty, SAL would have negative effects for the Bank's intended beneficiaries.

The Bank Breaks Down

As the 1970s drew to a close, there was a growing realization that the international development endeavor was at a critical juncture. Despite slower growth in many developed countries, the gap between the North and South remained wide. Developing countries accounted for 16 percent of global output in 1970, but nine years later this figure had risen to just 19 percent, with most of the gains attributable to increased oil revenues.[3] Rather than leading to greater cooperation, global inequality caused developing countries to reiterate their demands for a New International Economic Order. Meanwhile, the foreign aid levels of developed countries declined to around 0.3 percent of their income in the late 1970s, a far cry from the 0.7 percent the Pearson Report had called for a decade earlier.[4]

These trends reflected and reinforced the decline of development economics as an intellectual endeavor. In the mid-twentieth century, development

had been an influential discipline within economics. Development economists studied challenges poor countries faced in trying to stimulate growth
and tended to argue that government intervention was critical to this process. The economist Paul Rosenstein-Rodan, for instance, famously advocated for large-scale public investment programs in developing countries,
arguing that only a "big push" could overcome structural deficiencies in
these economies and foster sustained growth.[5] As noted earlier, the idea that
developing economies faced unique challenges in fostering growth, as well
as the notion that government intervention was a prescription for these ills,
went out of fashion in the 1970s. Reflecting the broader rejection of Keynesian approaches during the time, economists concluded that the problems of
development, not unlike the stagnation then afflicting many developed
countries, was a product of bloated public sectors and that governments were
generally incapable of intervening productively in the economy. Contributing to these trends, development economists struggled to translate their
ideas into the mathematical models that were becoming popular in economics departments.[6] As a result, by the late 1970s, scholars began to speak
about the "death of development economics."[7]

   Morale in the Bank was at a low point, as well. Staff members were frustrated by waning U.S. support for the Bank and the difficulties they faced in
trying to promote development.[8] For his part, McNamara was aware that,
despite his success in increasing the Bank's size, in key respects the organization was weaker than it had ever been. Although it had devoted a greater
amount of attention to advising developing country officials, partnering with
private banks, and expanding its research and publication programs, the
availability of private capital—in 1979, private lenders committed fifteen
times as much money to developing countries as did the Bank, up from just
two times as much at the beginning of the decade—rendered the Bank less
relevant as a development financier.[9] It was also becoming clear that the Bank
was having mixed success promoting development. While some of the
organization's projects had yielded impressive results, evidence began to ac-
cumulate that many had failed to meet their objectives. Developing countries
struggled to mobilize their share of funds for large infrastructure projects,
and many projects intended to alleviate poverty and promote bottom-up
growth had crumbled.

   While these problems were not entirely the Bank's fault, they signaled
that the organization had overextended itself. McNamara's drive to increase

the Bank's lending strained an organization that had long operated in a conservative fashion. The introduction of quantitative lending targets created a constant pressure to lend, and in McNamara's first years the Bank began to have trouble processing and supervising its loans. One internal Bank study found that 45 percent of projects presented to the Board in the Bank's 1973 fiscal year were either poorly prepared or lacked a strong justification.[10] In 1974, Bank managers noted that "programming and budgeting exercises" had "place[d] undue emphasis on speed . . . in completing programs," and officials in developing countries complained about a "general deterioration of Bank operations."[11]

These concerns grew more pronounced as the decade progressed. In 1975, the Bank's Operations Evaluation Department reported growing delays between the time the Bank signed a loan agreement with a borrowing country and when the loan was disbursed.[12] The following year, Japan's representative to the Bank resigned his post claiming that McNamara's drive to expand lending had caused a decline in the quality of Bank projects.[13] The representative of the Scandinavian countries at the Bank echoed these concerns by criticizing the "excessive demands" that were placed on staff to come up with projects to fund.[14] As an internal Bank report noted, "staff felt that nobody at the beginning of the year admitted that the program could not be fulfilled and that management did not listen when they argued that the project was not ready."[15] Pressure to lend consequently forced staff to "invent numbers," and some laughed when asked how often supervisors listened to these concerns.[16]

World Bankers were particularly frustrated by McNamara's emphasis on quantitative analysis. "There was cynicism among staff as to the reliability of the figures used in measurements of absolute and relative poverty," a Bank official noted. Despite the fact that various "standards and reporting procedures had been designed and frequently . . . carried out before project implementation," staff were convinced that the "quantification of project targets was subject to a large margin of error and involved a cascade of assumptions; even the best estimate was not very good . . . results tended not to be comparable and staff were uncomfortable about aggregation of figures."[17] As a result, staff began to demonstrate "a serious lack of confidence" in McNamara. Shahid Husain, head of the Bank's East Asia and Pacific Department, informed McNamara of complaints about his "excessive obsession with control" and the "one-way flow of ideas from the top to the bottom."

"Sometimes I have the funny feeling that the lunch lines are getting a bit longer."

Figure 9. "Sometimes I have the funny feeling that the lunch lines are getting a bit longer." *Bank Notes*, April 1978, 7, World Bank Group Archives.

Staff considered the organization "autocratic," complained that they were "overworked," and felt that the focus on meeting quantitative targets made them feel as if they were "factory workers on an assembly line."[18]

Despite such concerns, McNamara remained fixated on increasing Bank lending. He dismissed reports of declining staff morale, deteriorating project quality, and overprogramming by arguing that the organization had an obligation to lend as much money to as many countries as rapidly as possible. "The Bank exists only to the extent that it can serve the purposes of development," he told the President's Council.[19] "The development assistance needs of the country, and not staff or budget constraints, should be the determining factor" in lending decisions.[20] McNamara thus resisted efforts to reign in the Bank, at one point threatening to resign when the Colombian representative to the organization proposed a special committee to investigate problems relating to the procurement of materials for Bank-financed projects.[21]

Still, many in the Bank continued to criticize the direction McNamara was taking the organization. The governments of Germany and Japan complained that they had little input in selecting Bank projects, and in January

1977 an internal Bank investigation reported a precipitous decline in staff morale.[22] In addition to complaints about deteriorating project quality, staff felt that the organization was plagued by "serious lateral communications problems."[23] The Bank's managers corroborated these findings. "There was no voluntary spirit of cooperation" in the organization, they informed McNamara. Staff "felt left out of the decision-making process." The Bank's programming systems had "led to overcontrol." And "loan officers were too often caving into time and pressure."[24]

McNamara downplayed these reports. Informed that the Board was frustrated by its inability to review projects, he responded that the situation was "inevitable" given the nature of the organization's work. Developing countries "need and can absorb far more resources than the Bank can provide," he explained, and "operations must be over-programmed if maximum available resources are to be provided."[25] As a result, concerns about deteriorating project quality were overblown. As Warren Baum, vice president of the Bank's Projects Department, argued, "projects were riskier than in the past but they were also reaching the right beneficiaries."[26]

More than project quality, Bank officials were concerned about their ability to induce policy change in developing countries. They attributed some of these difficulties to the organization's procedures. Mechanisms such as the Country Program Paper (CPP), created by McNamara in 1969 to coordinate Bank operations by country, had led to a dilemma. In order to increase their power, the regional departments in charge of drafting CPPs tended to inflate their requests for funds. Additionally, quantitative planning limited the organization's leverage, since the Bank could not easily reduce or increase lending to punish or reward borrowers for their behavior. The organization was operating on a "dual system," Willi Wapenhans, head of the East Africa Department, complained to McNamara in 1977. Instead of serving as an "instrument of planning" with governments, CPPs had "become an instrument of resource allocation and hence an advocacy document for the region[al]" departments. Other Bank officials noted that "forecasts in CPPs often were too optimistic" and that this hamstrung the organization's relations with borrowing governments. "The Bank-wide lending program should not be a summation of CPP programs," they argued. Reliance on inflated country plans had led to an "improper, overconstrained and overloaded ... programming system."[27]

McNamara was also worried about the organization's ability to channel capital to countries on a rapid basis. The Bank disbursed funds only after a

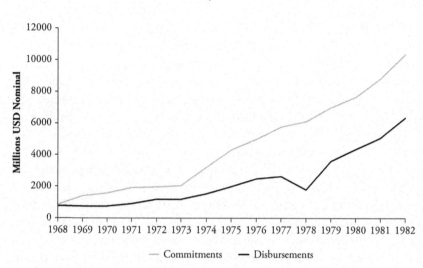

Figure 10. IBRD/IDA commitments and disbursements, 1969–1981. Source: IBRD/IDA, *Annual Reports*, 1968–1981.

project had been appraised and approved. The growing complexity of projects increased the time needed for such preparation, and as a result the organization's lending pipeline became backlogged. In the late 1970s, annual disbursements averaged about half of annual commitments. In fiscal year 1978, for instance, the Bank's Board approved $6.1 billion in new IBRD loans, but the organization disbursed just $2.8 billion.[28] McNamara felt the Bank had an "obligation" to maximize lending to developing countries.[29] In 1978, he told Bank managers that he was "not comfortable with the [organization's] disbursement performance" and began to look for ways to enhance the organization's ability to channel capital to borrowers.[30]

McNamara was concerned about disbursements because they drew attention to the fact that, when taking into account repayments on outstanding loans, the Bank was channeling increasingly fewer resources to developing countries. In the second half of 1970s, the ratio of repayments on outstanding Bank loans to dispersals steadily increased. In 1980, for instance, the Bank disbursed $5.8 billion and collected $3.1 billion in interest and amortization payments on previous loans, meaning that it transferred only $2.7 billion to borrowing governments that year.[31] Net transfers became a considerable source of consternation for Bank management in the late 1970s, drawing criticism from the Board and raising questions about McNamara's demand that wealthy governments increase their contributions to the organization. "People [saw] all this money piled up in the Bank, immobilized and not being put to constructive use," Burke Knapp, the Bank's chief of operations, later recalled. "We were under a great deal of pressure."[32]

Inventing Adjustment

The need to speed up lending, combined with the desire to influence the policies of developing countries, led McNamara to create structural adjustment. Formulated in discussions among the Bank's senior management in 1978, unveiled by McNamara in 1979, and approved by the organization's Board of Executive Directors in 1980, SAL was portrayed as a means to augment the Bank's project lending and policy advising operations by providing program loans to developing countries on the condition that they institute Bank-prescribed reforms. The Bank made its first structural adjustment loans to Kenya and Turkey in March 1980, and as the balance of payments positions of developing countries worsened over the coming years, SAL became a centerpiece of the organization's work.

Program lending was not a new concept at the Bank. As noted earlier, the organization's first loans to Western Europe in 1947 for postwar reconstruction were program loans. While project lending eventually came to dominate the organization's portfolio, the Bank made a number of program loans during the 1950s and 1960s, usually to countries suffering budgetary shortfalls. The primary benefit of program loans was that they were quick disbursing. Unlike project loans, which required identification, development, and assessment of a particular project, program loans provided general budgetary support. Accordingly, these funds could be transferred quickly. The Bank had also experimented with conditionality before embarking on SAL. The Bank's founders were intent on avoiding the sort of unaccountable lending typical of the interwar period, so Bank project loans often contained clauses governing implementation.[33]

The Bank continued to make non-project loans during McNamara's presidency. Because the Articles of Agreement permitted the use of non-project loans in "special circumstances," the organization wielded program lending as a tool to deal with certain emergency situations.[34] For example, most of McNamara's initial focus at the Bank was on India's need for assistance to finance food and energy imports.[35] In the winter of 1968–69 he pushed through a $125 million program loan to the government because of its inability to afford these critical imports.³⁶ Similarly, in 1971 the Bank issued a program loan to the government of Nigeria for reconstruction after the country's civil war.³⁷ The Bank also provided program loans to several nations adversely affected by the 1973–74 oil crisis.³⁸ And, though described as project loans, the organization issued quick-disbursing assistance to Romania after floods in 1976 and Lebanon in 1977 after its civil war.³⁹

Nevertheless, project lending remained the Bank's primary focus, not only in adherence to its governing documents but also because of a sense that the financial community might view program lending as a riskier use of Bank funds, thereby making it more costly for the organization to sell its bonds.⁴⁰ External factors further slowed the shift to program loans. For most of McNamara's tenure, developing country calls for increases in the Bank's program lending—seen as favorable because they went toward general budgetary support—encountered opposition from the U.S. government and the Bank's other powerful members, who argued that "lending for anything other than specific projects would lead to a loss of control over the Bank's loan funds and an attendant loss of confidence by bondholders in the organization."⁴¹ As a result, non-project lending declined as a percentage of the Bank's portfolio under McNamara, dropping from 13 percent of total Bank lending through 1968 to just 4 percent in 1979.⁴²

It was only as the limits of project loans as a means of channeling capital to developing countries became evident that McNamara came to support increasing the Bank's program lending. McNamara first voiced his frustrations about the Bank's ability to transfer large sums of capital to developing countries during discussions over the organization's fiscal year 1979 budget, when he told the President's Council that he was "not comfortable with the [Bank's] disbursement performance."⁴³ The Bank's staff had projected a significant reduction in net transfers to developing countries in the coming year, which McNamara considered a "serious" problem that "could lead to the conclusion by [the Board] that commitments should also be slowed."⁴⁴ In response, the head of the Bank's Programming and Budgeting Department floated the idea that the organization "change the mix of lending toward fast-disbursing programs." Meanwhile, McNamara reiterated his desire to increase the Bank's lending despite arguments that the organization was having trouble effectively processing its loans and despite indications that there were limits on how much developing countries could borrow.⁴⁵ In response to worries that "there was clearly a short-term problem of absorptive capacity in a number of countries," McNamara replied that he "could not believe that countries . . . could not absorb a high level of resource transfers, if their finance ministers got to work." To help them in this task, he told his aides that "rather than cutting back on lending programs the Bank should talk to the governments concerned."[46]

Indeed, at the same time that McNamara was growing frustrated by the disbursal problem, he was becoming more open to using Bank loans as a vehicle for inducing policy change. In May 1978, he noted his agreement with one senior Bank official's recommendation that the organization look to "combine the two aspects of projects and policy work," and shortly thereafter he ordered Bank managers to search out new ways of giving "economic policy advice" to borrowers.[47] Ernest Stern, who took over from Burke Knapp as the Bank's head of operations in July 1978, pushed McNamara in this direction. Stern adamantly believed in the importance of economic reform in developing countries.[48] He presented McNamara with several compelling arguments for greater conditionality: that developing countries needed to adopt market-oriented reforms (such as reductions in government expenditures and relaxation of price controls) in order to maintain growth rates; that the Bank's traditional methods of influencing borrower behavior (through informal country dialogues) were ineffective; and that the Bank's projects were failing because of the misguided policies of borrowing nations.[49] In May 1979, Stern sent McNamara a memorandum outlining the need for "macro-economic conditioning" in the Bank's loans. He insisted that the Bank's efforts to promote poverty alleviation and growth would become "increasingly inadequate unless we can also say that we are satisfied with their general development strategy and overall economic management." He also noted that some of the Bank's previous program loans had included reform conditions. "But," he concluded, "why should we wait until countries are in difficulty before we take such an approach?"[50]

Stern was not the only proponent of policy-conditioned lending. By 1979, the Bank's management had come to believe that the organization needed to change the way it did business. In a President's Council meeting that April, Shahid Husain, head of the Bank's East Asia and the Pacific Department, argued that the organization's lending and advising operations were significantly flawed. The Bank's country missions had proven to be "an act of diminishing returns," since governments simply ignored the organization's advice.[51] In addition, the Bank's ability to transfer funds to developing countries had been "more difficult than expected." Indeed, the Bank had reached the limits of project lending. "Experience now indicated that the [lending] pipeline could not be improved by simply adding more staff and financial resources," he explained, since "the Bank's program in many countries and sectors relied heavily on repeater projects which in turn depend on the implementation of previous projects."[52]

To address this problem, Husain asked "whether the same amounts could not be lent through fewer projects." By increasing the average size of Bank loans the organization would be able to lend more money more rapidly. McNamara concurred. "There were many reasons for increasing project size," he noted, especially the fact that it was "difficult . . . to believe that the envisaged increments in lending could not be absorbed by the developing countries."[53] To this effect, McNamara explained that he and Stern had already concluded that the Bank would institute an across-the-board increase of 7 percent on the price of its loans. McNamara also argued that the organization should focus more attention on its policy reform efforts. The "non-lending contributions of the Bank had expanded dramatically" in the recent past, he said, and he was "anxious to increase the Bank's non-lending activities and to get the recognition and acceptance of governments of this work" in the coming years."

McNamara proposed SAL at the fifth meeting of UNCTAD in Manila the following month. He initially hoped to use the occasion to call on wealthy nations to make it easier for developing country exporters to access their markets. Attila Karaosmonoglu, a director of one of the country divisions in the Bank's Europe, Middle East, and North Africa Department, encouraged McNamara to bolster his calls by signaling that the organization would simultaneously help developing countries expand their export sectors.[54] McNamara agreed, and in his speech to UNCTAD announced that "in order to benefit fully from an improved trade environment developing countries will need to carry out structural adjustments favoring their export sectors." This, he went on, would require "both appropriate domestic policies and adequate external help." McNamara declared that he was "prepared to recommend to the Executive Directors that the World Bank consider such requests for assistance, and that it make available program lending in appropriate cases."[55]

Less than a week later, Stern sent McNamara a memorandum detailing the form this lending might take. The Bank should "better condition its country lending programs by linking them, more explicitly, to the macroeconomic policies of our member governments," Stern wrote. Specifically, the organization should extend program loans to countries, to be disbursed in stages over three to five years, to help them cope with a deteriorating balance of payments. Unlike the Bank's regular program loans, however, these loans would be conditioned on the borrowing government agreeing to a range of Bank-prescribed economic policy changes. Stern acknowledged that this might "be strongly resisted by the developing countries." As such, he argued that these loans should initially be undertaken in only "a few countries annually after a considerable effort at preparation."[56]

The chain of events triggered by the Iranian revolution lent further momentum to SAL. The destabilization caused by the Shah's downfall in January 1979 led to another round of oil price increases. As a result, oil-importing developing countries soon faced increased financing needs. In a joint response to this crisis, staff at the Bank and the IMF issued a report calling on the two institutions to channel more capital to oil-importing developing countries.[57] The report focused particular attention on the need for "expanded sector and program lending by the World Bank . . . in support of adjustment measures taken by developing countries both in situations of extreme balance of payments difficulties . . . as well as adjustment measures taken in less difficult circumstances to encourage domestic production in line with the borrower's comparative advantage."[58] In so doing, the report argued that the Bank could complement IMF efforts to promote macroeconomic stability in developing countries. Although this level of conditionality would bring the Bank into the IMF's territory, the Bank could play an important role in these "parallel" efforts, since it had the unique ability to "dialogue with governments on their public investment programs," which was vital to ensuring that "the necessary adjustment policies were carried out."[59]

By the fall of 1979, McNamara was convinced that a large program of adjustment lending was needed. In President's Council meetings leading up to the Bank-IMF annual meeting, to be held in Belgrade in October, he remarked that developing countries' primary requirement over the coming years was "new funds connected with program-type lending in order to finance the necessary adjustment process."[60] For the Bank, the major question to be resolved at the annual meeting was simply whether such assistance would be "additional or a substitute for project financing."[61] Meanwhile, other Bank officials began to recognize the advantages of SAL as a policymaking tool. As Moeen Qureshi, the Bank's vice president of finance, explained, "in the case of long-term structural problems governments were inclined to hope that they would go away or that the succeeding government would deal with them. The Bank could help in making the political costs of addressing long-term structural problems more acceptable to governments and in ensuring sufficient support for such long-term measures."[62]

On the plane ride from Washington to Belgrade, McNamara and Stern hammered out the specifics of SAL, which McNamara announced in his speech to the opening session of the conference.[63] A "new international development strategy" was needed, he declared. Only through a series of "interconnected actions," including increased flows of capital to developing countries, would these nations be able to overcome adverse conditions in the world economy and accelerate their growth in the coming years. Success also hinged on leaders in developing countries making "hard decisions." Without specifying what these entailed, McNamara announced that the Bank was ready to provide financial and technical assistance to developing countries that were willing to undertake "difficult structural adjustments."[64]

After the speech, McNamara's focus shifted to securing the approval of the Bank's Board. He argued that large and growing current account deficits in developing countries constituted the "special conditions" required by the Articles of Agreement for non-project lending. As he told his aides, "the Bank should decide that the doubling of the balance of payments deficits of the developing countries over the next few years had created a new situation which required an expanded Bank mandate to help undertake the structural adjustments needed to overcome these deficits." In other words, SAL would be a "pre-crisis program loan."[65]

Some were skeptical. Roger Chaufournier, head of the Europe, Middle East and North Africa Department, told McNamara that "no dent could be made in the problems of the poorest countries through program lending," and, as such, the organization "should not entertain excessive expectations that program lending to the poorest countries as budgetary support would be forthcoming." For his part, Bank Treasurer Eugene Rotberg warned McNamara that "the financial world considered [SAL] to be a major shift in Bank policy."[66] Whereas the organization's focus on funding discreet projects had allowed it to establish its creditworthiness, some viewed McNamara's announcement of SAL as a sign that "IBRD money would now be channeled to non-creditworthy countries."[67] Longtime World Banker Bernard Chadenet, then head of the organization's Projects Department, worried that "new activity would stretch the Bank's functions and make them overlap more with the IMF" and questioned the organization's ability to prescribe policy reforms. The Bank "had obviously made mistakes in the past in dealing with simple projects and sector-level matters," and it would be "prone to making more serious mistakes in imposing conditions for structural adjustment lending based on macroeconomic models developed by the 'dismal science.'"[68]

Bank management dismissed these concerns. Hollis Chenery, the Bank's chief economist, stated that, while economics was "indeed an incomplete and imperfect science," this was no reason for "leaving the Africans alone." Shahid Husain added that SAL was "badly needed in order to enable the Bank to continue high levels of project lending." As Baum put it, "without structural adjustment, an increasing number of countries would have only a very limited ability to absorb new project lending."[69] McNamara also brushed aside concerns about the market's response to SAL, telling Rotberg that "IDA resources would continue to go to IDA countries and IBRD funds would continue to go to IBRD countries." He further stated that policy-conditioned lending would be more than a short-term fix. Rather, he told the President's Council the day after his speech in Belgrade, that SAL was "a major and new initiative" that would define the organization over the coming years.[70]

As senior Bank officials reiterated their concerns about the organization's ability to channel capital to and influence the economic policies of developing countries—a 1979 OED report noted that the organization had failed to "supervis[e]" its borrowers, and in January 1980 McNamara admitted that "the Bank's projects were becoming too complex and overstrained the administrative capabilities of governments"—governments expressed doubts about SAL.[71] In early 1979, nine members of the Bank's twenty-person Board argued that it was the IMF's job to promote adjustment.[72] And the conservative government of Margaret Thatcher considered SAL "money down the drain."[73] To stave off criticism, McNamara told his aides to keep the details of SAL secret by demanding that they "not go too far in spelling out this issue" in the paper on SAL being drafted for Board approval. Instead, the proposal "should be finessed for the time being."[74]

McNamara thus secured the Board's approval for SAL in February 1979 by assuring them that it "was to be a short-lived program to meet immediate needs."[75] The following month, the Board approved the Bank's first structural adjustment loans, a $55 million IDA credit to the government of Kenya to reform its "foreign trade and industrial structure" and a $300 million IBRD loan to the government of Turkey to "improve its capacity to earn foreign exchange through industrial and agro-industrial exports."[76] These were followed by a $50 million structural adjustment loan to Bolivia in June, a $200 million structural adjustment loan to the Philippines in September, and a $60 million structural adjustment credit to Senegal in December.

The U.S. government supported these efforts. Members of the Carter administration noted that SAL would give the Bank an "important, flexible capability to respond to near-term financial needs of [developing countries] with constructive longer-term results."[77] U.S. support for Bank adjustment lending increased after Ronald Reagan assumed the presidency the following year. Although Reagan officials were suspicious of foreign aid, they soon came to view SAL as an effective tool for promoting free market reforms in developing countries.

But this support should not be mistaken as a cause. Rather than the result of pressure from the U.S. government, SAL emerged as a response to factors internal to the Bank. McNamara created SAL as a means to solve interrelated problems that had been building up over the course of his tenure and that found their expression in the loan dispersal and net transfer crisis at the end of the 1970s. In some ways, SAL was attributable to McNamara's desire to increase the Bank's prestige. "McNamara was very . . . publicly minded," Burke Knapp remembered.

> He wanted the Bank to look like it was expanding its activities at a great rate . . . that was part of the whole game of building up the reputation and the power of the Bank, both in developing countries and in the donor countries . . . When he caught up with reality and realized that the actual impact we were having on net disbursements, it would dismay him. He would say, 'My God! What's happening here? We've got to accelerate disbursements!' You can't accelerate disbursements very much on project lending . . . The shift to policy-based lending was driven very much by the desire to accelerate disbursements.[78]

Negotiating Adjustment

Signed in September 1980, the Bank's $200 million structural adjustment loan to the Philippines highlighted key aspects of SAL. These included the specific policies the Bank advocated, the relative roles of the Bank and IMF in promoting policy reform, the ways adjustment lending was being considered well before McNamara formally announced the proposal, and the manner in which these loans allowed the Bank to intervene in the politics of developing countries.[79]

The Bank played a significant role in the Philippines prior to the 1980 structural adjustment loan. Early in McNamara's tenure, he remarked that Philippine President Ferdinand Marcos was "an impressive leader," and lending to the country increased significantly in the late 1960s.[80] The Bank stepped up its operations in the Philippines after Marcos declared martial law in 1972.

In addition to the Bank, the Philippines borrowed heavily from the IMF during this time. The two organizations divided their labors in the first half of the decade, with the Bank largely focused on rural and urban development and the IMF playing the dominant role in economic policy advising. In 1976, the Philippines agreed to borrow $250 million from the IMF over three years from its Extended Fund Facility (EFF), which the IMF had created in the wake of the oil crisis to augment its regular lending.[81] As part of this agreement, the IMF called on the government to eliminate certain policies that protected domestic industry, such as import restrictions. However, Marcos hesitated to carry out some of these measures for fear that they would reduce his political support.[82]

Meanwhile, the Bank began to take an interest in Philippine policy. In 1976, a Bank staffer working out of the country's National Economic and Development Authority (NEDA) drew up a "basic economic report" of the long-term prospects of the Philippine economy. In 1977, the Bank sponsored an influential study at the University of the Philippines that detailed the gains that the country could make through trade liberalization. And shortly thereafter, the organization drafted a detailed report on the nation's industrial sector that advocated liberalizing import and export controls.[83]

With the EFF winding down, the Bank sought to influence Philippine policy directly. The 1978 CPP for the Philippines noted that the "major objective" of Bank operations in the country would be to encourage "policy improvements."[84] Bank officials reiterated the view that import controls should be lifted and that the government should seek to expand the manufacture of labor-intensive products[85] A Bank mission then went to Manila to secure "a comprehensive understanding . . . at the highest levels on the objectives that could be reached through a series of staged industrial policy

reforms."[86] Bank staff proposed making a loan to the government that
would be conditioned on undertaking these measures. "Graduated action
by the government to implement industrial and financial policy improvements would provide the basis for substantially expanded World Bank support for the industrial sector over the next few years," a summary of the
negotiations read.[87] "The Bank laid it on the line," a Philippine official involved in the negotiations recalled. "No policy announcements, no new legislation, no loan."[88]

Philippine officials agreed to the proposal, and the government began to
implement some of the recommendations shortly thereafter. A few weeks
after the Bank mission left Manila, Marcos announced efforts to expand the
export of labor-intensive manufactured goods, as the Bank had required.[89]
The Bank's management subsequently declared that "most of the reforms
discussed during the review of the industrial report are either satisfactorily
accomplished or progressing as rapidly as could reasonably be expected,"
and the Board unanimously approved the first structural adjustment loan to
the Philippines.[90]

One reason for the Bank's ability to convince the government to adopt
reforms that had been rejected when proposed by the IMF was its ability to
navigate Philippine politics. In negotiating the structural adjustment loan,
the Bank worked with and bolstered the positions of likeminded officials in
the Philippine government. "Whereas the IMF had dealt almost exclusively
with a Central Bank not yet dominated by new technocratic elements," one
observer noted,

> the World Bank turned its back on these "old boys." Instead, it fo-
> cused on strengthening the positions and furthering the viewpoints
> of sympathetic technocrats in ministries that could be played off
> [the] Central Bank. Furthermore, the Bank learned from the IMF's
> mistakes and consciously strove for a different sort of image in the
> Philippines. Pervasive among government officials was the feeling
> that the IMF stood as a "watchdog disciplinarian," to be approached
> with caution. In contrast, World Bank missions moved in and out with
> ease, maintaining relative freedom to contact whomever they wanted
> directly without seeking highest-level Philippine government approval
> first—and vice versa. At any given time, went the standard joke among
> Philippine technocrats, there were at least five World Bank missions
> somewhere in-country.[91]

As the Philippine loan demonstrates, SAL entailed a significant expansion of Bank conditionality. Whereas the organization had long limited its loan conditions to the level of specific projects or sectors, with SAL the Bank began to engage in macroeconomic conditionality. This made the conditions of great importance. Although differing in the specifics, the Bank's early structural adjustment loans encouraged borrowers to liberalize trade and reduce government spending. The Bank's first structural adjustment loan to Turkey, for instance, aimed to promote "greater reliance on market forces and less on direct state intervention and control" by devaluing the lira, reducing import controls, and creating incentives for export promotion.[92] The Bank's initial structural adjustment loan to Bolivia called for privatizing state-owned enterprises as well as currency devaluation.[93] And early structural adjustment loans to Kenya and Senegal required reductions of agricultural price controls and import restrictions. As such, SAL gave operational significance to the emergent notion at the Bank, detailed in Chapter 5, that developing countries needed to reduce government intervention in their economies.

SAL marked the culmination of ongoing changes in the organization's conception of the development process and its role therein. Specifically, it formalized the Bank's shift, underway before McNamara's arrival but accelerated as a result of his leadership, from a focus on project financing to policy advising. As the Bank adopted a more interventionist posture—viewing its mandate as improving conditions *within* developing countries as opposed to improving conditions *of* those countries—its operations began to expand, and by the mid-1970s many of its projects encompassed countrywide economic sectors. In a sense, SAL enabled the Bank to extend the definition of a "project" to encompass an entire country. As one Bank official later explained, under McNamara the Bank moved "from a narrow project approach to a broader sector approach and then to a broad economic approach."[94]

In this way, SAL can be seen as a product of organizational learning. Over the course of the 1970s McNamara and others in the Bank became convinced that the success of the organization's projects depended upon the policy "environment" or "framework" in which they were carried out.[95] As McNamara explained in 1980, in order to promote development the Bank would have to grapple with "fundamental issues of national policy" and not concentrate "solely on investment projects."[96] This belief meshed with the organization's adoption of a more consultative orientation. "Here you had this institution that was building up a tremendous analytical capacity during the 1970s," a former Bank staff member explained. "But project loans are not very good vehicles really for this kind of general macro-policy advice because you are trying to carry too much other baggage with the project on the project side." As a result, "when the second oil shock came and there was this need for quick, fast-disbursing money, . . . this was really an opportunity for getting your policy advice listened to.[97]

SAL thus offered the Bank a novel tool with which to promote development. Freed from the constraint of lending for specific projects, the Bank was now able to put major resources behind its policy advising work, which itself came to include a greater range of issues. As Stern noted approvingly, "structural adjustment lending enables the Bank to address basic issues of economic management and development strategy more directly and more urgently than before."[98] McNamara was equally optimistic. "Structural adjustment lending opens new fields of opportunities," he told Bank managers in 1981. "The main difference between the 80s and that of the 70s will be in the intellectual contribution of the Bank."[99]

But these opportunities would come at great cost. Although the impact of SAL continues to be debated, evidence suggests that these operations largely failed to achieve their objectives.[100] While the financial assistance that developing countries received afforded them a greater degree of economic stability than would have otherwise been the case, the broad-based growth that was intended to result did not come to fruition.[101] Some researchers have even concluded that the Bank's initial structural adjustment loans depressed growth.[102] What is more clear is that requirements to cut spending tended to reduce borrowing governments' ability to provide public services.[103] As a result, early structural adjustment loans generally harmed low-income groups, something the Bank has admitted.[104]

Many observers have argued that the reason for these failures lies in the specific adjustment policies pursued.[105] Yet conditionality was never that strong in practice. Instead of undertaking the full range of prescribed measures, officials tended to adopt only those reforms that were easiest to implement. For instance, public opposition often hamstrung efforts to privatize state-owned industries, and fear of alienating domestic constituencies meant that protectionist measures often remained in place.[106]

Even so, SAL demonstrated considerable staying power. Rather than serving as a solution to temporary problems, SAL became an enduring part of the Bank's work. By 1989, the organization had issued over 200 adjustment loans, and some countries made yearly requests for aid.[107] The popularity of adjustment lending, in fact, was evidence of its failure—had the programs worked as intended, there would be little reason to continue them. As the economist William Easterly, a former Bank staffer, has concluded, "there is not much evidence that structural adjustment lending generated either adjustment or growth."[108]

Conclusion

On the morning of June 9, 1980, Robert McNamara informed the World Bank's Board of Executive Directors that he would be leaving the organization in one year's time. The announcement came as a surprise given that he would still have two years left in his third five-year term as president. The Board asked McNamara to reconsider, but he declined.[1] In a letter to staff, he explained that he had chosen to step down early because most "unresolved problems of the Bank's future" had been settled.[2] The previous months had seen a flurry of activity that had set the Bank up for continued growth. In late 1979, the organization's members came to terms on an unprecedented $12 billion replenishment of IDA, and the following January they nearly doubled the Bank's authorized capital stock to $85 billion. A month later, the Board approved McNamara's proposal to begin structural adjustment lending, and shortly thereafter Willy Brandt's Independent Commission on International Development Issues, which McNamara had organized in response to the impasse over the New International Economic Order (NIEO), released its report.[3]

Then, on May 15, the People's Republic of China joined the Bank. China's entry was the culmination of months of negotiations between Bank and Chinese officials, including a meeting between McNamara and Chinese leader Deng Xiaoping in Beijing on April 15, 1980.[4] China's membership immediately doubled the Bank's developing country population.[5] When McNamara announced his retirement a few weeks later, the organization appeared to have become the global institution he had envisioned twelve years earlier.

But these achievements masked significant problems. At the beginning of the 1980s, morale in the Bank was at a low point. Staff complained about the deteriorating quality of lending and management's apparent lack of concern. For his part, McNamara was aware that for all he had done to increase the Bank's power, the organization had made little headway in the fight against global poverty.[6] The Bank's new projects had largely failed to achieve their objectives, and developing country debs mounted. The Bank also struggled to convince borrowing governments to heed its policy advice. And U.S. support, which remained critical to the organization, continued to erode: in 1980 Congress failed to fill the Carter administration's annual request for Bank funding.[7] "The problems of providing finance to the third world," McNamara complained to his aides, "were getting more and more difficult."[8]

Things were about to get worse. That summer, Ronald Reagan, former governor of California, secured the Republican nomination for the upcoming U.S. presidential election. Like many conservatives, Reagan opposed both foreign aid and international organizations—a bad combination for the World Bank. In 1978, he dismissed aid as a "sieve" that drained taxpayer funds, and years earlier he had referred to the UN as a "moral[ly] bankrupt" institution.[9] As the race for the presidency heated up, the U.S.-Bank relationship looked like it was about to deteriorate even further. The Republican Party platform called for greater reliance on bilateral funding in the provision of foreign aid, as well an increased focus on military, as opposed to development, assistance.[10] Meanwhile, many on the left continued to criticize the Bank over its human rights and environmental record.

Because McNamara's resignation would take place before the election, he sought to identify a successor who would be acceptable to both Carter and Reagan. He settled on A. W. "Tom" Clausen, the fifty-seven-year-old president of the Bank of America.[11] McNamara had met Clausen, a moderate Republican, as the Bank forged closer ties with private banks during the 1970s, and the two discussed the Bank presidency in the months before McNamara's departure.[12] The Carter administration was impressed by Clausen's "experience and stature," and after running his name by Reagan's camp offered him the position in October, one month before the election.[13] In a private meeting, Carter told Clausen he wanted to proceed quickly, "before a movement develops among other key members [of the Bank] to nominate a non-American," which Carter felt might further reduce congressional support of the organization.[14] Clausen accepted. Carter informed other heads of state of his decision. And on November 25, 1980, the Bank's Board formally appointed him to succeed McNamara.[15]

Clausen's appointment lacked the drama of McNamara's thirteen years earlier. Still, the choice fit the times. Clausen had been a key figure in the financial globalization of the 1970s. At the end of his ten years as head of the Bank of America, 40 percent of company profits came from overseas.[16] Clausen was also, in the words of Carter officials, a "political and economic centrist" who believed the Bank could play a positive role in promoting market-oriented development.[17]

Clausen's bona fides did little to mollify American conservatives. After Reagan defeated Carter in November, the incoming administration voiced plans for significant cutbacks in U.S. funding of the Bank. David Stockman, the brash director of the Office of Management and Budget, led this charge. Stockman was determined to use his position as chief author of the Reagan budget to put an end to what he called "permanent government." In January 1981, he leaked a memo outlining a 50 percent reduction in the U.S. contribution to IDA. Stockman also proposed that instead of providing capital to the Bank, the U.S. government use that money to guarantee private loans to developing countries.[18] In justifying this functional withdrawal from the Bank, Stockman reiterated conservative charges that the organization had failed to advance U.S. interests. He claimed the Bank had not sufficiently pressured borrowing governments to liberalize and criticized the organization for lending to socialist governments.[19]

As we have seen, this was not the first time U.S. conservatives had chided the Bank on these grounds. But Stockman's ability to make good on his threats, combined with the rise of conservative governments in other wealthy nations, alarmed McNamara. Shortly after Reagan's election, he complained to his aides about the "very strong movement in the U.S., the UK, and Japan toward selfishness."[20] Other leaders of international agencies echoed McNamara's concerns. A few days after Stockman's memo became public, the heads of the UN Children's Fund and the UNDP, which were also on Reagan's chopping block, expressed "their gravest concern" to McNamara about the possibility of significant reductions in U.S. contributions to their organizations.[21]

Fortunately for the Bank, Stockman's position was too radical for his colleagues. Concerned about the international uproar that would ensue if the proposed cuts went through, Secretary of State Alexander Haig proposed more modest reductions in U.S. contributions to the Bank.[22] A Treasury Department report released in the fall of 1981 that argued that the Bank in fact did serve U.S. interests bolstered Haig's position.[23] The report noted that Bank loans and policy advice facilitated private investment in developing countries and, as such, the organization had been "effective in contributing to the achievement of [U.S.] global economic objectives."[24] The report also found that, while McNamara had failed to respond to some U.S. directives, the Bank had "contributed significantly to the achievement of U.S. long and medium term political/strategic interests" by financing anticommunist governments in the Philippines, Indonesia, and Brazil.[25]

Accordingly, the Reagan administration decided that rather than withdraw support from the Bank, it would seek to increase its power within the organization. Stockman's plan was discarded, and the administration requested that Congress increase U.S. funding of the Bank.[26] In so doing, however, Reagan officials made it clear that they wanted the Bank to more aggressively push developing countries to reduce the level of government intervention in their economies, an approach they felt "represented the best approach to poverty alleviation."[27]

*   *   *

Robert McNamara left the World Bank on June 30, 1981, just as these events were taking place. A few days before his retirement, the Bank's Board and senior management gathered for a farewell reception at the Kennedy Center. After praising McNamara for his "dynamic" leadership and "outstanding work" at the Bank, the Board presented him with a clock to signify the precision with which he ran their meetings and announced the publication of a book of his major speeches as Bank president to demonstrate his role as a "serious development thinker."[28] The participants credited McNamara with having "redefined" the concept of development during his tenure and for turning the Bank into "one of the most effective instruments ever devised to fulfill the human aspiration for progress."[29]

Despite the rhetoric, sadness permeated the proceedings. A few months earlier, McNamara's wife Margaret had died of cancer. The loss was a tremendous personal blow and a factor in his decision to leave the Bank. Margaret had repeatedly encouraged her husband to direct the Bank's resources to the fight against global poverty. In this way, her influence recalled the activist vision of the 1960s, when many Americans believed in the power of government to promote economic progress and social welfare. By the time of Margaret's death, however, a growing number of people—including the new president of the United States—had come to view government as the cause, rather than the solution, to such problems.

The radicalness of the new approach emerged shortly after McNamara's retirement, when the Reagan administration nixed one of his last major proposals for the Bank. Concerned about the vulnerability of oil-importing developing countries to continued fluctuations in oil prices, in January 1979 McNamara convinced the Bank's Board to approve the creation of an "energy affiliate" that would use contributions from wealthy countries to support domestic energy production in oil-importing developing nations.[30] The effects of the second oil crisis made the importance of such a program evident, and in 1980 Bank members encouraged management to proceed with the plan.[31] Right before the program was to launch, however, the Reagan administration voiced its opposition on the grounds that some funds would go to state-owned energy companies. In leading the effort to overturn the Board's decision, U.S. officials demanded that the Bank instead focus its efforts on "foster[ing] private sector involvement in energy development."[32] The Bank's management was unable to overcome U.S. resistance, and the proposal died.

The demise of the energy affiliate represented a repudiation of the Bank's basic approach under McNamara. Although the organization continued to support the expansion of capitalism in the developing world, the Bank demonstrated a considerable degree of openness to government interventionism throughout the 1970s. McNamara never focused on whether a country followed a public or private-led development strategy.[33] Instead, he considered the main issue whether local officials appeared serious about development. This may have been one of the things that attracted him to governments, like those in Indonesia and the Philippines, which pursued authoritarian development strategies. It was also why, despite repeated setbacks, he tried to foster public solutions to challenges like the oil crisis. McNamara's belief that progress could be engineered owed a great deal to his personal sensibilities. He was a quintessential technocrat and had a natural affinity for planning. Yet the focus on working with and through governments was also in line with development orthodoxy. Since its emergence as an intellectual and policy domain, development had been synonymous with state-led efforts to accelerate economic expansion. Indeed, the very idea that development needed to be planned constituted a rejection of the belief that market forces, left to their own devices, would lead to progress.

This understanding had changed significantly by the early 1980s. Economists increasingly argued that economic growth was the surest route to growth. At the same time, the prospect that developing countries could catch up to developed ones and create robust social welfare states, a widely shared goal during the postwar decades, seemed dimmer than ever.

McNamara's retirement from the Bank came at the precise time that this change was taking place. As such, his presidency marked a moment of transition in the history of development. As we have seen, the Bank began to embrace a more neoliberal conception of development during the 1970s. The organization's policy and research documents increasingly stressed the need for developing countries to reduce trade barriers, price controls, and government spending, as well as to privatize state-owned enterprises. The onset of structural adjustment lending in 1980 gave these ideas teeth.

McNamara's successor accelerated this shift. A few months after taking office, Clausen gave a speech in which he stated that the Bank "was not in the business of redistributing wealth from one set of countries to another." Under his leadership, the organization also reduced its poverty-oriented lending while expanding structural adjustment.[34] Clausen's appointment of Anne Krueger, a leading critic of state-led development efforts, as the Bank's chief economist in 1982 further entrenched the Bank's move to the right.

At the same time, the Reagan administration adopted an increasingly confrontational posture toward the developing world. Speaking at the World Bank-IMF annual meetings in Washington, D.C. in September 1981, Reagan argued strongly against state-led development efforts. "The societies which have achieved the most spectacular broad-based economic progress in the shortest period of time are not the most tightly controlled, not necessarily the biggest in size, or the wealthiest in natural resources," he declared. "What unites them all is their willingness to believe in the magic of the marketplace."[35] The following month, Reagan squashed any remaining hopes for the NIEO by informing developing country leaders at a summit in Cancún, Mexico, that the United States was firmly opposed to Southern demands.[36]

World events soon brought the Bank and the United States even closer. When the government of Mexico suspended payments on its external debt and touched off an international debt crisis in 1982, the Reagan administration looked to the Bank to help manage the aftermath.[37] Although American officials were primarily concerned about ensuring the stability of the U.S. financial system, they saw the crisis as an opportunity to promote free market reforms in developing countries. Consequently, they pushed the Bank to expand its structural adjustment activities. Bank management obliged, and an organization that had demonstrated considerable independence from the U.S. government during the 1970s soon emerged as a tool in the Reagan administration's efforts to roll back the state in the developing world.[38]

The Bank's response to the debt crisis, which proceeded in parallel with the IMF's stabilization and adjustment efforts, was a disaster. Over the course of the 1980s, the adoption of adjustment measures became a condition for bailout funds.[39] Instead of debt relief or growth, the period was marked by economic stagnation. According to Bank researchers, in Latin America, the epicenter of the crisis, per capita income declined by an average of 0.5 percent per year during the 1980s, down from a yearly average of 2.5 to 3 percent between 1940 and 1980.[40] Latin America's "Lost Decade" extended well into the 1990s; not until 1994 did the region's per capita income recover to its pre-crisis level.[41] Adjustment was painful in other parts of the world, as well. Beginning in 1980, per capita growth in sub-Saharan Africa fell to nearly 1 percent per year, and by the end of the century most countries on the continent were poorer than they had been at the start of the crisis.[42] Yet growth was not the only thing that was lost during this time. Although they were rarely implemented fully, structural adjustment measures marked a repudiation of development approaches that envisioned a role for government as a guarantor of social welfare, which had long a central goal of development.[43]

*   *   *

The structural adjustment era was a fitting postscript to Robert McNamara's presidency of the World Bank. In establishing a program of conditional lending, he entrenched the view that policy advising was the critical component of the organization's work. Although the Bank may have evolved in a similar way under a different president, McNamara accelerated the Bank's transformation into a more interventionist institution.

McNamara's impact extended in other directions, as well. The former Harvard Business School professor, Ford executive, and secretary of defense helped change the way the Bank thought about its work. Like a growing number of people in the late 1960s, McNamara recognized that economic growth did not inexorably result in improved living standards, and he used the Bank presidency to provide rhetorical, financial, and institutional support to those advocating for greater attention to the human aspects of development. Reducing poverty had always been an implicit goal of the Bank's, and others had tried to get the organization to expand in this direction. But it was not until McNamara that the Bank started speaking about the centrality of poverty to development, funding projects that sought to reduce poverty, and channeling a significant share of its resources to the world's poorest countries. Since McNamara, every World Bank president has spoken extensively about poverty alleviation. Today, it is the organization's main goal.

The poverty focus not only put the Bank at the forefront of the international development field but also served as an umbrella under which the organization justified its growth. At the same time that McNamara was having the Bank embark on new forms of rural and urban development, the organization initiated and broadened its work in education, nutrition, technical assistance, and tourism, among other fields. McNamara also used the Bank's resources to coordinate multiparty initiatives, such as the Consultative Group on International Agricultural Research and the Onchocerciasis Control Program. He entrenched the idea that the Bank could best understand complex phenomena like poverty through economic analysis. And he presided over a tremendous expansion of the organization's research and publications program, including the creation of the *World Development Report*.

In expanding the Bank's work in these ways, McNamara set the organization on a path in which its activities proliferated. Although the Bank had expanded significantly before McNamara—transitioning from European reconstruction to Latin American development in the late 1940s, beginning to lend significantly to South Asia in the 1950s, and starting to branch out from infrastructure lending in the 1960s—it was a minor player in the world stage before McNamara arrived. In large part, this was because it tended to behave as a conservative financial institution focused on maintaining its reputation as a sound investment in the capital markets in which it raised money. McNamara felt that development challenges could result in global conflagration if left unaddressed, and upon assuming the Bank presidency he sought to shed the organization's conservatism. Under his direction, the Bank increased and diversified its lending and borrowing programs and emerged as a center of development research. Coming at the same time that the foreign aid budgets of major Western nations were shrinking, McNamara's active management thrust the organization into a leadership position in development. Nevertheless, the Bank's growth came at a price. Most notably, the establishment of country lending targets incentivized staff to move money out the door. This marked a shift from the restrained style in which Bank previously operated and placed a significant strain on both the organization and its borrowers.

For all McNamara did to increase the Bank's reach, it is worth considering some of the things that the organization did not do during his tenure.

Despite the fact that many people inside and outside the organization had become aware of the adverse ecological impacts of some of its projects, the Bank under McNamara never incorporated environmental concerns into its lending practices. The Bank also failed to respond to concerns about human rights. Many countries wanted the organization to avoid the issue, and Mc-Namara was happy to oblige. These experiences demonstrated a major constraint under which the Bank operated: governments still had to approve major decisions. Indeed, even though Bank staff and management were aware of corruption, tax evasion, and other forms of illicit behavior in borrowing countries, they had a difficult time addressing such issues. The limits on the Bank's behavior were perhaps most evident in McNamara's failure to make lending for population control a significant part of the Bank's work. Despite his concerns about global population growth, his efforts to have the organization support population control efforts ran into opposition from developing country officials who saw it as a form of neocolonialism, as well as from Bank staff who felt that proposed loans were too inexpensive to justify their attention.

Despite such difficulties, the McNamara years demonstrate the critical role that Bank presidents have played in the organization's history. During his brief tenure as the Bank's second president, John J. McCloy managed to convince the U.S. government to vest significant power in the hands of the Bank's president. Eugene Black established the organization's creditworthiness, and George Woods took the first steps in moving the Bank beyond infrastructure lending. McNamara built upon these efforts in a number of ways—and not surprisingly, his departure left a void. Although Tom Clausen initially enjoyed close relations with the U.S. government, he ran into problems with the Reagan administration and decided to step down after just one term. Barber Conable, a Republican congressman from New York, replaced Clausen in 1986. Conable's tenure was also rocky. While he oversaw a significant increase in the activities of the International Finance Corporation, the Bank's private sector investment arm, the Bank faced significant criticism over structural adjustment lending during his watch. Things went poorly inside the Bank as well. Like many U.S. conservatives, Conable thought the Bank was too large, and he pushed through a poorly executed reorganization in which 400 members of the Bank's staff were fired.[44] The effects of Conable's reorganization were still being felt when Lewis Preston, a long-time executive at J.P. Morgan who took over from Conable in 1991, passed away four years into his term.

James Wolfensohn, an Australian-born financier who had become a naturalized U.S. citizen in 1980, took over shortly after Preston's death. Even as he was making a fortune in the burgeoning Eurobond market in the 1970s, Wolfensohn eyed the Bank presidency (hence his obtaining U.S. citizenship). Inspired by McNamara, during his ten years at the helm of the Bank he pushed the organization to refocus its efforts on poverty reduction.[45] Under Wolfensohn, the Bank started to speak openly about the challenges of corruption in developing nations, forgave some of the debt that continued to plague many of its borrowers, and began to incorporate gender and environmental concerns into its work. Wolfensohn's active response to the bevy of global challenges during the time, from the street protests that greeted the yearly IMF-Word Bank meetings to the outbreak of the HIV/AIDs crisis, endeared him to many observers and provided some relief to an institution that had stagnated for more than a decade. Even so, Wolfensohn's tenure had its downsides. His volatile management style, in which he punished internal dissent and threatened to resign when things did not go as planned, rubbed many people the wrong way, and his efforts to expand the Bank's activities enlarged its bureaucracy.[46]

Wolfensohn resembled McNamara in his missionary zeal, his success in pushing the Bank in new directions, and the mix of enmity and admiration that he inspired inside and outside the organization. For other reasons, his successor also drew comparisons to McNamara. In 2005, U.S. President George W. Bush tapped Paul Wolfowitz to take over from Wolfensohn. Wolfowitz had been a zealous advocate of the Iraq War as U.S. deputy secretary of defense, and his appointment to the Bank presidency—just as it was becoming clear that the war was turning into a disaster—evoked memories of McNamara's transition from the Pentagon to the Bank four decades earlier. But while both McNamara and Wolfowitz came to the Bank from failed wars, the comparisons ended there. Whereas McNamara went on to an eventful thirteen-year tenure, Wolfowitz, who lacked management experience, became embroiled in a conflict-of-interest scandal and resigned from the Bank after just two years.

The Wolfowitz debacle ignited calls to reform the process for selecting the Bank president. Remarkably, the organization's Articles of Agreement do not specify how the organization's president is to be chosen. Instead, under an informal agreement by which European countries select the IMF managing director, the United States chooses the Bank president. As a result, each president has been a U.S. citizen (and, it should be added, a man). Although this situation helps ensure congressional support for the Bank, the process is anachronistic. The lack of a more equitable and transparent means of selecting the Bank's head also deprives developing countries of a say over the organization's most important position, which contributes to the Bank's democratic deficit.[47]

The absence of meaningful governance reforms makes understanding the internal workings of the Bank all the more important. Although focusing on leadership is only one way of analyzing an institution as large and complex as the World Bank, McNamara's presidency offers a window into top-level decision-making in international organizations, an approach that remains lacking in global governance scholarship.[48] Similarly, it makes sense to consider the role of staff. In the case of McNamara's Bank, staff was instrumental, at points even derailing managerial decisions. We have also seen how the Bank's organizational dynamics can exert a strong influence on its operations. During McNamara's tenure, the impetus for growth shaped the way in which the organization defined and addressed development. Early in McNamara's presidency, this manifested itself in the creation of capital-intensive rural and urban development projects. Later, the need to create lending instruments that could rapidly channel large amounts of funds to developing countries drove the creation of structural adjustment lending.

More broadly, McNamara's presidency of the Bank demonstrates the important role that international organizations can play in world affairs. The belief that multilateral bodies are passive agents of major countries is pervasive. Yet McNamara's experience at the Bank provides an example of an international organization that occasionally acted against the wishes of its most powerful member. This history upends views of the Bank as a monolithic tool of U.S. foreign policy. The belief that international organizations have little real world influence is also common. Yet in addition to the thousands of projects that it carries out, the Bank has been instrumental in shaping the meaning of development. It is hard to imagine a more impactful institution.

McNamara's presidency of the Bank further challenges our understanding of the history of development. For well over a decade, scholars have devoted considerable attention to documenting how development emerged and evolved as a domestic and international policy goal, practice, and discourse. This work has provided much-needed context for current development approaches and enriched our understanding of the past.[49] Nevertheless, historians have largely failed to explore the institutions that have formulated and executed development, as well as to consider how the field evolved after the 1960s.[50] McNamara's presidency of the Bank shows that the transition away from state-centric development was rooted in the economic, political, and intellectual upheavals of the 1970s. It also demonstrates how organizational dynamics shaped the specific mechanisms of post-1980s development, such as structural adjustment.

As the Whiz Kid architect of the Vietnam War, Robert McNamara has long personified some of the contradictions of modern American history. McNamara is the straight-laced bureaucrat who lied through his teeth, the corporate manager emboldened and constrained by his systems of analysis, the quantifier whose numbers failed to add up.[51] To some, McNamara even embodies the demise of postwar American liberalism. However, because his presidency of the World Bank has escaped scholarly and popular attention, our understanding of the man has remained incomplete.

These pages have shown that McNamara's attempt to tackle global poverty should not be viewed as a break with Vietnam. Instead, there were clear continuities between his approach at the Bank and his tenure at the Defense Department. These include not just the specific techniques he used to manage each institution but also his interventionist logic. At the Pentagon, McNamara was an early proponent of escalation in Vietnam. When he realized that intervention was failing, he refused to speak out. At the Bank, McNamara sought to lend more money, to more countries, and for more projects than ever before. Yet he kept quiet even after realizing that there were limits to how much the Bank could lend and developing countries could borrow. On a more personal level, McNamara could never escape the ghosts of Vietnam. Even when at the Bank, those close to him described him as "a deeply wounded" man.[52] Compounding his grief was the fact that he was aware that, for all his success in remaking the Bank, the organization made little headway in reducing global poverty. This failure is perhaps one reason why McNamara rarely spoke about his time at the Bank after leaving in 1981.[53]

Nevertheless, McNamara's presidency continues to shape the organization. The Bank's focus on maximizing lending is one of his more prominent legacies. Contemporary observers have detailed how the Bank is often more focused on making loans than ensuring that its funds are used productively. In detailing this "culture of disbursement," critics are identifying a phenomenon that can be traced to McNamara.[54] McNamara's ability to expand Bank lending without sacrificing its ability to borrow also created a situation in which Bank presidents have felt comfortable placing an ever wider range of initiatives onto the organization's agenda This tendency toward "mission creep" had been evident since the Bank's first days and characterizes many organizations.[55] Still, McNamara helped lay the groundwork by which the Bank's agenda—which now encompasses climate change, corruption, biodiversity, tax reform, money laundering, disaster management, technology transfer, cultural preservation, and many other important issues— has continued to expand. In sum, McNamara was instrumental in turning the World Bank into the the vexed institution that it is today: an organization supreme in the development field but which remains unable to solve the increasing number of problems it puts on its plate.

NOTES

Introduction

1. Video of the ceremony is included in the documentary film *The Fog of War: Eleven Lessons from the Life of Robert S. McNamara* (Sony Pictures Classics, 2004).

2. Lyndon B. Johnson, "Remarks Upon Presenting the Medal of Freedom to Robert S. McNamara, February 28, 1968," in *Public Papers of the Presidents of the United States: Lyndon B. Johnson, 1968–69, Book I–January 1 to June 30, 1968*, 290–92 (Washington, D.C.: Government Printing Office, 1970).

3. Robert S. McNamara with Brian VanDeMark, *In Retrospect: The Tragedy and Lessons of Vietnam* (New York: Vintage, 1996), xx.

4. Although this is the first full-length study of McNamara's presidency of the Bank, detailed accounts may also be found in Devesh Kapur, John P. Lewis, and Richard Webb, *The World Bank: Its First Half Century*, vol. 1, *History* (Washington, D.C.: Brookings Institution, 1997), 215–329 and Deborah Shapley, *Promise and Power: The Life and Times of Robert McNamara* (New York: Little, Brown, 1993), 463–582.

5. See Michael O'Brien, *John F. Kennedy: A Biography* (New York: St. Martin's, 2005), 505.

6. Robert S. McNamara, "To the Board of Governors, Washington D.C., September 30, 1968," in McNamara, *The McNamara Years at the World Bank: Major Policy Addresses of Robert S. McNamara, 1968–1981* (Baltimore: Johns Hopkins University Press, 1981), 3, 5.

7. On the history of development and its relationship to U.S. foreign relations, see Michael E. Latham, *The Right Kind of Revolution: Modernization, Development, and U.S. Foreign Policy from the Cold War to the Present* (Ithaca, N.Y.: Cornell University Press, 2011); Nick Cullather, *The Hungry World: America's Cold War Battle Against Poverty in Asia* (Cambridge, Mass.: Harvard University Press, 2010); David Ekbladh, *The Great American Mission: Modernization and the Construction of an American World Order* (Princeton, N.J.: Princeton University Press, 2010). For a recent overview of scholarship on the history of development generally, see Joseph Morgan Hodge, "Writing the History of Development (Part 1: The First Wave)," *Humanity* 6, 3 (Winter 2015): 429–63, and "Writing the History of Development (Part 2: Longer, Deeper, Wider)," *Humanity* 7, 1 (Spring 2016): 125–74.

8. E. F. Schumacher, "Intermediate Technology: The Missing Factor in Foreign Aid," *Oxford Diocesan Magazine* (July 1970), in Records of the Office of the President, Records of President Robert S. McNamara (hereafter McNamara Papers), Chronological file (outgoing)—19, World Bank Group Archives (hereafter WBGA).

9. See William R. Easterly, *The Elusive Quest for Growth: Economists' Adventures and Misadventures in the Tropics* (Cambridge, Mass.: MIT Press, 2001).

10. David Halberstam, *The Best and the Brightest* (New York: Ballantine, 1992), 245. On McNamara's tenure as secretary of defense, see Lawrence S. Kaplan, Ronald D. Landa, and Edward J. Drea, *The McNamara Ascendancy, 1961–1965* (Washington, D.C.: Historical Office, Office of the Secretary of Defense, 2006) and Drea, *McNamara, Clifford, and the Burdens of Vietnam, 1965–1969* (Washington, D.C.: Historical Office, Office of the Secretary of Defense, 2011).

11. On the international history of the 1970s, see Niall Ferguson, Charles S. Maier, Erez Manela, and Daniel Sargent, eds., *The Shock of the Global: The 1970s in Perspective* (Cambridge, Mass.: Belknap Press of Harvard University Press, 2011). On changes in U.S. foreign relations during this time, see Sargent, *A Superpower Transformed: The Remaking of American Foreign Relations in the 1970s* (Oxford: Oxford University Press, 2015).

12. Scholarship on the history of development in the 1970s is still in its infancy. For a general overview of the U.S. experience during this time, see Latham, *The Right Kind of Revolution*, 157–85.

13. On the historical significance of international organizations, see Akira Iriye, *Global Community: The Role of International Organizations in the Making of the Contemporary World* (Berkeley: University of California Press, 2004).

Chapter 1. An Unlikely World Banker

1. John Blaxall, interview with author.

2. Harry Dexter White, "Proposal for a United Nations Stabilization Fund and a Bank for Reconstruction," April 1942, cited in Edward S. Mason and Robert E. Asher, *The World Bank Since Bretton Woods* (Washington, D.C.: Brookings Institution, 1973), 15.

3. Mason and Asher, *The World Bank Since Bretton Woods*, 17–18.

4. White's April 1942 plan called for the Bank to "help strengthen the monetary and credit structures of the member countries by redistributing the world gold supply . . . stabilize the prices of essential raw materials and other important commodities [and] . . . provide for the financing and distribution of foodstuffs and other essential commodities needed for the relief of populations devastated by war conditions." Cited in Mason and Asher, *The World Bank Since Bretton Woods*, 16. Also see Donald Babai, "Between Hegemony and Poverty: The World Bank in the World Economy" (Ph.D. dissertation, University of California, Berkeley, 1984), 157–60.

5. Henry Morgenthau, Jr., memorandum attached to the "Preliminary Draft Outline of a Proposal for a United Nations Bank for Reconstruction and Development," November 1943. Cited in Mason and Asher, *The World Bank Since Bretton Woods*, 18.

6. The preliminary draft outline for the Bank called for votes to be divided according to government contributions, with no single country controlling more than 25 percent of the votes. Mason and Asher, *The World Bank Since Bretton Woods*, 17.

7. See Michael D. Bordo, *The Gold Standard and Related Regimes: Collected Essays* (Cambridge: Cambridge University Press, 1999), 427.

8. Robert Skidelsky, *John Maynard Keynes: Fighting for Freedom, 1937–1946* (New York: Penguin, 2002), 307. Instead, Keynes and the British delegation supported creation of an "International Development Corporation," as well as a commodity stabilization and buffer stock mechanism (307–9); Kapur et al., *The World Bank*, 197 ff. Also see Roy Harrod, *Life of John Maynard Keynes* (New York: Norton, 1983), 525–85.

9. Elizabeth Borgwardt, *A New Deal for the World: America's Vision for Human Rights* (Cambridge, Mass.: Harvard University Press, 2005), 25–26.

10. Mason and Asher, *The World Bank Since Bretton Woods*, 13.

11. Ibid., 21–22.

12. *Articles of Agreement, International Monetary Fund and International Bank for Reconstruction and Development, United Nations Monetary and Financial Conference, Bretton Woods, N.H., July 1 to 22, 1944*, III(4)(vii); III(3); I(ii); II(1)(a), http://siteresources.worldbank.org/EXTARCHIVES/Resources/IBRD_Articles_of_Agreement.pdf.

13. Mason and Asher, *The World Bank Since Bretton Woods*, 23–24.

14. IBRD, *Articles of Agreement*, IV(10).

15. Harrod, *Life of Keynes*, 540.

16. U.S. Department of State, *Proceedings and Documents*, vol. 1, 1101.

17. See Craig N. Murphy, *International Organizations and Industrial Change: Global Governance Since 1850* (New York: Oxford University Press, 1994); David Armstrong, Lorna Lloyd, and John Redmond, *From Versailles to Maastricht: International Organisation in the Twentieth Century* (New York: St. Martin's, 1996), 7–61.

18. In 1920, the prime minister of Belgium proposed that an "International Bank of Issue" be created to provide investment capital to governments on favorable terms, and two years later German officials suggested establishment of a "Bank of Nations" that would do the same. See Rich, *Mortgaging the Earth*, 51; Dean Elizabeth Traynor, "International Monetary and Financial Conferences in the Interwar Period" (Ph.D. dissertation, Catholic University of America, 1949).

19. Frank Costigliola, "The Other Side of Isolationism: The Establishment of the First World Bank, 1929–30," *Journal of American History* 59, 3 (1972): 602–20. The BIS role as a manager of World War I reparations fell by the wayside shortly after establishment as a result of the onset of the Depression. It soon evolved into a body for central bank coordination, a role it continues to play.

20. See Eric Helleiner, *Forgotten Foundations of Bretton Woods: International Development and the Making of the Postwar Order* (Ithaca, N.Y.: Cornell University Press, 2014), 52–79.

21. William Appleman Williams, *The Tragedy of American Diplomacy*, rev. ed. (New York: Norton, 1988); Walter LaFeber, *The American Age: United States Foreign Policy at Home and Abroad, 1750 to the Present*, 2nd ed. (New York: Norton, 1994); Emily S. Rosenberg, *Financial Missionaries to the World: The Politics and Culture of Dollar Diplomacy, 1900–1930* (Durham, N.C.: Duke University Press, 2003); Rosenberg, *Spreading the American Dream: American Economic and Cultural Expansion, 1890–1945* (New York: Hill and Wang, 1982).

22. Franklin Delano Roosevelt, "Message to Congress on the Bretton Woods Agreements," February 12, 1945, *Public Papers of the Presidents*, American Presidency Project (hereafter APP), http://www.presidency.ucsb.edu/ws/?pid=16588.

23. Borgwardt, *A New Deal for the World*.

24. John G. Ruggie, "International Regimes, Transactions, and Change: Embedded Liberalism in the Postwar Economic Order," *International Organization* 36, 2 (Spring 1982): 379–415. On the role of the state in the postwar order, see also Helleiner, *States and the Reemergence of Global Finance* (25) and Jacob Viner, "International Finance in the Postwar World," *Journal of Political Economy* 65, 2 (April 1947): 97–107.

25. In his closing remarks to the Bretton Woods conference, for instance, Morgenthau declared that the Bank would "drive the usurious money lenders from the temple of international finance." U.S. Department of State, *Proceedings and Documents*, vol. 2, 1227.

26. Anastasia Xenias, "Wartime Financial Diplomacy and the Transition to the Treasury System, 1939–1947," in David M. Andrews, ed., *Orderly Change: International Monetary Relations Since Bretton Woods* (Ithaca, N.Y.: Cornell University Press, 2008), 41–50; Raymond F. Mikesell, *Foreign Adventures of an Economist* (Eugene: University of Oregon Press, 2000), 63–66; Richard N. Gardner, *Sterling-Dollar Diplomacy: Anglo-American Collaboration in the Reconstruction of Multilateral Trade* (Oxford: Clarendon, 1956); Borgwardt, *A New Deal for the World*, 127–40; Theodore R. Libby, "The Ideology and Power of the World Bank" (Ph.D. dissertation, University of Washington, 1975), 18–20.

27. The Bank's Articles of Agreement formally came into effect on December 31, 1945, after signature by twenty-eight governments.

28. IBRD, *Third Annual Report, 1947–1948*.

29. Jeffrey M. Chwieroth, "International Liquidity Provision: The IMF and the World Bank in the Treasury and Marshall Systems, 1942–1957," in Edwards, ed., *Orderly Change*, 53.

30. Ibid., 56–60.

31. Ibid., 71.

32. Also see Chwieroth, "Organizational Change 'From Within': Exploring the World Bank's Early Lending Practices," *Review of International Political Economy* 15, 4 (2008): 481–505.

33. Chwieroth, "International Liquidity Provision," 72; Catherine Gwin, "U.S. Relations with the World Bank, 1945–1992" in Kapur et al., *The World Bank*, vol. 2, 253–54; Valerie J. Assetto, *The Soviet Bloc in the IMF and IBRD* (Boulder, Colo.: Westview, 1988), 70–73.

34. IBRD, *Third Annual Report, 1947–1948*. The report of the Colombia mission was published as IBRD, *The Basis of a Development Program for Colombia* (Baltimore: Johns Hopkins University Press, 1950). For more on the Colombia mission and the Bank's turn to development see Alacevich, *The Political Economy of the World Bank*, 11–63.

35. Kapur et al., *The World Bank*, vol. 1, 57.

36. IBRD, *Articles of Agreement*, I(i); Kapur et al., *The World Bank*, vol. 1, 59–61.

37. Keynes, "Opening Remarks at the First Meeting of the Second Commission on the Bank for Reconstruction and Development," in U.S. Department of State, *Proceedings and Documents*, 84. For a view of the proceedings that stresses the centrality of development in the discussions over the IMF and World Bank, see Helleiner, *Forgotten Foundations*.

38. Cooper, "Modernizing Bureaucrats, Backward Africans, and the Development Concept," in Cooper and Packard, eds., *International Development and the Social Sciences*, 64.

39. On the colonial origins of development see Joseph Morgan Hodge *Triumph of the Expert: Agrarian Doctrines of Development and the Legacies of British Colonialism* (Athens: Ohio University Press, 2007) and Frederick Cooper, *Decolonization and African Society: The Labor Question in French and British Africa* (Cambridge: Cambridge University Press, 1996), among others.

40. Mason and Asher, *The World Bank Since Bretton Woods*, 491–537.

41. Libby, "The Ideology and Power of the World Bank," 26–32.

42. Warren Baum, *The Project Cycle* (Washington, D.C.: World Bank Group, 1982); Kapur et al., *The World Bank*, vol. 1, 85–138.

43. Kapur et al., *The World Bank*, vol. 1, 8; Chwieroth, "International Liquidity Provision," 74, and "Organizational Change 'From Within,'" 497–501.

44. Mason and Asher, *The World Bank Since Bretton Woods*, 124–46.

45. On the Bank's creation of "client constituencies," see Libby, "The Ideology and Power of the World Bank," 40–62.

46. List of closed projects by approval date, World Bank Projects Database, www .worldbank.org/projects.

47. The Bank's management pushed for creation of the IFC as a means to counter competition from the U.S. Export-Import Bank in financing private enterprises in developing countries. See Libby, "The Ideology and Power of the World Bank," 73–86.

48. Mason and Asher, *The World Bank Since Bretton Woods*, 72–87.

49. IDA, *Articles of Agreement*, V(1)(b).

50. On the creation of IDA see Mason and Asher, *The World Bank Since Bretton Woods*, 382–89; Gwin, "U.S. Relations with the World Bank," in Kapur et al., *The World Bank*, vol. 2, 206; Guia Migani, *La France et l'Afrique sub-saharienne, 1957–1963: Histoire d'une décolonisation entre idéaux eurafricains et politique de puissance* (Bern: Peter Lang, 2008), 207–21; Libby, "The Ideology and Power of the World Bank," 87–105.

51. Mason and Asher, *The World Bank Since Bretton Woods*, 62–63. On the power of the Bank's president also see Andrew Shonfield, "The World Bank," in Evan Luard., ed., *The Evolution of International Organizations* (New York: Praeger, 1966), 235–36, and Theodore H. Cohn, "Influence of the Less Developed Countries in the World Bank Group" (Ph.D. dissertation, University of Michigan, 1972), 61–76.

52. Chwieroth, "International Liquidity Provision," 75.

53. The Bank's focus on projects was also the result of the predilections of Robert Garner, who as chair of the organization's loan committee was able to make his personal preference for infrastructure projects Bank policy. Chwieroth, "Organizational Change 'From Within,'" 497.

54. Amy L. S. Staples, "Seeing Diplomacy Through Bankers' Eyes: The World Bank, the Anglo-American Oil Crisis, and the Aswan High Dam," *Diplomatic History* 26, 3 (Summer 2002): 397–418.

55. Robert W. Oliver, *George Woods and the World Bank* (Boulder, Colo.: Lynne Reinner, 1995).

56. Mason and Asher, *The World Bank Since Bretton Woods*, 136; World Bank Archives, "Robert Strange McNamara: 5th President of the World Bank Group, 1968–1981.

57. Praveen K. Chaudhry, Vijay L. Kelkar, and Vikash Yadav, "The Evolution of 'Home-grown Conditionality' in India: IMF Relations," *Journal of Development Studies* 40, 6 (August 2004): 59–81.

58. Kaplan et al., *The McNamara Ascendancy*, 547.

59. The most comprehensive biography of McNamara is Deborah Shapley, *Promise and Power: The Life and Times of Robert McNamara* (Boston: Little, Brown, 1993). Also see Paul Hendrickson, *The Living and the Dead: Robert McNamara and Five Lives of a Lost War* (New York: Knopf, 1996) and Henry L. Trewhitt, *McNamara* (New York: Harper & Row, 1971).

60. Shapley, *Promise and Power*, 1–19.

61. Ibid., 24.

62. Ibid., 20–27.

63. Ibid., 28–38.

64. John R. Davis, quoted in Allan Nevins and Frank Ernest Hill, *Ford: Decline and Rebirth, 1933–1962* (New York: Scribner's, 1962), 294.

65. Shapley, *Promise and Power*, 45–49. Paul Hendrickson has described how McNamara's accounting system went beyond traditional methods of data collection by trying to determine new metrics for the company, such as "cost centers and budget centers and profit centers," and using this information to plan business decisions. See Hendrickson, *The Living and the Dead*, 83–86. On GM's decentralization, see Robert F. Freeland, "The Struggle for Control of the Modern Corporation: Organizational Change at General Motors, 1924–1958," *Business and Economic History* 25, 1 (Fall 1996): 32–37.

66. Shapley, *Promise and Power*, 59–80.

67. On Kennedy's recruitment of McNamara, see Shapley, *Promise and Power*, 82–86, and Hendrickson, *The Living and the Dead*, 108–15.

68. On the history of the U.S. Department of Defense, see James Carroll, *House of War: The Pentagon and the Disastrous Rise of American Power* (New York: Houghton Mifflin, 2006).

69. Kaplan et al., *The McNamara Ascendancy*, 72–95.

70. In 1963, for instance, *Time* Magazine wrote about McNamara's "brilliance and dedication" in overcoming the military's opposition to his management programs. See "The Dilemma & the Design," *Time*, February 15, 1963.

71. On McNamara's role in the Bay of Pigs, see Shapley, *Promise and Power*, 114–16 and Trewhitt, *McNamara*, 97–98. On his role in the Cuban Missile Crisis, see Shapley, *Promise and Power*, 165–89.

72. Shapley, *Promise and Power*, 75–265.

73. Herring, *America's Longest War*, 102.

74. Kevin Ruane, *The Vietnam Wars* (New York: St. Martin's, 2000), xiii.

75. "Rusk-McNamara Report to Kennedy on South Vietnam, November 11, 1961," in Neil Sheehan et al., *The Pentagon Papers: As Published by the New York Times, Based on Investigative Reporting by Neil Sheehan* (New York: Quadrangle, 1971), 150–53; Kaplan et al., *The McNamara Ascendancy*, 276.

76. Kaplan et al., *The McNamara Ascendancy*, 517–24.

77. Herring, *America's Longest War*, 164. For a detailed account of Johnson administration decision-making in 1965 and 1966, see Drea, *McNamara, Clifford, and the Burdens of Vietnam*, 21–82.

78. The classic critique of McNamara's management of the war is found in Halberstam, *The Best and the Brightest*. Also see H. R. McMaster, *Dereliction of Duty: Lyndon Johnson, Robert McNamara, the Joint Chiefs of Staff, and the Lies That Led to Vietnam* (New York: HarperCollins, 1997).

79. Shapley, *Promise and Power*, 247–360.

80. The speech was reprinted in Robert S. McNamara, *The Essence of Security: Reflections in Office* (New York: Harper & Row, 1968), 141–58.

81. James Reston, "Washington: The Computer That Turned Philosopher," *New York Times*, May 22, 1966, 12E.

82. Mary McGrory, *Omaha World Herald*, May 25, 1966, cited in Shapley, *Promise and Power*, 383.

83. Reston, "The Computer That Turned Philosopher."

84. *The Fog of War*.

85. McNamara, "On Gaps and Bridges," in McNamara, *The Essence of Security*, 109.

86. On "helping the largest number," see Shapley, *Promise and Power*, 18. On McNamara's safety efforts at Ford, see *The Fog of War*, and Michael R. Lemov, *Car Safety Wars: One Hundred Years of Technology, Politics, and Death* (Madison, N.J.: Farleigh Dickinson University Press, 2015), 61. On Project 100,000, see Christian G. Appy, *Working-Class War: American Combat Soldiers and Vietnam* (Chapel Hill: University of North Carolina Press, 1993), 32–37.

87. For example, in 1963 McNamara told John Kennedy that initiatives to relocate South Vietnamese civilians to military-controlled "strategic hamlets" would give them "an identity as citizens of a community." Quoted in Latham, *Modernization as Ideology*, 189.

88. On Point Four see McVety, "Truman's Point Four Program."

89. Harry S. Truman, "Inaugural Address, January 20, 1949," http://www.presidency.ucsb.edu/ws/?pid=13282.

90. On U.S. aid in the 1960s and its relationship with the Vietnam War, see Ekbladh, *The Great American Mission*, 190–225.

91. Latham, *Modernization as Ideology*; Gilman, *Mandarins of the Future*, 203–76; Ekbladh, *The Great American Mission*, 226–256.

92. Shapley, *Promise and Power*, 323; Herring, *America's Longest War*, 214–15.

93. Trewhitt, *McNamara*, 235.

94. McNamara, *In Retrospect*, 266–271.

95. "McNamara to Johnson, May 19, 1967," in Sheehan et al., *The Pentagon Papers*, 580.

96. Robert Dallek, *Flawed Giant: Lyndon Johnson and His Times, 1961–1973* (New York: Oxford University Press, 1998), 391–442.

97. Quoted in Halberstam, *The Best and the Brightest*, 645.

98. Shapley, *Promise and Power*, 424.

99. John Roche in Shapley, *Promise and Power*, 426.

100. Robert Dallek, *Lyndon B. Johnson: Portrait of a President* (New York: Oxford University Press, 2004), 319.

101. Robert McNamara, interview with Errol Morris, December 11–12, 2001, 247–50, II:116, Robert S. McNamara Papers, Manuscript Division, Library of Congress, Washington, D.C. (hereafter RSM, LOC)

102. Shapley, *Promise and Power*, 427–28; McNamara, *In Retrospect*, 312–13; Hendrickson, *The Living and the Dead*, 338–39.

103. "List of possible choices, listed in alphabetical order of names, that have been suggested to succeed Mr. George D. Woods upon his retirement as President of the World Bank," undated, International Classified Material: World Bank 1967, Papers of Henry Fowler, Box 40, Lyndon Baines Johnson Library (hereafter LBJL). The list included five Americans: David E. Bell, Douglas C. Dillon, Thomas S. Gates, William McChesney Martin, Jr., and David Rockefeller.

104. Office Memorandum, Livingston T. Merchant to Henry H. Fowler, Subject: World Bank Presidency Succession, May 22, 1967, International Classified Material: World Bank 1967, Papers of Henry Fowler, Box 40, LBJL.

105. Shapley, *Promise and Power*, 436–37.

106. Ibid., 437–40.

Chapter 2. Modernizing the Bank

1. This story is recounted in Shapley, *Promise and Power*, 464.

2. Greg Votaw, interview with author.

3. John Blaxall, interview with author.

4. There was some precedent for automobile executives moving into development. Paul Hoffman, who served as director of the Economic Cooperation Administration, which administered the Marshall Plan, from 1948 to 1950 and headed the UNDP from 1959 to 1972, was president of Studebaker from 1935 to 1948. See Alan R. Raucher, *Paul G. Hoffman: Architect of Foreign Aid* (Lexington: University Press of Kentucky, 1985).

5. Minutes of the President's Council meeting (hereafter PC), April 1, 1968, McNamara Papers, President's Council Minutes. The quote comes from Clark, *From Three Worlds*, 239.

6. Clark, *From Three Worlds*, 239.

7. Quoted in Shapley, *Promise and Power*, 465.

8. Clark, "Reconsiderations," 168.

9. Ibid.

10. J. Burke Knapp, World Bank Oral History (hereafter WBOH), 83.

11. Weiss, "Science and Technology at the World Bank," 82.

12. Clark, "Reconsiderations," 168.

13. On the protests of 1968 and their relationship with global political and economic change, see Jeremi Suri, *Power and Protest: Global Revolution and the Rise of Detente* (Cambridge, Mass.: Harvard University Press, 2003).

14. *Partners in Development: Report of the Commission on International Development*, ed. L. B. Pearson (London: Pall Mall Press, 1969), 138.

15. Ibid. 138–39.

16. Ibid., 72–73.

17. Ibid., 3.

18. McNamara, List of Projects, May 25, 1968, RSM Chronological Files, Personal, Box 1.

19. Quoted in Shapley, *Promise and Power*, 471.

20. IBRD/IDA, *Annual Report*, 1968, 25.

21. PC, April 1, 1968, April 15, 1968, McNamara Papers, President's Council Minutes, Box 1.

22. Shapley, *Promise and Power*, 471.

23. McNamara, "To the Board of Governors, September 30, 1968," in McNamara, *The McNamara Years*, 8; Kapur et al., *The World Bank*, vol. 1, 957.

24. Rotberg, WBOH; Rotberg, "The Job Interview-1968," *The Memory Bank: World Bank Stories and Revelations* (1818 Society 30th Anniversary Publication, 2008), 6–7. Rotberg accepted the position on November 9, 1968. Cable, McNamara to Siem Aldewereld, November 9, 1968, in IBRD/IDA 03-04-09S, Box 1. He was named treasurer on November 20. Kapur et al., *The World Bank*, vol. 1, 957.

25. Shapley, *Promise and Power*, 472.

26. On the globalization of finance in the 1960s and 1970s see Eric Helleiner, *States and the Reemergence of Global Finance: From Bretton Woods to the 1990s* (Ithaca, N.Y.: Cornell University Press, 1994).

27. Cary Reich, "The World's Greatest Borrower (as Told by Himself)," *Institutional Investor* (July 1984): 57–69; Kapur et al., *The World Bank*, vol. 1, 957.

28. Eugene Rotberg, interview with author.

29. PC, July 14, 1969, McNamara Papers, President's Council Minutes, Box 1.

30. "McNamara Statement on Kennedy Role," *New York Times*, April 14, 1968, 62.

31. Shapley, *Promise and Power*, 466–67.

32. IBRD Articles of Agreement, IV (10).

33. "Indiscretion," *New York Times*, April 16, 1968, 46; "McNamara Assailed for Kennedy Acclaim," *Los Angeles Times*, April 15, 1968, 17.

34. Catherine Gwin, "U.S. Relations with the World Bank," in Kapur et al., *The World Bank*, vol. 2, 205–7.

35. Oliver, *George Woods*, 204–8.

36. Warren Unna, "IDA Nations Move to Replenish Funds," *Washington Post*, December 22, 1967.

37. PC, May 6, 1968, September 23, 1968, McNamara Papers, President's Council Minutes, Box 1.

38. IBRD/IDA, *Annual Report*, 1968, 26.

39. Eric Owen-Smith, *The German Economy* (London: Routledge, 1994), 505.

40. Rotberg, interview with author.

41. Memorandum of Conversation, Mr. McNamara's Visit with Finance Minister Strauss on Monday, July 1, 9:00 a.m., Bonn, Germany, July 17, 1968, in IBRD/IDA 03-04-09S, Box 1; Memorandum of Conversation, Mr. McNamara's Meeting with Minister Schiller, Monday, July 1, 11:30 a.m., Bonn, July 19, 1968 in IBRD/IDA 03-04-09S, Box 1.

42. "World Bank Borrows $100 Million from Bank in Dusseldorf, Germany," *Wall Street Journal*, July 1, 1968, 27; Kapur et al., *The World Bank*, vol. 1, 1223; Edwin L. Dale, Jr., "World Bank's Aid to Be Increased to Offset U.S. Cut," *New York Times*, August 7, 1968, 1.

43. PC, December 20, 1968.

44. On McNamara's reaction to Robert Kennedy's assassination, see Shapley, *Promise and Power*, 473–74.

45. "World Bank Issue Is Sold in Kuwait," *New York Times*, August 15, 1968, 55.

46. PC, March 10, March 24, 1969, McNamara Papers, President's Council Minutes, Box 1.

47. On the Japanese "miracle" see Gary D. Allinson, *Japan's Postwar History* (Ithaca, N.Y.: Cornell University Press, 1997).

48. PC, May 26, 1969, McNamara Papers, President's Council Minutes, Box 1.

49. PC, October 1, 1969, McNamara Papers, President's Council Minutes, Box 1. On the Bank-Japanese relationship during this time see Ming Wan, "Spending Strategies in World Politics: How Japan Used Its Economic Power, 1952–1992" (Ph.D. dissertation, Harvard University, 1993), 228–36.

50. Letter, McNamara to Takeo Fukuda, Minister of Finance, Japan, November 21, 1969, in IBRD/IDA 03-04-09S, Box 1.

51. Letter, McNamara to Aldewereld, reporting on McNamara's meeting with Minister Kashiwagi, July 6, 1970 in IBRD/IDA 03-04-09S, Box 2; Wan, "Spending Strategies in World Politics" 233–34; Kapur et al., *World Bank*, vol. 1, 1224; World Bank Group Historical Chronology (hereafter WBGHC), 1970–79; http://go.worldbank.org/847R4CBE80.

52. Letter from McNamara to Fowler, July 25, 1968, cited in Mason and Ascher, *The World Bank Since Bretton Woods*, 137.

53. John H. Allan, "World Bank Floats $250 Million," *New York Times*, September 18, 1968, 59.

54. McNamara, "To the Bond Club of New York, New York, May 14, 1969," in McNamara, *The McNamara Years*, 55–56.

55. Clark, "Reconsiderations," 170.

56. IBRD/IDA, *Annual Report*, 1974, 69.

57. Frank C. Porter, "World Bank Readies Bold New Efforts to Aid Poorer Nations," *Los Angeles Times*, September 30, 1968, B10.

58. Halberstam, *The Best and the Brightest*.

59. McNamara, Memorandum for the Record, January 10, 1969, in IBRD/IDA 03-04-09S, Box 1.

60. Rotberg, "The Job Interview," 7.

61. Robert McNamara interview with Errol Morris, December 11–12, 2001, pp. 378–79 II:116, RSM, LOC.

62. The Bank was not completely uninvolved in Indonesian history. Funds from its 1948 postwar reconstruction loan to the Dutch government were widely believed at the time to have gone to support the war against Indonesian nationalists. See Rich, *Mortgaging the Earth*, 69–70.

63. Quoted in ibid., 227.

64. Ibid., 127–28. Also see Jeremy Kuzmarov, "Modernizing Repression: Police Training, Political Violence, and Nation-Building in the 'American Century,'" *Diplomatic History* 33, 2 (April 2009): 191–21.

65. Shapley, *Promise and Power*, 475; Mason and Asher, *The World Bank Since Bretton Woods*, 678.

66. Shapley, *Promise and Power*, 476. On the Indonesian killings of 1965–66, see Robert Cribb, "Genocide in Indonesia, 1965–66," *Journal of Genocide Research* 3, 2 (2001), 219–39.

67. McNamara, Statement at Press Conference, Djakarta, June 15, 1968, IBRD/IDA 03-04-12S Box 1.

68. On the Bank's role in Indonesia in the 1970s see Miftah Wirahadikusma, "The Rise and Development of the Indonesian New Order Regime" (Ph.D. dissertation, University of Hawaii, 1990) and Brad Simpson, "Indonesia's 'Accelerated Modernization' and the Global Discourse of Development, 1960–1975," *Diplomatic History* 33, 3 (June 2009): 467–86.

69. PC, April 15, 1968, McNamara Papers, President's Council Minutes, Box 1.

70. "Calcutta Mobs Protest Visit by McNamara," *Los Angeles Times*, November 21, 1968, 8.

71. Katherine Marshall, interview with author.

72. Clark, "Dr. McNamara, I Presume," *Bank Notes*, December 1972, 2, WBGA.

73. Memorandum of Conversation, Participants: The President (Richard Nixon), President Leopold Senghor of Senegal, Marshall Wright, NSC, Jose Deseabra, Interpreter, June 18, 1971, 9:30 a.m., Oval Office, June 23, 1971, Foreign Relations of the United States (hereafter FRUS), 1969–1976, vol. E-5, Documents on Africa, 1969–1972; Clark, "Reconsiderations," 175–76.

74. McNamara, "To the Board of Governors, September 30, 1968," 6.

75. IBRD/IDA, *Annual Reports*, 1968–1981.

76. Richard Nixon, "Special Message to the Congress Proposing Reform of the Foreign Assistance Program September 15, 1970," http://www.presidency.ucsb.edu/ws/?pid=2661; Carol Lancaster, *Foreign Aid: Diplomacy, Development, Domestic Politics* (Chicago: University of Chicago Press, 2007), 75.

77. Roger D. Hansen and the Staff of the Overseas Development Council, *The U.S. and World Development: Agenda for Action, 1976* (New York: Praeger, 1976), Table E-11.

78. OECD, Development Cooperation (Paris: OECD, annual issues), in Michael E. Akins, "United States Control over World Bank Group Decision-Making" (Ph.D. dissertation, University of Pennsylvania, 1981), 64.

79. Edwin L. Dale, Jr., "World Bank's Aid to Be Increased to Offset U.S. Cut."

80. McNamara, "To the Board of Governors, Washington, D.C., September 30, 1968," 15.

81. IBRD, *The Program for Selecting Young Professionals for Careers with the World Bank Group* (Washington, D.C.: IBRD, 1970).

82. IBRD/IDA, *Annual Reports*, 1968–1981.

83. McNamara, List of Projects, May 25, 1968, in RSM Chronological Files, Personal, Box 1; McNamara, "To the Board of Governors, Washington, D.C., September 30, 1968," 9.

84. IDA, *50 Questions and Answers* (May 1970), cited in Cohn, "Influence of the Less Developed Countries," 160.

85. Visvanathan Rajagopalan, WBOH.

86. See Mitsuo Ezaki, "On the Two-Gap Analysis of Foreign Aid," *Journal of Southeast Asian Studies* 6, 2 (September 1975), 151–63.

87. Kapur et al., *The World Bank*, vol. 1, 17.

88. John G. Gurley, Book Review: Structural Change and Development Policy, *Journal of Asian Studies* 40, 2 (February 1981): 329.

89. According to one former staffer, McNamara "had his first influence on the Bank before he actually got there." Before McNamara's arrival, the Bank "had no programming or budgeting of any sort . . . we had six months [from announcement of his appointment until beginning of his term]. . . . So people started saying 'oh my God, what are we going to do? We can't have McNamara coming in here and finding out we don't know what the hell we're doing. So we better start adding things up' . . . all the country people started rushing around trying to write up for each country a description of the country and its economics and what it was that we were supposed to be doing there with a sort of forward looking program of loans that we were making. And all this was done in an absolute mad rush." Stephen Eccles, interview with author.

90. John Blaxall, "The World Bank's Management Control Systems: A Brief History," World Bank Working Paper (August 2006).

91. Ibid.

92. Ibid.

93. Eccles, interview with author.

94. Blaxall, interview with author.

95. McNamara, PC, April 1, 1968, McNamara Papers, President's Council Minutes, Box 1. McNamara's initial agenda included a call to "replace the present procedure in which unrelated project loans, considered in isolation from one another, filter up through the levels with a five-year program based on systems analysis and overall development strategy, taking account of relative priorities among countries and within sectors of each country, is directed from the top." McNamara, List of Projects, May 25, 1968.

96. Clark, "Reconsiderations," 168.

97. Blaxall, "The World Bank's Management Control Systems."

98. Blaxall, interview with author.

99. PC, May 27, 1968, McNamara Papers, President's Council Minutes, Box 1.

100. Blaxall, "The World Bank's Management Control Systems."

101. Blaxall, interview with author.

102. Knapp, WBOH, 9.

103. Blaxall, "The World Bank's Management Control Systems."

104. Kaplan et al., *The McNamara Ascendency*, 72–95.

105. Ibid., 92.

106. Blaxall, "The World Bank's Management Control Systems."

107. Blaxall, interview with author.

108. Blaxall, "The World Bank's Management Control Systems."

109. Knapp, WBOH, 71.

110. PC, April 9, 1968, McNamara Papers, President's Council Minutes, Box 1.

111. Ibid.

112. PC, February 23, 1972, McNamara Papers, President's Council Minutes, Box 1.

113. Quoted in Shapley, *Promise and Power*, 459.

114. PC, May 14, 1968, McNamara Papers, President's Council Minutes, Box 1.

115. PC, June 2, 1969," McNamara Papers, President's Council Minutes, Box 1; Memorandum, John H. Adler to Area Department Directors and Deputies, "Forecast of Board Action," October 8, 1970, in IBRD/IDA 03-04-09S Box 2, WBGA.

116. PC, May 6, 1968, June 7, 1971, McNamara Papers, President's Council Minutes, Box 1

117. PC, March 27, 1972, McNamara Papers, President's Council Minutes, Box 1.

118. Blaxall, interview with author.

119. PC, April 1, 1968, McNamara Papers, President's Council Minutes, Box 1.

120. PC, April 14, 1969, April 13, 1970, April 1, 1968, March 15, 1971, McNamara Papers, President's Council Minutes, Box 1.

121. These had resulted in publications such as James Morris, *The Road to Huddersfield: A Journey to Five Continents* (New York: Pantheon, 1963) and Albert O. Hirschman, *Development Projects Observed* (Washington, D.C.: Brookings Institution, 1967).

122. McNamara, List of Projects, May 25, 1968.

123. The P&B Department carried out limited evaluation work during this time. See Christopher Willoughby, "First Experiments in Operations Evaluation: Roots, Hopes, and Gaps," in World Bank, OED, *The First 30 Years* (Washington, D.C.: World Bank, 2003), 3–4.

124. PC, December 15, 1969, McNamara Papers, President's Council Minutes, Box 1.

125. PC, June 8, 1970, McNamara Papers, President's Council Minutes, Box 1.

126. PC, December 15, 1969, McNamara Papers, President's Council Minutes, Box 1.

127. PC, August 31, 1970, November 16, 1970, McNamara Papers, President's Council Minutes, Box 1; OED, *The First 30 Years*, 165.

128. OED, *The First 30 Years*, 166.

129. GAO, Comptroller General, "Report to the Congress: More Effective United States Participation Needed in World Bank and International Development Association," February 14, 1973.

130. PC, April 3, 1972, McNamara Papers, President's Council Minutes, Box 1.

131. PC, February 26, 1973, McNamara Papers, President's Council Minutes; OED, *The First 30 Years*, 166.

132. OED, *The First 30 Years*, 7, 167.

133. PC, May 6, 1968, McNamara Papers, President's Council Minutes; IBRD/IDA, *Annual Report*, 1970, 28.

134. Letter, McNamara to K.A. Busia, Prime Minister of Ghana, July 7, 1971 in IBRD/IDA 03-04-09S Box 2.

135. PC, March 3, 1969, June 30, 1969, July 7, 1969, McNamara Papers, President's Council Minutes, Box 1.

136. Letter, McNamara to Sir Robert Jackson, Commissioner, UNDP Capacity Study, July 21, 1969 in IBRD/IDA 03-04-09S Box 1.

137. McNamara, List of Projects, May 25, 1968.

138. IBRD/IDA, *Annual Reports*, 1970–1973.

139. PC, May 13, 1968, McNamara Papers, President's Council Minutes, Box 1; Craig N. Murphy, *The United Nations Development Programme: A Better Way?* (Cambridge: Cambridge University Press, 2006), 24.

140. Leif Christoffersen, interview with author.

141. PC, December 16, 1968, July 14, 1969, McNamara Papers, President's Council Minutes, Box 1.

142. PC, January 26, 1970, McNamara Papers, President's Council Minutes, Box 1.

143. PC, February 8, 1971, McNamara Papers, President's Council Minutes, Box 1.

144. PC, February 15, 1971, McNamara Papers, President's Council Minutes, Box 1.

145. Quoted in Libby, "The Ideology and Power," 181.

146. OECD, Query Wizard for International Development Statistics, https://stats.oecd.org/qwids/.

147. Quoted in Libby, "The Ideology and Power," 186.

148. Ibid., 181.

149. Letter, McNamara to C. A. Doxiadis, President, Athens Center of Ekistics, April 28, 1970 in IBRD/IDA 03-04-09S, Box 1; PC, November 30, 1970, McNamara Papers, President's Council Minutes, Box 1; McNamara, Remarks at Board Meeting Regarding Future Lending and Borrowing, February 10, 1972 in IBRD/IDA 03-04-12S Box 1, March 20, 1972, McNamara Papers, President's Council Minutes, Box 1.

150. PC, October 14, 1974, McNamara Papers, President's Council Minutes.

151. PC, December 18, 1972, McNamara Papers, President's Council Minutes.

152. Office Memorandum: Staff Morale, H. B. Ripman to Robert S. McNamara, January 8, 1971, I:22, RSM, LOC.

153. Mohamed Shoaib, quoted in Louis Galambos and David Milobsky, "Organizing and Reorganizing the World Bank," *Business History Review*, 69, 2 (Summer 1995): 177–78.

154. "World Bank Cites Shift in Divisions," *New York Times*, November 18, 1968, 71.

155. McKinsey & Company, "Recommended Organization Structure: The World Bank Group" July 1972, II: 4, RSM, LOC; Galambos and Milobsky, "Organizing and Reorganizing the World Bank,"180.

156. McNamara called for a "decentralization of authority and responsibility" in his initial agenda. McNamara, List of Projects, May 25, 1968.

157. Eccles, interview with author.

158. Kapur et al., *The World Bank*, vol. 1, 246. Also see Oshiba, "Resource Allocation," 67.

159. President's Council Meeting to Discuss Organizational Changes, August 7, 1972, McNamara Papers, President's Council Minutes, Box 1.

160. Marshall, interview with author.

161. Votaw, interview with author.

162. Marshall, interview with author.

163. PC, June 11, 1973, January 29, 1973, McNamara Papers, President's Council Minutes, Box 1.

164. Sudanese official quoted in Libby, "The Ideology and Power of the World Bank," 193.

165. Quoted in ibid., 193.

166. Ethiopian official quoted in ibid., 193.

167. Quoted in ibid., 194.

Chapter 3. Developing Development

1. Katherine Marshall, *The World Bank: From Reconstruction to Development to Equity* (London: Routledge, 2008), 54.

2. Robert S. McNamara, "To the Board of Governors, Nairobi, Kenya, September 24, 1973," in McNamara, *The McNamara Years at the World Bank: Major Policy Addresses of Robert S. McNamara, 1968–1981* (Baltimore: Johns Hopkins University Press, 1981), 230–63.

3. For a useful summary of economists' concerns and their relation to the Bank's work, see Nicholas Stern with Francisco Ferreira, "The World Bank as 'Intellectual Actor,'" in Kauper et al., *The World Bank*, vol. 2, 530–31.

4. George Woods, Gabriel Silver Memorial Lecture, Columbia University, April 13, 1967, excerpted in IBRD/IDA, *Annual Report*, 1967, 1.

5. McNamara, *The Essence of Security*, 150.

6. McNamara, "To the Board of Governors, Washington, D.C., September 30, 1968," in *The McNamara Years*, 15.

7. McNamara, "To the Inter-American Press Association, Buenos Aires, October 18, 1968," in ibid., 22.

8. McNamara, "To the University of Notre Dame, Indiana, May 1, 1969," in ibid., 40.

9. McNamara, Arrival Statement in Addis Ababa, November 18, 1970, in IBRD/IDA 03-04-12S Box 1.

10. McNamara, Draft Reply to Toast at President Ahidjo's Formal Dinner at Yaounde, January 15, 1971, in IBRD/IDA 03-04-12S Box 1.

11. Robert McNamara Remarks at Dinner, Dakar, February 9, 1969, in ibid.

12. Agronsky Interview (University of Georgia), December 2, 1971, in ibid.

13. Shapley, *Promise and Power*, 18.

14. *The Fog of War*.

15. McNamara with VanDeMark, *In Retrospect*, 324.

16. Shapley, *Promise and Power*, 523.

17. Ford Foundation, *Annual Report, 1968*, http://www.fordfound.org/archives/item /1968/text/21. On the influence of U.S. foundations in development policy generally see Inderjeet Parmar, *Foundations of the American Century: The Ford, Carnegie, and Rockefeller Foundations and the Rise of American Power* (New York: Columbia University Press, 2012).

18. Letter, McNamara to Barbara Ward (Lady Jackson), July 13, 1970, in IBRD/IDA 03-04-09S Box 2; McNamara, "An Eloquent Evangelist for the Poor," *Washington Post*, June 3, 1981; McNamara, "Miscellaneous Comments by Barbara Ward," undated (probably 1968/69) I:31, Robert S. McNamara Papers, LOC. Also see "Barbara Ward: Correspondence, I:18, Robert S. McNamara Papers, LOC.

19. Mahbub ul Haq, World Bank Oral History, December 3, 1982.

20. Ul Haq, *The Poverty Curtain: Choices for the Third World* (New York: Columbia University Press, 1976), 1.

21. Ul Haq, World Bank Oral History, 2–3.

22. For a summary of the first UN Decade for Development see United Nations, *Toward Accelerated Development: Proposals for the Second United Nations Development Decade* (New York: UN, 1970).

23. Dudley Seers, "The Meaning of Development," *International Development Review* 11 (December 1969): 2–6.

24. David Morse, "The Employment Problem in Developing Countries," speech at the Seventh Cambridge Conference on Development, September 1970, in Ronald Robinson and Peter Johnson, eds., *Prospects for Employment Opportunities in the Nineteen Seventies* (London: Cambridge University Overseas Study Committee, 1971), 5–13.

25. E. F. Schumacher, "Intermediate Technology: The Missing Factor in Foreign Aid," *Oxford Diocesan Magazine* (July 1970).

26. PC, August 12, 1968, McNamara Papers, President's Council Minutes, Box 1.

27. McNamara, letter to Lester Pearson, July 17, 1968, in IBRD/IDA 03-04-09S Box 1. On McNamara's interest in the Pearson Report as a public relations document also see PC August 4, 1969, McNamara Papers, President's Council Minutes, Box 1.

28. *Partners in Development*, 18. On the production of the Pearson Report and the surrounding debates, see Michael A. Clemens and Todd J. Moss, "Ghost of 0.7%: Origins and Relevance of the International Aid Target," Center for Global Development Working Paper 68 (September 2005).

29. PC, August 4, 1969, McNamara Papers, President's Council Minutes, Box 1.

30. Barbara Ward, J. D. Runnalls, and Lenore D'Anjou, eds., *The Widening Gap: Development in the 1970's: A Report on the Columbia Conference on International Development, Williamsburg, Virginia, and New York, February 15–21, 1970* (New York: Columbia University Press, 1971).

31. Ibid., 11.

32. Ibid., 13.

33. Ibid., 12–13.

34. Shapley, *Promise and Power*, 507–8; Ekbladh, *The Great American Mission*, 226.

35. McNamara, "To the Columbia University Conference on International Economic Development, New York, February 20, 1970," in McNamara, *The McNamara Years*, 104.

36. Richard Jolly, UNOH, http://www.unhistory.org/CD/PDFs/Jolly.pdf.

37. Matthew Connelly, *Fatal Misconception: The Struggle to Control World Population* (Cambridge, Mass.: Belknap Press of Harvard University Press, 2008), 155–236; Population Division, Department of Economic and Social Affairs, UN Secretariat, *The World at Six Billion* (12 October 1999), ESA/P/WP.154, 5.

38. Cohn, "Influence of the Less Developed Countries," 248–49.

39. Quoted in Asher Brynes, "Charity Begins at Home, *The Nation*, October 1, 1973, 307.

40. McNamara, List of Projects, May 25, 1968, in RSM Chronological Files, Personal, Box 1. Both Eugene Black and George Woods called attention to the issue of overpopulation during their presidencies, but neither took any steps to move the organization into the field. Similarly, Bank staff had long drawn attention to population growth as part of the development process (the 1949 mission to Colombia stated that "the population is completely out of

balance with other factors"), but the organization did not make any population loans nor encourage governments to adopt population control programs prior to McNamara's arrival. See Cohn, "Influence of the Less Developed Countries," 227–28, 256.

41. PC, May 6, 1968, October 7, 1968, October 7, 1968, McNamara Papers, President's Council Minutes; McNamara, Memorandum for Mr. Friedman, October 12, 1968, in IBRD/IDA 03-04-09S Box 1.

42. McNamara, "To the Board of Governors, September 30, 1968," in *The McNamara Years*, 12–14.

43. McNamara, "To the Inter-American Press Association," in *The McNamara Years*, 21–27.

44. Statement by Mr. Robert S. McNamara, President of the World Bank, on leaving India, Sunday, November 24, 1968 in IBRD/IDA 03-04-12S Box 1.

45. McNamara, "To the University of Notre Dame," in *The McNamara Years*, 31–52; IBRD/IDA, *Annual Report*, 1970.

46. "Economic aspects of population and labor force growth in Brazil," World Bank Staff Working Paper, 1970; "Problems of applying stable population techniques in estimating demographic measures for Arab countries," World Bank Staff Working Paper, 1971. Also see George C. Zaidan, "The Costs and Benefits of Family Planning Programs," World Bank Staff Occasional Paper Number 12, 1971. The most comprehensive statement of the Bank's population policy was "Population Planning," World Bank Sector Working Paper, 1972.

47. For instance, three years after the Bank issued a $4.8 million loan to the government of Tunisia for the construction of maternity hospitals and an extension of family planning services, the government requested another $3.8 million to complete the project. Memorandum, from the President to the Executive Directors, Subject: TUNISIA—Population Project, July 29, 1974, in J. Burke Knapp Papers, Hoover Institution Archives (hereafter HIA).

48. Meet the Press, March 24, 1974, in IBRD/IDA 03-04-12S Box 2.

49. Memorandum for the Record, Meeting to Discuss Population, July 18, 1975.

50. On the population control movement generally, see Connelly, *Fatal Misconception*, 276–340. On developing country opposition to Bank population programs, see Cohn, "Influence of the Less Developed Countries," 213–64; Edmundo Flores, "The Desperation of Calcutta," *The Nation*, May 24, 1971, 653; and David Gordon, "The World Bank: New Directions in Africa," *African Affairs* 68, 2 (July 1969): 241. On staff resistance, see Michael Walden, interview with author; PC, December 2, 1974, May 17, 1976, McNamara Papers, President's Council Minutes, Box 1; and Robert McNamara, WBOH, October 3, 1991. For more on the Bank's failure to develop a population lending program see Barbara Crane and Jason Finkle, "Organizational Impediments to Development Assistance: The World Bank's Population Program," *World Politics* 33, 4 (July 1981): 516–53.

51. PC, March 3, 1969, McNamara Papers, President's Council Minutes, Box 1.

52. Letter, McNamara to Prince Sadruddin Aga Khan, High Commissioner for Refugees, Office of the UN High Commission for Refugees, February 11, 1970, in IBRD/IDA 03-04-09S Box 1.

53. McNamara, letter to Mr. Mohamed Nassim Kochman, Subject: Community Development, May 1, 1969, in IBRD/IDA 03-04-09S Box 1.

54. PC, April 22, 1974, April 23, 1979, McNamara Papers, President's Council Minutes, Box 1; PC, April 23, 1979, Box 2; Jennifer Prah Rugger, "The Changing Role of the World Bank in Global Health," *American Journal of Public Health* 95, 1 (January 2005): 65.

55. Hollis B. Chenery and Alan M. Strout, "Foreign Assistance and Economic Development," *American Economic Review* 56, 1 (September 1966): 679–733.

56. McNamara, "To the Board of Governors, Washington, D.C., September 25, 1972," in *The McNamara Years*, 228.

57. For instance, in the early 1970s the Bank began to issue "sector study papers" on agriculture, water supply and sewerage, forestry, education, and telecommunications, among other topics.

58. Weiss and Jéquier, eds., *Technology, Finance, and Development*, 261.

59. Though Bank staff had been assisting other international agencies in trying to address the issue since the early 1960s, it was not until McNamara and his wife came across victims of the disease on a trip to Mali that the Bank took up the cause. In April 1972, McNamara proposed that the Bank enlist other donors in a cooperative effort to limit river blindness. A few months later, the Bank summoned the first meeting of the Onchocerciasis Control Program (OCP), and the program commenced spraying in 1974. Jesse Bump, "The Lion's Gaze: African River Blindness from Tropical Curiosity to International Development (Ph.D. dissertation, Johns Hopkins University, 2005), 306–72; Shapley, *Promise and Power*, 523; Bernard H. Liese, John Wilson, Bruce Benton, and Douglas Marr, "The Onchocerciasis Control Program in West Africa: A Long-Term Commitment to Success," World Bank Staff Working Paper (August 1991); Ellie Tragakes, "The Political Economy of National and International Agricultural Research" (Ph.D. dissertation, University of Maryland, College Park, 1987), 261; John K. Coulter, "The Consultative Group on International Agricultural Research," in Weiss and Jéquier, *Technology, Finance, and Development*, 267. In addition to the OCP and CGIAR the Bank's support of development research institutes included co-sponsorship of the Special Program for Research and Training in Tropical Diseases, created by the World Health Organization in 1977. See Adetokunbo O. Lucas, "The Tropical Diseases Research Program," in Weiss and Jéquier, *Technology, Finance, and Development*, 283–94.

60. Statement by McNamara on leaving India.

61. PC, March 24, 1969, McNamara Papers, President's Council Minutes, Box 1.

62. McNamara, "To the Board of Governors, September 30, 1968," in *The McNamara Years*, 11; Kapur et al., *The World Bank*, vol. 1, 405.

63. PC, October 4, 1971, December 13, 1971, McNamara Papers, President's Council Minutes, Box 1.

64. Uma Lele, *The Design of Rural Development: Lessons from Africa* (Baltimore: Johns Hopkins Press, 1975), 6. Also see Albert Waterston, "A Viable Model for Rural Development," *Finance and Development* 11, 4 (December 1974): 22–25.

65. For an overview of the Bank's urban development approach before, during, and after the McNamara years see Cecilia Zanetta, "The Evolution of the World Bank's Urban Lending in Latin America: From Sites and Services to Municipal Reform and Beyond," *Habitat International* 25, 4 (December 2001): 513–33.

66. Commission on International Development, *Partners in Development*, 60–61.

67. World Bank, *Urbanization Sector Working Paper* (Washington, D.C.: World Bank, 1972).

68. McNamara, "To the Board of Governors, Washington, D.C., September 1, 1975," in *McNamara Years*, 316.

69. On the Bank's failure to lend for urban development before the McNamara years, see Edward Ramsamy, "From Projects to Policy: The World Bank and Housing in the Developing World" (Ph.D. dissertation, Rutgers University, 2002), 147; PC, February 23, 1971, McNamara Papers, President's Council Minutes, Box 1; Letter, McNamara to Senator John Sparkman, Chairman of the Committee on Banking and Currency, Subcommittee on Housing and Urban Affairs, April 14, 1971 in IBRD/IDA 03-04-09S Box 2.

70. Ramsamy, "From Projects to Policy," 175.

71. PC, January 6, 1969, May 15, 1972, McNamara Papers, President's Council Minutes; William Ascher, "New Development Approaches and the Adaptability of International Agencies: The Case of the World Bank," *International Organization* 37, 3 (Summer 1983), 432.

72. Ascher, "New Development Approaches," 433.

73. Ibid., 428–34.

74. John Blaxall, interview with author.

75. Office Memorandum: Summary of Special Meeting with Agricultural Staff, From Montague Yudelman to Robert S. McNamara, October 28, 1976, I: 20, Robert S. McNamara Papers, LOC.

76. Katherine Marshall, interview with author.

77. In 1973, Hollis Chenery broached the idea of creating a system to determine the "distributional effects of Bank projects," and McNamara promised the Bank should devote greater attention to assessing the social impacts of its projects during his speech to the Bank and IMF Board of Governors that fall. PC, May 7, 1973, McNamara Papers, President's Council Minutes, Box 1.

78. Ascher, "New Development Approaches," 428–33.

79. Knapp, WBOH, 59.

80. IBRD/IDA, *Annual Report*, 1973, 6; Mahbub ul Haq, "Changing Emphasis of the Bank's Lending Policies," *Finance and Development* 15, 2 (September 1978): 10–21.

81. McNamara, "To the Board of Governors, Nairobi, Kenya, September 24, 1973," in *The McNamara Years*, 242.

82. McNamara, "To the Board of Governors, Washington, D.C., September 25, 1972," in ibid., 220–22.

83. Ul Haq, WBOH, 3–4.

84. Hollis Chenery et al., *Redistribution with Growth: Policies to Improve Income Distribution in Developing Countries in the Context of Economic Growth: A Joint Study by the World Bank's Development Research Center and the Institute of Development Studies at the University of Sussex* (Oxford: Oxford University Press, 1974). The report was based on papers delivered at a conference held at the Rockefeller Foundation's Bellagio estate in April 1973.

85. Ibid., v.

86. Ibid., xiii.

87. Ibid., 10. The authors did not include mainland China or the Soviet Union in their analysis.

88. Ibid., xiii, 38.

89. Ibid., 48–49.

90. Ibid., 48.

91. Ibid., 47.

92. Ibid., xv.

93. McNamara, "To the Board of Governors, September 29, 1969," in *The McNamara Years*, 73.

94. "Concluding Remarks by Robert S. McNamara, President of the International Bank for Reconstruction and Development and Affiliates, at the Closing Session, September 28, 1973," World Bank press release 82; McNamara, Remarks upon Departure from Mauritania, January 21, 1971, in IBRD/IDA 03-04-12S Box 1.

95. John Blaxall, interview with author, January 2008.

96. Finnemore, "Redefining Development," 203–27.

97. See Paul Streeten and Shahid Javed Burki, "Basic Needs: Some Issues," *World Development* 6, 3 (March 1978): 411–21.

98. PC, October 20, 1975, McNamara Papers, President's Council Minutes, Box 2.

99. Ayers, *Banking on the Poor*, 79.

100. Kapur in Knapp, WBOH, 72.

101. Nancy Birdsall and Juan Luis Londono, "Asset Inequality Matters: An Assessment of the World Bank's Approach to Poverty Reduction," *American Economic Review: Papers and Proceedings of the Hundred and Fourth Annual Meeting of the American Economic Association* 87, 2 (May 1997): 33.

102. McNamara, "To the Board of Governors, Washington, D.C., September 1 1975," in *The McNamara Years*, 309–10.

103. Robert McNamara, WBOH, October 3, 1991.

104. Babai, "Between Hegemony and Poverty," 391.

105. Mr. McNamara's Remarks at State Dinner in Colombia, June 4, 1970, in IBRD/IDA 03-04-12S Box 1.

106. Letter, McNamara to Jose Figueres Ferrer, President, Costa Rica, December 18, 1970, in IBRD/IDA 03-04-09S Box 2.

107. Letter, McNamara to Jean-Bédel Bokassa, President, Central African Republic, December 15, 1971, in ibid.

108. McNamara, Agronsky Interview (University of Georgia), December 2, 1971, in ibid.

109. Escott Reid, "McNamara's World Bank," *Foreign Affairs* 51, 4 (July 1973), 795.

110. McNamara, David Spanier Interview (London Times and EUROPA), February 4, 1975, in ibid.

111. Tanzanian official quoted in Libby, "Ideology and Power," 49.

112. Ceylonese official quoted in ibid., 198.

113. Eugene Black, "Development Revisited," *International Development Review* 13, 4 (1970): 2–8.

114. Michael Hoffman, "The Challenges of the 1970s and the Present Institutional Structure," in John P. Lewis and Ishan Kapur, eds., *The World Bank Group, Multilateral Aid, and the 1970s* (Lexington, Mass.: Lexington, 1973), 17.

115. Jennifer Light, *From Warfare to Welfare: Defense Intellectuals and Urban Problems in Cold War America* (Baltimore: Johns Hopkins University Press, 2003).

116. G. H. R. to Robert McNamara, February 1975, I:20, Robert S. McNamara Papers, LOC.

117. Shaun Farragher to Robert McNamara, September 28, 1977, I:20, Robert S. McNamara Papers, LOC.

118. Blaxall, interview with author.

119. Shapley, *Promise and Power*, 491; William Safire, *Before the Fall: An Inside View of the Pre-Watergate White House* (Garden City, N.Y.: Doubleday, 1975), 192; "Kissinger and World Bank President Robert McNamara, 3 January 1973, 5:45 p.m.," Nixon Presidential Materials Project, Henry A. Kissinger Telephone Conversations Transcripts, Chronological File, Box 17, 1973 2–6, National Security Archive (NSA); McNamara to Kissinger, October 15, 1972, I:26, Robert S. McNamara Papers, LOC.

120. Shapley, *Promise and Power*, 491; Safire, *Before the Fall*, 192; "Kissinger and World Bank President Robert McNamara, 3 January 1973"; PC, April 7, 1969, June 30, 1969, McNamara Papers, President's Council Minutes. Also see the folder "Mekong Basin dam project" in I: 30, Robert S. McNamara Papers, LOC.

121. Letter, McNamara to Tran-Thien-Khiem, Prime Minister of Vietnam, April 19, 1971, RSM, Chronological Files (Outgoing), Box 2.

122. PC, January 22, 1973, May 21, 1973, McNamara Papers, President's Council Minutes, Box 1.

123. Mark Selden, "Multinational Aid to Saigon," *The Nation*, April 6, 1974, 422–23.

124. Quoted in Sanford, *U.S. Foreign Policy*, 214.

125. Shapley, *Promise and Power*, 495.

126. Hendrickson, *The Living and the Dead*, 7–13.

127. On McNamara's early interest in Romania see Memorandum of Conversation, Mr. McNamara's Meeting with Minister Wischnewski and Dr. Dumke of Ministry for Economic Cooperation, Monday, June 1, 10:00 a.m., Bonn, July 19, 1968, in IBRD/IDA 03-04-09S Box 1; Assetto, *The Soviet Bloc in the IMF and IBRD*, 146.

128. IBRD, *Yugoslavia and the World Bank* (Washington, D.C.: IBRD, 1979), 34; Assetto, *The Soviet Bloc in the IMF and IBRD*, 108, 126–28. McNamara met with Yugoslavian officials early in his tenure to encourage them to borrow more from the Bank. See Memorandum for the Record, January 14, 1969 in IBRD/IDA 03-04-09S Box 1.

Chapter 4. Global Shocks

1. Robert S. McNamara, "To the Board of Governors, Nairobi, Kenya, September 24, 1973," in McNamara, *The McNamara Years*, 230–63.

2. McNamara, "To the Board of Governors, Nairobi, Kenya, September 24, 1973," in ibid., 230–63.

3. "IMF Overflows Nairobi's Hotels," *New York Times*, September 24, 1973, 49.

4. Charles N. Stabler, "Clamoring for 'Paper Gold,'" *Wall Street Journal*, September 24, 1973, 30.

5. For instance, Tajuddin Ahmad, the first Prime Minister of Bangladesh and a sometimes critic of the Bank, praised McNamara for shedding light on "number of disconcerting facts about the current international economic situation which are having very deleterious effects on the poorer nations such as continuous trade barriers against poor countries, considerable shortfall in official aid flow below the target 0.7 per cent of the GNP of the rich countries and the mounting external debt-service problem of the developing countries." See IBRD, *1973 Annual Meetings of the Boards of Governors: Summary Proceedings, Nairobi, Kenya, September 24–28, 1973* (Washington, D.C.: World Bank, 1973), 50.

6. Edwin L. Dale, Jr., "The Nairobi Talks: In Search of Stability; In Quest of Aid," *New York Times*, September 30, 1973, 208. See also "Innovative Aid Reform," *New York Times*, October 1, 1973, 34 and "The Impossibility of Isolation," *Los Angeles Times*, September 28, 1973, B6.

7. Ayres, *Banking on the Poor*, 4, 9; Leif Christoffersen, Sakiko Fukuda-Parr, interviews with author.

8. Nicholas Stern with Francisco Ferreira, "The World Bank as 'Intellectual Actor,'" in Kapur et al., *The World Bank*, vol. 2, 535, 549; Finnemore, "Redefining Development," 217; Escobar, *Encountering Development*, 160–62.

9. Maddux, *The Development Philosophy of Robert S. McNamara*, 19.

10. Clark, "Reconsiderations," 177.

11. Organization of Petroleum Exporting Countries, "Declaratory Statement of Petroleum Policy in Member Countries," Resolutions of Sixteenth OPEC Conference, Vienna, June 24–25, 1968.

12. On the origins, contours, and consequences of the 1973–74 oil crisis, see Daniel Yergin, *The Prize: The Epic Quest for Oil, Money, and Power* (New York: Free Press, 2008).

13. PC, December 10, 1973, McNamara Papers, President's Council Minutes, Box 1.

14. "Draft Report on FAO/IBRD Roundtable Discussion," February 21–22, 1974, FAO Investment Center, SF 4/1-UN 12/1, Archives of the Food and Agriculture Organization (hereafter FAO Archives).

15. PC, December 17, 1973, McNamara Papers, President's Council Minutes.

16. Munir P. Benjenk, "The Impact of New Oil Prices on Developing Countries," January 29, 1974, IMF Central Files Collection: Economics Subject Files S1184–1190, Box 383, IMF Archives.

17. PC, January 14, 1974, McNamara Papers, President's Council Minutes, Box 1.

18. PC, January 14, January 21, 1974, McNamara Papers, President's Council Minutes, Box 1.

19. PC, December 10, 1974, McNamara Papers, President's Council Minutes, Box 1.

20. PC, January 21, 1974, McNamara Papers, President's Council Minutes, Box 1.

21. Benjenk, "Impact of New Oil Prices," 2–3.

22. McNamara, List of Projects, May 25, 1968, in RSM Chronological Files, Personal, Box 1.

23. Kapur et al., *The World Bank*, vol. 1, 973.

24. PC, February 26, 1973, McNamara Papers, President's Council Minutes, Box 1.

25. Ibid.

26. Stephen S. Rosenfeld, "Robert S. McNamara and the Wiser Use of Power," *World* 2 (July 3, 1973): 18.

27. Shapley, *Promise and Power*, 516.

28. IBRD/IDA, *Annual Report*, 1974, 5-7.

29. Memo, Martin J. Paijmans to Burke Knapp, European Communities: Future Aid to Developing Countries, January 29, 1974, J. Burke Knapp Papers, HIA.

30. PC, February 4, 1974, McNamara Papers, President's Council Minutes, Box 1.

31. Memorandum for the Record, Meeting on Energy, January 22, 1974, McNamara Papers, Memoranda for the Record, Box 1.

32. Memorandum from J. J. Polak to Acting Managing Director, January 23, 1974, in S1780, IMF Archives; Memorandum for the Record, Meeting on Energy, January 22, 1974.

33. A. D. Crockett to Files, Memorandum, Subject: Financing Oil in the Medium Term, February 11, 1974, IMF Central Files: Economic Subject Files S1780 (1973-1974), Box 472, IMF Archives.

34. A. D. Crockett to Files, Memorandum, Subject: Financing Oil in the Medium Term, February 13, 1974, IMF Central Files: Economic Subject Files S1780 (1973-1974), Box 470, IMF Archives.

35. A. D. Crockett to Files, Memorandum, Subject: Managing Director's Conversation with Mr. McNamara, February 26, 1974, IMF Central Files: Economic Subject Files S1780 (1973-1974), Box 472, IMF Archives.

36. Ibid.

37. Press Conference, Tehran, Iran, February 21, 1974, in WBGA IBRD/IDA 03-04-12S Box 2.

38. Algerian officials thought the Bank often refused to lend to them because of French resistance. They also opposed the Bank's policy against financing energy projects, which according to McNamara made them "feel forced to deal with private firms they would have liked to avoid." PC, April 1, 1974, McNamara Papers, President's Council Minutes, Box 1.

39. IBRD/IDA, *Annual Report*, 1974, 67.

40. Ibid., 5.

41. IBRD/IDA, *Annual Report*, 1975, 76.

42. Kapur et al., *The World Bank*, vol. 1, 973.

43. Jahangir Amuzegar, *Oil Exporters' Economic Development in an Interdependent World* (Washington, D.C.: IMF, 1983), 62.

44. Ibid., 62-63; Kapur et al., *The World Bank*, vol. 1, 973-74.

45. Kapur et al., *The World Bank*, vol. 1, 973-74.

46. Ibid., 975-76; V. H. Oppenheim, "Whose World Bank?," *Foreign Policy* 19 (Summer 1975): 104.

47. Kapur et al., *The World Bank*, vol. 1, 977.

48. PC, September 9, 1974, McNamara Papers, President's Council Minutes, Box 1.

49. IBRD/IDA, *Annual Report*, 1975, 42.

50. Amuzegar, *Oil Exporters' Economic Development*, 62.

51. From 1977 and 1981 just 8 percent of the organization's borrowings came from OPEC members. Kapur et al., *The World Bank*, vol. 1, 973–74.

52. PC, June 10, 1974, McNamara Papers, President's Council Minutes, Box 1.

53. In the U.S., for instance, ODA increased from $2.34 billion in 1973 to just $2.5 billion the following year (in current dollars), while Japanese ODA actually declined between 1974 and 1976. World Bank, GDF.

54. Richard Nixon, "Special Message to the Congress Proposing Reform of the Foreign Assistance Program September 15, 1970," http://www.presidency.ucsb.edu/ws/?pid=2661; Carol Lancaster, *Foreign Aid: Diplomacy, Development, Domestic Politics* (Chicago: University of Chicago Press, 2007), 75.

55. Roger D. Hansen and the Staff of the Overseas Development Council, *The U.S. and World Development: Agenda for Action, 1976* (New York: Praeger, 1976), Table E-11.

56. Robert David Johnson, *Congress and the Cold War* (New York: Cambridge University Press, 2006), 72; Jeffrey F. Taffet, *Foreign Aid as Foreign Policy: The Alliance for Progress in Latin America* (New York: Routledge, 2007), 40; Randolph Jones, "Otto Passman and Foreign Aid: The Early Years," *Louisiana History* 26, 1 (Winter 1985): 53–62.

57. National Security Council Memorandum, Arnold Nachmanoff and Robert Hormats to General Haig, May 6, 1971, RG 56: Records Relating to International Financial Institutions, Box 9, National Archives and Records Administration (hereafter NARA); Jonathan E. Sanford, *U.S. Foreign Policy and Multilateral Development Banks* (Boulder, Colo.: Westview, 1982), 121; Babb, *Behind the Development Banks*, 67.

58. In Latin America alone, U.S.-owned companies were expropriated on at least twenty-two separate occasions between 1968 and 1976. See Hal Brands, "Richard Nixon and Economic Nationalism in Latin America: The Problem of Expropriations, 1969–1974," *Diplomacy and Statecraft* 18, 1 (January 2007), 216.

59. Brands, "Richard Nixon and Economic Nationalism," 221.

60. Memorandum for the Record, Meeting on Expropriation of Foreign Investments, October 21, 1971, McNamara Papers, Memoranda for the Record, Box 1.

61. "Expropriation Policy, 1969–1972," Editorial Note 148, *FRUS*, 1969–1976, IV, Foreign Assistance, International Development, Trade Policies, 1969–1972.

62. U.S. General Accounting Office, *More Effective United States Participation Needed in World Bank and International Development Association* (Washington, D.C.: Comptroller General of the United States, 1973), 2. These findings were echoed by a Congressional Research Service report issued the following year. See U.S. Congress, House, Committee on Foreign Affairs, *The United States and the Multilateral Development Banks*, by Margaret Goodman and Jonathan Sanford, A Report to the Committee on Foreign Affairs, 93rd Cong., 2nd sess., 1974, 210.

63. Gwin, "U.S. Relations," 219–20.

64. Memorandum of Conversation, November 17, 1969, White House Situation Room, Subject: Discussions of References to Increased Japanese Economic Development Assistance in President's Talks with Japanese Prime Minister Sato, Nixon Presidential Materials, National Security Council Files, Name Files, Box 828, NARA.

65. John Blaxall, interview with author, January 2008.

66. Memorandum of Conversation, Palm Springs, California, May 7, 1971, 2:50–5:45 p.m., Kissinger Office Files, Country Files, Middle East, Farland, Amb. (Pakistan), Nixon Presidential Materials, NSC Files, Box 138, NARA, cited in *FRUS, 1969–1976*, vol. 11, South Asia Crisis, 1971; Conversation among President Nixon, the president's assistant for National Security Affairs (Kissinger), and Attorney General Mitchell, Washington, D.C., December 8, 1971, 4:20–5:01 p.m., *FRUS, 1969–1976*, vol. E-7, Documents on South Asia, 1969–1972.

67. Memorandum of Conversation, Washington, July 23, 1971, 12:50–1:18 p.m., Country Files, Middle East, India/Pakistan, July 1971, Nixon Presidential Materials, NSC Files, Box 643, NARA, cited in *FRUS, 1969–1976*, vol. 11, South Asia Crisis, 1971; Memorandum of Conversation, Washington, July 30, 1971, 6 p.m., Geopolitical File, South Asia, Chronological File, Nov 69-July 1971, Kissinger Papers, Box CL 210, LOC, cited in *FRUS, 1969–1976*, vol. 11.

68. World Bank Office Memorandum to Mr. Lester Nurick, Subject: Cases of Nationalization Relevant to the Iraqi Dispute, June 10, 1972, RG 56, Records Relating to International Financial Institutions, Box 1, NARA.

69. William Clark, "Reconsiderations: Robert McNamara at the World Bank," *Foreign Affairs* 60, 1 (Fall 1981): 176; J. Burke Knapp, WBOH, Papers of J. Burke Knapp, HIA.

70. PC, March 5, 1973, McNamara Papers, President's Council Minutes, Box 1; "Lists of White House 'Enemies' and Memorandums Relating to Those Named," *New York Times*, June 28, 1973, 38.

71. PC, June 7, 1971, McNamara Papers, President's Council Minutes, Box 1.

72. Sanford, *U.S. Foreign Policy*, 62–63.

73. John M. Hennessy, Draft letter to Chairman of House Banking and Currency Committee, Senate Foreign Relations Committee, House and Senate Appropriations Sub-Committees on Foreign Operations, undated, RG 56, Office of International Development Banks, Chronological File, Box 1, NARA.

74. Memorandum for Secretary Shultz from John M. Hennessy, Assistant Secretary for International Affairs, Subject: "Stretch-out" U.S. Contribution to IDA, April 16, 1973, William E. Simon Papers (microfiche), Series IIIA Subject Files (D.S.) Drawer 14 Federal Energy Office Folders 14:1 thru 14:64, Gerald Ford Library (hereafter GFL).

75. PC, September 23, 1973, McNamara Papers, President's Council Minutes.

76. Gwin, "U.S. Relations," 215.

77. On the decline in U.S. support for foreign aid see David Ekbladh, *The Great American Mission: Modernization and the Construction of an American World Order* (Princeton, N.J.: Princeton University Press, 2010), 226–56.

78. Randall Bennett Woods, *J. William Fulbright, Vietnam, and the Search for a Cold War Foreign Policy* (New York: Cambridge University Press, 1998), 255; PL 93–189 (December 17, 1973).

79. Selig S. Harrison, "Administration Plans New Aid Fund Attempt," *Washington Post*, February 10, 1974, A17.

80. On responses to the oil crisis see G. John Ikenberry, "The Irony of State Strength: Comparative Responses to the Oil Shocks in the 1970s," *International Organization* 40, 1 (Winter 1986): 105–37.

81. Memorandum for the Record, Meeting on Energy, January 22, 1974, McNamara Papers, Memoranda for the Record, Box 1; Memorandum for the Record, Meeting on Energy, January 28, 1974, McNamara Papers, Memoranda for the Record, Box 1; Memorandum for the Record, Meeting with Mr. Ullberg, Minister Counsellor, Norwegian Embassy, March 1, 1974, McNamara Papers, Memoranda for the Record, Box 1. On the U.S. response to the oil crisis generally see David E. Spiro, *The Hidden Hand of American Hegemony: Petrodollar Recycling and International Markets* (Ithaca, N.Y.: Cornell University Press, 1999).

82. Oppenheim, "Whose World Bank?" 106–8.

83. Quoted in Gwin, "U.S. Relations with the World Bank," 217.

84. Prominent among these critics was British economist P. T. Bauer, whose *Dissent on Development* (Cambridge, Mass.: Harvard University Press, 1972) argued that post-World War II foreign aid had not achieved its development objectives for a variety of reasons, including the inability of government planners to identify productive investments. For a sympathetic review of Bauer's work, see Andrei Shleifer, "Peter Bauer and the Failure of Foreign Aid," *Cato Journal* 29, 3 (Fall 2009): 379–90.

85. PC, February 2, 1976, McNamara Papers, President's Council Minutes, Box 2.

86. PC, December 16, 1974, McNamara Papers, President's Council Minutes, Box 1.

87. McNamara initially sought to get around U.S. hesitancy to increase its capital contribution to the Bank by reaching out to oil-producers. In January 1975, he asked OPEC officials to consider increasing their share of capital subscriptions to the Bank from 4 to 15 percent, an "extraordinary offer," the Bank's historians note, "given the record of the extreme difficulties in changing relative voting power in the IBRD." Yet here too McNamara was rebuffed. PC, January 6, 1975, McNamara Papers, President's Council Minutes, Box 2; Kapur et al., *The World Bank*, vol. 1, 973.

88. Charles F. Schwartz, Memorandum to the Managing Director and the Deputy Managing Director, Subject: Board Meeting at the World Bank, March 21, 1974, IMF Central Files- Economic Subject Files S1780 (1973–1974), Box 470, IMF archives; PC, July 8, 1974, McNamara Papers, President's Council Minutes, Box 1. Meanwhile, the U.S. opposed IMF efforts to expand its oil facility. See Daniel Sargent, "The United States and Globalization in the 1970s," in Ferguson et al., *The Shock of the Global*, 59.

89. By contrast, the U.S. put up 41 percent of the Bank's initial capital and held 25 percent in 1975. Akins, "U.S. Control over World Bank Group Decision-Making," 147–55.

90. PC, July 1, 1974, McNamara Papers, President's Council Minutes, Box 1.

91. Kapur et al., *The World Bank*, vol. 1. A similar proposal for an "Interest Equalization Fund" had been put forward in 1962 by David Horowitz, the Israeli governor to the Bank. See James H. Weaver, *The International Development Association* (New York: Praeger, 1965), 179.

92. Memorandum for the President from William E. Simon, Subject: Results of International Meetings this Week on Monetary and Development Issues, January 18, 1975, White House Central Files, Subject Files IT 10–20, Box 2, GFL; Memorandum to Ms. Marian Bradley from Bernard Zinman, Subject: Comments on DDC Policy Paper No. 1, May 30, 1975, Office of International Development Banks, Chronological File, Box 3, RG 56, NARA; IBRD/IDA, *Annual Report*, 1975, 14.

93. Kapur et al., *The World Bank*, vol. 1, 1984.

94. Declaration on the Establishment of a New International Economic Order, Resolution adopted by the General Assembly, May 1, 1974, A/RES/S-6/3201.

95. Guiliano Garavini, *After Empires: European Integration, Decolonization, and the Challenge from the Global South, 1957–1986*, trans. Richard R. Nybakken (Oxford: Oxford University Press, 2012), 178.

96. PC, May 6, 1974, McNamara Papers, President's Council Minutes, Box 1. McNamara had flirted with a number of "pro-South" positions before. Aside from continuing the Bank's longstanding support for reductions in developed country import barriers and increased foreign assistance levels, in 1972 he argued for allocating SDRs to developing countries as a means to supplement regular aid flows. In 1969 McNamara also pushed through a proposal to have the Bank provide developing countries with supplementary financing in case of sudden commodity price drops.

97. PC, December 4, 1978, McNamara Papers, President's Council Minutes, Box 2.

98. On U.S. responses to the NIEO see John Toye and Richard Toye, "From New Era to Neo-Liberalism: U.S. Strategy on Trade, Finance, and Development in the United Nations, 1964–1982," *Forum for Development Studies* 1, 32 (June 2005): 151–80.

99. Henry Kissinger, *Global Consensus and Economic Development, Speech Delivered to the Seventh Special Session of the United Nations General Assembly, September 1, 1975* (Washington, D.C.: U.S. Department of State, Bureau of Public Affairs, 1975); Peter Dickson, *Kissinger and the Meaning of History* (Cambridge: Cambridge University Press, 1978), 181; PC, April 26, 1976, McNamara Papers, President's Council Minutes, Box 2.

100. Robert Hormats, National Security Council memorandum for Brent Scowcroft, January 20, 1976, Subject: Nigeria: Treasury Intends to Oppose IBRD Lending, *FRUS*, 1969–1976, vol. E-6, Documents on Africa, 1973–1976.

101. On Kissinger's growing appreciation for the role of economics in international affairs see Daniel J. Sargent, "The United States and Globalization in the 1970s," in Ferguson et al., *The Shock of the Global*, 49–51.

102. Kissinger to Simon, March 3, 1976, *FRUS*, 1969–1976, vol. E-6.

103. PC, February 2, 1976, McNamara Papers, President's Council Minutes, Box 2.

104. Raul Prebisch, *The Economic Development of Latin America and Its Principal Problems* (New York: UN, 1950); H. W. Singer, "The Distribution of Gains between Investing and Borrowing Countries," *American Economic Review* 40, 2, Papers and Proceedings of the Sixty-Second Annual Meeting of the American Economic Association (May 1950): 473–85.

105. Paul A. Baran, *The Political Economy of Growth* (New York: Monthly Review Press, 1957); Celso Furtado, *Desenvolvimento e subdesenvolvimento* (Rio de Janeiro: Editora Fundo de Cultura, 1961); Samir Amin, *L'accumulation à l'échelle mondiale* (Dakar: IFAN, 1970); Andre Gunder Frank, *Capitalism and Underdevelopment in Latin America: Historical Studies of Chile and Brazil* (New York: Monthly Review Press, 1967).

106. Frank, "The Development of Underdevelopment," *Monthly Review Press* 18, 4 (September 1966): 17–31.

107. For a representative dependency theory approach, see Frank, *Capitalism and Underdevelopment in Latin America*.

108. Teresa Hayter, *Aid as Imperialism* (Middlesex: Penguin, 1971). As described in the following chapter, the Bank initially sponsored Hayter's study but then tried to prevent its publication.

109. Ernest Feder, "McNamara's Little Green Revolution: World Bank Scheme for Self-Liquidation of Third World Peasantry," *Economic and Political Weekly* 11, 14 (April 3, 1976): 538. See also Rosemary Galli, "Rural Development as Social Control: International Agencies and Class Struggle in the Colombian Countryside," *Latin American Perspectives* 5, 4 (Autumn 1978): 86. At times critics took such complaints directly to the Bank. In 1976, for instance, a Bank staff noted that European scholars had "viciously attacked the organization on the grounds that it serves as a "pathfinder for multinational corporations [and] proleterized small farmers through its rural development program so that their land could be taken over by multinational agribusinesses." PC, March 15, 1976, McNamara Papers, President's Council Minutes, Box 2.

110. Bertram Gross, "Destructive Decision-Making in Developing Countries," *Policy Sciences* 5, 2 (June 1974): 236.

111. Aart J. M. van de Laar, "The World Bank: Which Way?" *Development and Change* 7 (1976): 93. Also see van de Laar, "The World Bank and the World's Poor," *World Development* 4, 10–11 (1976): 837–51.

112. Gordon H. Ball, "Man and His Parasites in the Tropics," *American Biology Teacher* 30, 5 (May 1968): 429; Thayer Scudder, "The Human Ecology of Big Projects: River Basin Development and Resettlement," *Annual Review of Anthropology* 2 (1973): 45–55; M. Taghi Farvar and John P. Milton, eds., *The Careless Technology: Ecology and International Development* (New York: Doubleday, 1972).

113. Brynes, "Charity Begins at Home," 307.

114. Donella H. Meadows, Dennis L. Meadows, Jørgen Randers, and William W. Behrens III, *The Limits to Growth: A Report for the Club of Rome's Project on the Predicament of Mankind* (New York: Universe, 1972). On the rise of environmental concerns about development, see Stephen J. Macekura, *Of Limits and Growth: The Rise of Sustainable Development in the Twentieth Century* (New York: Cambridge University Press, 2015).

115. E. F. Schumacher, *Small Is Beautiful: A Study of Economics as if People Mattered* (London: Blond & Briggs, 1973). For a contemporary perspective on the environmentalist critique of foreign aid, see Richard Critchfield, "The New Environment of Foreign Aid," *The Nation*, May 15, 1972, 622.

116. On opposition to the Chico Dam project, see Sanjeev Khagram, *Dams and Development: Transnational Struggles for Water and Power* (Ithaca, N.Y., Cornell University Press, 2004), 191–92, and "The Cordillera Under Siege: An Interview with Victoria Tauli Corpuz," *Multinational Monitor* (September 1992).

117. Peter Winn, "Why Letelier Died Now," *The Nation*, October 9, 1976, 327.

118. PC, December 13, 1976, McNamara Papers, President's Council Minutes, Box 2.

119. Well-known development economist William Arthur Lewis, for instance, argued that economic development would lead to a greater prevalence of nuclear families, which would give women more freedom to enter the formal workforce. See W. Arthur Lewis, *The Theory of Economic Growth* (London: Allen and Unwin, 1955), 48–50. On early views of the

role of women in development, see Maureen Woodhall, "Investment in Women: A Reappraisal of the Concept of Human Capital," *International Review of Education* 19, 1 (March 1973): 10.

120. See Arvonne S. Fraser and Irene Tinker, eds., *Developing Power: How Women Transformed International Development* (New York: Feminist Press at the City University of New York, 2004); Robyn G. Isserles, "Ideology, Rhetoric and the Politics of Bureaucracy: Exploring Women and Development" (Ph.D. dissertation: City University of New York, 2002); Jane L. Parpart, M. Patricia Connelly, and V. Eudine Barriteau, eds., *Theoretical Perspectives on Gender and Development* (Ottawa: International Development Research Centre, 2000); Nuket Kardam, *Bringing Women In: Women's Issues in International Development Programs* (Boulder, Colo.: Lynne Rienner, 1991).

121. Ester Boserup, *Woman's Role in Economic Development* (London: Allen and Unwin, 1970).

122. For a sampling of the emerging scholarship on women in development, see Lourdes Arizpe, "Women in the Informal Labor Sector: The Case of Mexico City," *SIGNS* 3, 1 (August 1977): 25–37; Kathleen Staudt, "Agricultural Productivity Gaps: A Case Study of Male Preference in Policy Implementation," *Development and Change* 9, 3 (July 1978): 439–57; Ruth Dixon, *Rural Women at Work: Strategies for Development in South Asia* (Baltimore: Johns Hopkins University Press, 1978); Barbara Rogers, *The Domestication of Women: Discrimination in Developing Societies* (New York: St. Martin's, 1979); Roslyn Dauber and Melinda Cain, eds., *Women and Technological Change in Developing Countries* (Boulder, Colo.: Westview, 1981); Barbara Lewis, ed., *Invisible Farmers: Women and the Crisis in Agriculture* (Washington, D.C.: Women in Development Office, Agency for International Development, 1981).

123. Irene Tinker, "Challenging Wisdom, Changing Policies: The Women in Development Movement," in Fraser and Tinker, *Developing Power*, 70–72.

124. See Irene Tinker and Michele Bo Bramsen, eds., *Women and World Development* (Washington, D.C.: Overseas Development Council, 1976) for a collection of papers and a review of the proceedings of an American Association of Science Seminar on Women in Development held at the Mexico City Conference.

125. John Toye, *Dilemmas of Development: Reflections on the Counter-Revolution in Development Theory and Policy* (New York: Blackwell, 1987).

126. P. T. Bauer, *United States Aid and Indian Economic Development* (Washington, D.C.: American Enterprise Association, 1959), 115.

127. P. T. Bauer and B. S. Yamey, "The Economics of the Pearson Report," *Journal of Development Studies* 8, 2 (January 1972): 322, 325.

128. On Johnson's views on development see Arnold C. Harberger and David Wall, "Harry G. Johnson as a Development Economist," *Journal of Political Economy* 92, 4 (August 1984): 616–41. For a critique of Johnson's arguments see Toye, *Dilemmas of Development*, 47.

129. Harry Johnson, "Thrust and Response: The Multinational Corporation as a Development Agent," *Columbia Journal of World Business* 5, 3 (May–June 1970): 25–30; Johnson, "Economic Growth and Economic Policy," in Johnson, *The Canadian Quandary: Economic Problems and Policies* (Toronto: McGraw-Hill, 1963), 61–63.

130. Bella Balassa, *The Structure of Protection in Developing Countries* (Baltimore: Johns Hopkins University Press, 1971).

131. Anne O. Krueger, "The Political Economy of the Rent-Seeking Society," *American Economic Review* 64, 3 (June 1974): 291–303.

132. Ian Little, Tibor Scitovsky and Maurice Scott, *Industry and Trade in Some Developing Countries: A Comparative Study* (London: Oxford University Press, 1970).

133. Arthur M. Okun, *Equality and Efficiency: The Big Tradeoff* (Washington, D.C.: Brookings Institution Press, 1975).

Chapter 5. Navigating Turbulence

1. PC, February 27, 1978, McNamara Papers, President's Council Minutes, Box 2.

2. Ibid.

3. PC, March 31, 1975, McNamara Papers, President's Council Minutes, Box 1.

4. IBRD/IDA, *Annual Report*, 1976, 5.

5. IBRD/IDA, *Annual Report*, 1977, 5.

6. Daniel Yergin and Joseph Stanislaw, *The Commanding Heights: The Battle for the World Economy* (New York: Touchstone, 2002), 113–14.

7. PC, January 14, 1974, McNamara Papers, President's Council Minutes, Box 1.

8. PC, July 8, 1974, McNamara Papers, President's Council Minutes, Box 1.

9. McNamara, Remarks at the Commerce Department, June 17, 1976, in WBGA IBRD/IDA 03-04-12S Box 2.

10. PC, June 10, July 8, 1974, McNamara Papers, President's Council Minutes, Box 1.

11. World Bank, International Debt Statistics.

12. J. Burke Knapp, WBOH, 88.

13. A few factors complicate our ability to document this change. Not only was much of the Bank's advisory work informal and, as such, undocumented, but the Bank continued to grow as both a bank and a development agency during these years. In nominal terms, annual IBRD lending commitments more than doubled between 1974 and 1980, while IDA credits nearly tripled. At the same time, loans for rural development, primary education, population, health and nutrition, small-scale industry, water supply and sewerage, and urban development, jumped from 5 percent of the organization's portfolio between 1968 and 1970 to 27.4 percent between 1975 and 1978. See Hirosato, "Changing Policies of the World Bank for Educational Intervention," 187–88.

14. Between 1969 and 1974, the percentage of IBRD and IDA loans with a distinct technical assistance component increased from 45 to 64 percent. See IBRD/IDA, *Annual Report*, 1974, 58.

15. IBRD/IDA, *Annual Report*, 1972, 9.

16. IBRD/IDA, *Annual Report*, 1974, 58.

17. Ibid., 31.

18. Ibid., 31–32.

19. IBRD/IDA, *Annual Report*, 1975, 43.

20. IBRD/IDA, *Annual Report*, 1974, 58.

21. For example, Bank loans with a technical assistance component rose from 112 in 1974 to 139 in 1975 and 152 in 1976. See IBRD/IDA, *Annual Report*, 1975, 67; 1976, 73.

22. For background, see Mason and Asher, *The World Bank Since Bretton Woods*, 528–35.

23. World Bank, *Review of World Bank Co-Financing with Private Financial Institutions* (Washington, D.C.: World Bank, 1980), 1–3.

24. Babai, "Between Hegemony and Poverty," 257.

25. World Bank, *Review of World Bank Co-Financing*, 4–5.

26. For instance, when McNamara visited officials at the Bank of America to discuss co-financing in 1977, he sought to "outline the advantage for commercial banks to participate in financing [developing country] growth [and] . . . give assurance that [the Bank] would inform the Bank of America of the countries and projects where we were contemplating lending." See Memorandum for the Record, Meeting to Discuss IBRD Capital Increase and Cofinancing, September 19, 1977, IBRD/IDA 03-04. Office of the President, Records of President Robert S. McNamara, Series 07: Memoranda for the Record, Box 2.

27. Babai, "Between Hegemony and Poverty," 266.

28. "Nordic Cable, Report of Board Meeting January 11, 1976," 065-1, E-3-B: Motereff, Box 43, Riksarkivet, Oslo.

29. Anonymous Brazilian journalist quoted in Office Memorandum: Visit to Brazil, from Dinesh Bahl to John E. Merriam, November 10, 1978, I:20, Robert S. McNamara Papers, LOC.

30. PC, October 30, 1978, McNamara Papers, President's Council Minutes, Box 2, WBGA; Hans Janssen, "Bank has undergone significant changes," *Bank Notes*, September 1978, 6, WGBA.

31. PC, July 12, 1976, McNamara Papers, President's Council Minutes, Box 2.

32. PC, January 9, 1978, McNamara Papers, President's Council Minutes, Box 2. Some developing country officials had voiced these concerns earlier.

33. Ibid.

34. Edwin L. Dale, Jr., "McNamara Asks for Poverty Group," *New York Times*, January 15, 1977, 38; Barbara Ward Jackson to William Clarke, January 25, 1976, I:20, Robert S. McNamara Papers, LOC.

35. PC, March 7, 1977, McNamara Papers, President's Council Minutes, Box 2.

36. Statement by McNamara to the Executive Directors' Meeting, June 23, 1977, in IBRD/IDA 03-04-12S Box 2.

37. Ibid.

38. Ibid.

39. McNamara, "To the Board of Governors, Washington, D.C., September 26, 1977," in *The McNamara Years*, 468–69.

40. PC, January 9, 1978, McNamara Papers, President's Council Minutes, Box 2.

41. Bruno S. Frey and Friedrich Schneider, "Competing Models of International Lending Activity," *Journal of Development Economics* 20, 2 (March 1986): 225–45.

42. Cheryl Payer, *The World Bank: A Critical Analysis* (New York: Monthly Review Press, 1982).

43. PC, November 16, 1970, McNamara Papers, President's Council Minutes, Box 1.

44. On the United States and Allende see Tanya Harmer, *Allende's Chile and the Inter-American Cold War* (Chapel Hill: University of North Carolina Press, 2011) and Lubna Z. Qureshi, *Nixon, Kissinger, and Allende: U.S. Involvement in the 1973 Coup in Chile* (Lanham, Md.: Lexington, 2009).

45. John Hugh Crimmins, Acting Chairman, Ad Hoc Interagency Working Group on Chile, Memorandum for Mr. Henry A. Kissinger, December 4, 1970, in "Chile and the United States: Declassified Documents Relating to the Military Coup, 1970–1976," National Security Archive, http://www.gwu.edu/~nsarchiv/NSAEBB/NSAEBB8/nsaebb8.htm.

46. On Allende's economic policies see Edward Boorstein, *Allende's Chile: An Inside View* (New York: International, 1977).

47. Memorandum, Richard Dosik to files, "Chile- Mr. Knapp's Meeting with Delegation," October 4, 1971, in Kapur et al., *The World Bank*, vol. 1, 1007.

48. Quoted in "Chile and the World Bank," U.S. Congress, House, Committee on Foreign Affairs, United States and Chile During the Allende Years, 1970–1973, Hearings before the Subcommittee on Inter-American Affairs, a compilation (Washington, D.C.: GPO, 1975), 445.

49. For views that attribute the cutoff in Bank lending to pressure from the Nixon administration see Don M. Coerver and Linda B. Hall, *Tangled Destinies: Latin America and the United States* (Albuquerque: University of New Mexico Press, 1999), 140, and Michael Reid, *Forgotten Continent: The Battle for Latin America's Soul* (New Haven, Conn.: Yale University Press, 2007), 112.

50. PC, October 18, 1971, November 29, 1971, January 10, 1972, McNamara Papers, President's Council Minutes, Box 1.

51. Memorandum, Knapp to McNamara, January 6, 1972, in Kapur et al., *The World Bank*, vol. 1, 1007.

52. PC, October 2, 1972, McNamara Papers, President's Council Minutes, Box 1.

53. PC, January 22, 1973, McNamara Papers, President's Council Minutes, Box 1.

54. Kapur et al., *The World Bank*, vol. 1, 1008.

55. PC, July 16, 1973, McNamara Papers, President's Council Minutes, Box 1.

56. PC, June 18, 1973, McNamara Papers, President's Council Minutes, Box 1.

57. Although the Board approved the loans, the director representing the Norwegian countries repeatedly criticized Bank management for lending to Pinochet. See "Memorandum: The Nordic executive director's Position toward IBRD's Policies and Relationships with Chile," December 18, 1974, in 065-1, E-3-B: Motereff, Box 43, Riksarkivet, Oslo.

58. Mahbub ul Haq, "The Bank's Mistakes in Chile," April 26, 1976, in Kapur et al., *The World Bank*, vol. 1, 301.

59. Stephen Eccles, interview with author.

60. Quoted in Babb, *Behind the Development Banks*, 62–63.

61. Congressional Quarterly, *Congressional Quarterly Almanac 1976*, 787; Babb, *Behind the Development Banks*, 67.

62. Transcript of Robert S. McNamara Speaking to a Press Seminar in The World Bank on May 10, 1978, McNamara Papers, Statements, Speeches, and Interviews, Box 2. See also PC, September 28, 1977, April 17, 1978, McNamara Papers, President's Council Minutes, Box 2.

63. "Staff Compensation Policy: Recommendations of the Management of the Bank," April 1979 and Statement by the Managing Director on 1980 Staff Compensation Review, IMF Executive Board Meeting 81/85, June 5, 1981, Computer Database, Archives of the International Monetary Fund.

64. PC, April 17, 1978, McNamara Papers, President's Council Minutes, Box 2.

65. Clark, "Reconsiderations," 180.

66. PC, April 17, 1978, McNamara Papers, President's Council Minutes, Box 2.

67. James Grant, "Strings Attached: Will Congress Finally Hobble the World Bank?" *Barron's*, July 18, 1977.

68. See Samuel Moyn, *The Last Utopia: Human Rights in History* (Cambridge, Mass.: Belknap Press of Harvard University Press, 2010), 151–52.

69. See Clair Apodaca, "U.S. Human Rights Policy and Foreign Assistance: A Short History," *Ritsumeikan International Affairs* 3 (2005): 64.

70. Charles W. Yost, "Should U.S. Tie Aid to Human Rights?" *Christian Science Monitor*, November 28, 1975.

71. To Board of Governors from Ken Guenther, Subject: House Rejection of Conference Report, September 19, 1977, Arthur Burns Papers, 1969–1978, Federal Reserve Board Subject File: IMF/IBRD Meeting, Washington, Sept. 30–Oct. 4, 1974: Summary Proceedings, Box B71, GFL.

72. PC, March 14, 1977, McNamara Papers, President's Council Minutes, Box 2.

73. PC, October 25, 1977, McNamara Papers, President's Council Minutes, Box 2.

74. Transcript of Robert S. McNamara Speaking to a Press Seminar in The World Bank on May 10, 1978, McNamara Papers, Statements, Speeches, and Interviews, Box 2. On the Bank's response to the U.S. human rights position also see "Human Rights Issues and the Bank and IDA," November 29, 1977, I:28, Robert S. McNamara Papers, LOC.

75. *Congressional Quarterly Almanac* 33 (Washington, D.C.: Congressional Quarterly, 1977), 370–75.

76. PC, February 15, 1978, McNamara Papers, President's Council Minutes, Box 2.

77. U.S. Congress, Senate, Committee on Foreign Relations, *U.S. Policy and the Multilateral Banks: Politicization and Effectiveness*, by Jonathan E. Sanford, Staff Report to the Subcommittee on Foreign Assistance, 95th Cong., 1st sess., May 1977, 5.

78. Ibid., 10. The Senate Foreign Relations Committee repealed the law in March 1977. According to Senator Hubert Humphrey (D-Minn.) the restriction had been "an ineffectual message to India to 'drop dead.'" Quoted in *Washington Post*, March 31, 1977, A-24. Also see Akins, "U.S. Control," 222.

79. Sanford, *Multilateral Development Banks*, 31.

80. IBRD/IDA, *Annual Report*, 1981, 86; Clark, "Reconsiderations," 169, n. 1.

81. IBRD/IDA, *Annual Report*, 1968, 89; IBRD/IDA, *Annual Report*, 1981, 162.

82. Memorandum for the President from W. Michael Blumenthal, Subject: Robert McNamara's Serving Another Term as President of the World Bank, March 25, 1977, Presidential Papers of Jimmy Carter, White House Central File Subject File, IT-3, Jimmy Carter Library (hereafter JCL).

83. See, for example, McNamara, Remarks before Congressional Breakfast Audience, March 30, 1977, McNamara Papers, Statements, Speeches, and Interviews, Box 2.

84. Mahbub ul-Haq, quoted in Barbara Ward Jackson to William Clarke, January 25, 1976, I:20, Robert S. McNamara Papers, LOC.

85. World Bank Projects Database.

86. Babb, *Behind the Development Banks*, 67; Schoultz, "United States Participation," 566–67; House Would Bar World Bank Use of U.S. Funds to Aid Vietnam," *Washington Post*, July 19, 1979, A7.

87. PC, September 10, 1979, September 17, 1979, McNamara Papers, President's Council Minutes, Box 2.

88. PC, April 30, 1979, McNamara Papers, President's Council Minutes, Box 2.

89. Gwin, "U.S. Relations," 226

90. Clyde H. Farnsworth, "Legislative Snags Peril Foreign Aid," *New York Times*, December 10, 1979, D4; PC, September 10, 1979, September 17, 1979, McNamara Papers, President's Council Minutes, Box 2.

91. Shapley, *Promise and Power*, 571; Babb, *Behind the Development Banks*, 67; Schoultz, "United States Participation," 566–67.

92. Hayter, *Aid as Imperialism*, 193–213.

93. In April 1971, for instance, McNamara had the Bank's Public Affairs Department respond to critical newspaper editorials by drawing attention to the "shift of emphasis in Bank lending toward such [poor] areas as East Pakistan and Northeast Brazil." PC, April 5, 1971, McNamara Papers, President's Council Minutes, Box 1.

94. Wade, "Greening the Bank," 616.

95. McNamara, "To the United Nations Conference on the Human Environment, Stockholm, Sweden, June 8, 1972," in McNamara, *The McNamara Years*, 193–206. McNamara's Stockholm speech was one of the first times the head of an international development organization publicly addressed environmental concerns. Indeed, the organization played a key role in organizing the conference. The Bank's new environmental adviser, James Lee, helped draft the Conference agenda, and Mahbub ul Haq was instrumental in convincing developing countries, who feared that environmental concerns would give developed nations a reason to further reduce their foreign aid, to participate. See James Lee, WBOH; Wade, "Greening the Bank," 622–23. A preparatory meeting was held in Founex, Switzerland in the spring of 1971. The report from the Founex Conference, which served as the basis for the program at Stockholm, "was largely drafted inside the World Bank." Wade, "Greening the Bank," 623. Also see Philippe Le Prestre, *The World Bank and the Environmental Challenge* (London: Associated University Presses, 1989), 83.

96. Tom Stoel, "July–August 1976 Trip to Europe and Nairobi," August 26, 1976, Folder 4169, Box 696, RG 3.1, Rockefeller Brothers Fund Archives, Rockefeller Archive Center, Sleepy Hollow, N.Y. Stoel was citing the views of Raymond Dasmann of the International Union for the Conservation of Nature. Thanks to Paul Adler for locating this material.

97. Wade, "Greening the Bank," 620–21.

98. Ibid., 621.

99. Quoted in ibid., 616.

100. See generally Shahara Razavi and Carol Miller, *Gender Mainstreaming: A Study of Efforts by the UNDP, the World Bank, and the ILO to Institutionalize Gender Issues* (Geneva: UN Research Institute for Social Development, 1995), 33–34.

101. Gloria Scott, "Breaking New Ground at the UN and the World Bank," in Fraser and Tinker, eds., *Developing Power*, 14–25.

102. V. Rajagopalan, WBOH.

103. Razavi and Miller, *Gender Mainstreaming*, 35; Isserles, "Exploring Women and Development," 71, n. 11.

104. Razavi and Miller, *Gender Mainstreaming*, 35. According to the Bank's own evaluations, "progress in moving from rhetoric to action [in integrating women's concerns into Bank lending decisions] remained slow until the mid-1980s." World Bank, Independent Evaluation Group, "Gender Issues in World Bank Lending: An Overview," 1995.

105. Kapur et al., *The World Bank*, vol. 1, 480.

106. Jurgen Donges, "Incentive Policies and Economic Integration: Report of the Research Advisory Panel on Industrial Development and Trade," May 1, 1979, in Kapur et al., *The World Bank*, vol. 1, 484.

107. World Bank, *Accelerated Development in Sub-Saharan Africa: An Agenda for Action* (Washington, D.C.: World Bank, 1981), 1.

108. Ibid., 2.

109. Ibid., 4–7.

110. Ibid., 6.

111. Katherine Marshall, interview with author.

112. See, for instance, Ramgopal Agarwala, *Price Distortions and Growth in Developing Countries* (Washington, D.C.: World Bank, 1983).

113. See, e.g., Bela A. Balassa, *Policy Reform in Developing Countries* (Oxford: Pergamon, 1977). On Balassa's influence in the Bank, see Kapur et al., *The World Bank*, Vol. 1, 485.

114. These resulted in Deepak Lal, *The Poverty of "Development Economics"* (London: Institute of Economic Affairs, 1983); Lal and Paul Collier, *Labour and Poverty in Kenya, 1800– 1980* (Oxford: Clarendon, 1986); Lal, *The Hindu Equilibrium* (Oxford: Clarendon, 1989). See "Deepak Lal," in Roger E. Backhouse and Roger Middleton, eds., *Exemplary Economists*, vol. 2, *Europe, Asia, and Australia* (Northhampton, Mass.: Edward Elgar, 2000), 379–80.

115. Eccles, interview with author.

116. Marshall, interview with author.

Chapter 6. Fighting Poverty

1. On the difficulty in evaluating development interventions, see George Keith Pitman, Osvaldo N. Feinstein, and Gregory K. Ingram, eds., *Evaluating Development Effectiveness* (New Brunswick, N.J.: Transaction, 2005).

2. Robert Ayers, *Banking on the Poor: The World Bank and World Poverty* (Cambridge, Mass.: MIT Press, 1983) remains the best account of the organization's antipoverty initiatives during the McNamara era. Reports from the Bank's Operations Evaluation Department

(OED) provide another source of information on the impact of its projects. Unfortunately, most of these materials are classified, as are many documents pertaining to the Bank's policy discussions with developing country officials.

3. McNamara, "To the Board of Governors, September 24, 1973," 246.

4. PC, March 24, 1969, McNamara, President's Council Minutes, Box 1.

5. Montague Yudelman, "The Role of Agriculture in Integrated Rural Development Projects: The Experience of the World Bank," *Journal of the European Society for Rural Sociology* 16, 4 (November 1976): 308–24.

6. Ayers, *Banking on the Poor*, 99.

7. Daniel Noah Lindheim, "Regional Development and Deliberate Social Change: Integrated Rural Development in Mexico" (Ph.D. dissertation, University of California, Berkeley, 1986), 74.

8. Ibid., 120.

9. World Bank OED, "Appraisal of Integrated Rural Development Project—PIDER Mexico," April 16, 1975, ii.

10. Ibid., iii.

11. Lindheim, "Regional Development and Deliberate Social Change," 122–23.

12. Ibid., 171.

13. Ibid.," 174.

14. OED, Project Performance Audit Report (hereafter PPAR), "Mexico: Integrated Rural Development Project, Papaloapan Basin (Loan 1053-ME)," June 28, 1985, iii.

15. Ibid.

16. Ibid.

17. Ibid., 1985, iii–iv.

18. James K. Boyce and Betsy Hartmann, "View from a Bangladesh Village," *The Nation*, March 4, 1978, 239.

19. World Bank, Projects Database; Mohamed Ibn Chambas, "The Politics of Agricultural and Rural Development in the Upper Region of Ghana: Implications of Technocratic Ideology and Non-Participatory Development" (Ph.D. dissertation, Cornell University, 1980), 178–79.

20. Ernest Aryeetey, "Decentralization for Rural Development: Exogenous Factors and Semi-Autonomous Program Units in Ghana," *Community Development Journal* 25, 3 (January 1990): 206–14.

21. Letter of Managing Director, FASCOM, to Programme Manager, January 2, 1979, in Chambas, "Politics of Agricultural and Rural Development," 198.

22. Chambas, "Politics of Agricultural and Rural Development," 200.

23. Quoted in ibid., 213. Also see Christian Lund, *Local Politics and the Dynamics of Property in Africa* (New York: Cambridge University Press, 2008), 95–96.

24. Peter Uvin, *Aiding Violence: The Development Enterprise in Rwanda* (West Hartford, Conn.: Kumarian, 1998), 119.

25. Cited in ibid.

26. René Lemarchand, *The World Bank in Rwanda: The Case of the Office de Valorisation Agricole et Pastorale du Mutara (OVAPAM)* (Bloomington: African Studies Program, Indiana University, 1982), 18.

27. Ibid., 5.

28. OED reports cited in Uvin, *Aiding Violence*, 119–20.

29. Tina Wallace, "Agricultural Projects and Land in Northern Nigeria" *Review of African Political Economy* 17 (January–April 1980): 59–70. Also see Raufu Ayoade Dunmoye, "The State and the Peasantry: The Politics of Integrated Agricultural Development Projects in Nigeria" (Ph.D. dissertation, University of Toronto, 1986) and see Brian C. D'Silva and M. Rafique Raza, "Integrated Rural Development in Nigeria: The Funtua Project," *Food Policy* 5, 4 (November 1980): 282–97.

30. Quoted in Ayers, *Banking on the Poor*, 124–25. Also see Bello et al., *Development Debacle*, 84–88.

31. World Bank, OED, PPAR, "Malaysia-Johore Land Settlement Project," in Rich, *Mortgaging the Earth*, 94.

32. Ibid., 94–95.

33. Ibid., 27–29.

34. Cathy Ann Hoshour, "Relocating Development in Indonesia: A Look at the Logic and Contradictions of State-Directed Resettlement" (Ph.D. dissertation, Harvard University, 2000).

35. World Bank, Independent Evaluation Group (IEG), *Indonesia Transmigration Program: A Review of Five Bank-Supported Projects*, http://lnweb90.worldbank.org/oed/oeddoclib.nsf/ DocUNIDViewForJavaSearch/777331DDD0B6239C852567F5005CE5E2.

36. Barry Newman, "Missing the Mark: In Indonesia, Attempts by World Bank to Aid Poor Often Go Astray," *Wall Street Journal*, November 10, 1977, 26.

37. Ayers, *Banking on the Poor*, 122.

38. Newman, "Missing the Mark," 26.

39. Daniel Benor and James Q. Harrison, *Agricultural Extension: The Training and Visit System* (Washington, D.C.: World Bank, 1977).

40. Mick Moore, "Institutional Development, the World Bank, and India's New Agricultural Extension Programme," *Journal of Development Studies* 20, 4 (July 1984): 312.

41. Jaswinder Singh Brara, "The Political Economy of Rural Development: International Development Agencies and the Indian Context" (Ph.D. dissertation, University of Hawaii, 1980), 325.

42. Moore, "Institutional Development," 310.

43. Quoted in ibid., 307.

44. Frank Patrick Dall, "Education, Agricultural Extension and Peasant Farmer Marginalization: A Case Study in the High Amazon of Peru" (Ph.D. dissertation, Florida State University, 1987), 458.

45. Ibid., 459, 380–81.

46. World Bank, OED, "Agricultural Research and Extension: An Evaluation of World Bank's Experience," in Dall, "Education, Agricultural Extension and Peasant Farmer Marginalization," 11. Also see Tragakes, "The Political Economy of National and International Agricultural Research," 144.

47. World Bank, OED, *Annual Review of Project Performance Audit Results* (Washington, D.C.: World Bank, 1978).

208 Notes to Pages 123–125

48. "Notes on Board Meeting, March 21, 1978," 065-1, E-3-B: Motereff., Box 42, Riksarkivet, Oslo.

49. Ayers, *Banking on the Poor*, 129–30.

50. Ibid., 130.

51. Ibid., 131.

52. World Bank, OED, *Annual Review of Evaluation Results* (Washington, D.C.: World Bank, 1989), v.

53. Ibid., vii.

54. Paarlberg and Lipton, "Changing Missions," 483.

55. Ayers, *Banking on the Poor*, 126.

56. World Bank, OED, *Twelfth Annual Review of Project Performance Results* (Washington, D.C.: World Bank, 1987), 113, 160.

57. Ayers, *Banking on the Poor*, 113.

58. Ibid., 113–15.

59. For a more extended discussion see Tragakes, "Political Economy," 140–58.

60. World Bank Archives, "Robert Strange McNamara: Fifth President of the World Bank Group, 1968–1981," http://go.worldbank.org/44V9497H50.

61. Ayers, *Banking on the Poor*, 116–121.

62. Ibid., 107. Some of the Bank's executive directors also expressed frustration with what they felt were the Brazilian government's lack of attention to distributional issues, 065-1, E-3-B: Motereff, Box 42, Riksarkivet, Oslo.

63. World Bank, "Sites and Services Projects: A World Bank Paper" (Washington, D.C.: World Bank, April 1974).

64. Herbert H. Werlin, "Urban Shelter and Community Development," in Weiss and Jequier, eds., *Technology, Finance, and Development*, 141.

65. World Bank, "Sites and Services," 3.

66. Douglas H. Keare and Scott Parris, "Evaluation of Shelter Programs for the Urban Poor: Principal Findings," *World Bank Staff Working Paper* 547 (Washington, D.C.: World Bank, 1982), v.

67. Stephen K. Mayo and David J. Gross, "Sites and Services- and Subsidies: The Economics of Low-Cost Housing in Developing Countries," *World Bank Economic Review* 1, 2 (January 1987): 305.

68. Pieter J. M. Robben and Pieter A. van Stuijvenberg, "India's Urban Housing Crisis: Why the World Bank's Sites and Services Schemes Are Not Reaching the Poor in Madras," *Third World Planning Review* 8, 4 (1986): 335–51.

69. Horace Campbell, "Tanzania and the World Bank's Urban Shelter Project," *Review of African Political Economy* 42 (1988): 10–11.

70. World Bank, Completion Report: Tanzania: First National Sites and Services Project (Report no. 4941), East Africa Regional Office, 1984, in Campbell, "Tanzania and the World Bank's Urban Shelter Project," 12.

71. World Bank, OED, "Indonesia: Impact Evaluation Report, Enhancing the Quality of Life in Urban Indonesia: The Legacy of the Kampung Improvement Program" (June 29, 1995): 71; Ayers, *Banking on the Poor*, 188–89.

72. Newman, "Missing the Mark," 1.

73. World Bank, Project Database.

74. Bello et al., *Development Debacle*, 111–13.

75. Ibid., 107.

76. Mayo and Gross, "Sites and Services," 327–28.

77. Ibid., 332.

78. World Bank, *Better Urban Services: Finding the Right Incentives*, Development in Practice Series (Washington, D.C.: World Bank, 1995), 20.

79. Gerhard Pohl and Dubravko Mihaljek, "Project Evaluation and Uncertainty in Practice: A Statistical Analysis of Rate-of-Return Divergences of 1,015 World Bank Projects," *World Bank Economic Review* 6, 2 (May 1992): 273–74.

80. World Bank, OED, *Tenth Annual Review of Project Performance Audit Results* (Washington, D.C.: World Bank, 1984), 13.

81. "Report of the Committee on the Quality of Bank Lending," May 10, 1977 I: 23, McNamara Papers, LOC.

82. Benjamin King, quoted in Caufield, *Masters of Illusion*, 102.

83. Kapur et al., *The World Bank*, vol. 1, 454.

84. Ibid., 463–67.

85. IBRD/IDA Economic Committee, "Brazil: Country Program Paper," draft EC/O/69-125/1, November 25, 1969, in Kapur et al., *The World Bank*, vol. 1, 275.

86. Memorandum, Gerald Alter for the record, "Meeting of Mr. McNamara with the Minister of Interior of Brazil, Jose Costa Cavalcanti," February 17, 1970, in Kapur et al., *The World Bank*, vol. 1, 275.

87. Kapur et al., *The World Bank*, vol. 1, 276.

88. World Bank, "Notes on Brazil Country Program Review, December 2, 1971," December 9, 1971, in Kapur et al., *The World Bank*, vol. 1, 276.

89. Kapur et al., *The World Bank*, vol. 1, 277.

90. Memorandum, Hollis B. Chenery to Robert S. McNamara, "Brazil: Outstanding Policy Issues," February 16, 1973, in Kapur et al., *The World Bank*, vol. 1, 278.

91. Memorandum, Alexis E. Lachman to John H. Alder, attaching "Notes on Review of CPP on Brazil," February 28, 1973, in Kapur et al., *The World Bank*, vol. 1, 278.

92. Memorandum, Gerald Alter to Robert S. McNamara, "Brazil: Impressions Gained from Recent Visit to Brazil," June 10, 1974, 2 in Kapur et al., *The World Bank*, vol. 1, 279.

93. Memorandum, Robert S. McNamara to J. Burke Knapp, March 18, 1975, in Kapur et al., *The World Bank*, vol. 1, 279. Some of the Bank's directors were also frustrated by the Brazilian government's economic and social policies. See "Report of the Board Meeting Held October 21, 1975," in 065-1, E-3-B: Motereff., Box 42, Riksarkivet, Oslo.

94. Nevertheless, the Bank continued to fund significant poverty oriented lending in Brazil. In 1979, 57 percent of its lending to the country went toward small-farmer projects. Kapur et al., *The World Bank*, vol. 1, 280.

95. Memorandum, Mahbub ul Haq to Robert S. McNamara, "Brazil CPP: Major Policy Issues," May 29, 1981, in Kapur et al., *The World Bank*, vol. 1, 281.

96. Kapur, et al., *The World Bank*, vol. 1, 500.

97. Ibid., 501.

98. Robert McNamara, "Conversations with the Shah of Iran at Blair House," July 27, 1973, in ibid.

99. Ibid., 501–2.

100. Loh, "Foreign Technical Assistance to Malaysia"; Rene Salgado, "International Economic Organizations and Domestic Economic Policies: A Study of the Relationships of Colombia with the Economic Commission for Latin America, the World Bank and the International Monetary Fund" (Ph.D. dissertation, University of Maryland, Baltimore County, 1991).

101. Kapur et al., *The World Bank*, vol. 1, 283–84.

102. Robert S. McNamara, "Notes on Visit to India, November 6–12, 1976," 3 in Kapur et al., *The World Bank*, vol. 1, 295.

103. Memorandum, Alexis E. Lachman to John H. Alder, December 5, 1973, in Kapur et al., *The World Bank*, vol. 1, 296. Also see Praveen K. Chaudhry, "International Linkages, Economic Reforms, and Democracy: A Study of India's Political Economy" (Ph.D. dissertation, University of Pennsylvania, 2003).

104. PC, April 15, 1968, McNamara, President's Council Minutes, Box 1.

105. Cable, Bernard R. Bell to Robert S. McNamara, February 11, 1972, in Kapur et al., *The World Bank*, vol. 1, 490–94; Adrian Vickers, *A History of Modern Indonesia* (Cambridge: Cambridge University Press, 2005), 187.

106. Kapur et al., *The World Bank*, vol. 1, 494.

107. For instance, poverty concerns were largely absent in Bank discussions with the government of Bangladesh. See Abdul Halim, "Lending Policy of the World Bank with Special Reference to Its Contribution to the Economic Development of Bangladesh, 1972–1978" (M.A. thesis, Carleton University, 1979), 83–101; Kapur et al., *The World Bank*, vol. 1, 299–300.

108. Bello et al., *Development Debacle*, 127–64. The study was based on classified documents leaked by Bank staff.

109. Ibid., 134–35.

110. Ibid., 137.

111. World Bank, "Priorities and Prospects for Development," vol. 1, Confidential Draft, Washington, D.C., 1976, 1, in ibid., 139.

112. World Bank, "Priorities and Prospects," 139.

113. World Bank, "Philippines: Review of the Philippines and Bank Activities," Memo from David Steel, July 8, 1977, 1, in Bello et al., *Development Debacle*, 147.

114. World Bank, "Meeting of the Consultative Group for the Philippines, December 13 and 14, 1979," in Bello et al., *Development Debacle*, 148.

115. World Bank, GDF.

116. Quoted in Karin Lissakers, *Banks, Borrowers, and the Establishment: A Revisionist Account of the International Debt Crisis* (New York: Basic, 1991).

117. PC, June 19, 1969, McNamara Papers, President's Council Minutes, Box 1. Also see PC, April 20, 1970, McNamara Papers, President's Council Minutes, Box 1.

118. Letter, McNamara to Aleke K. Banda, Minister of Finance, Malawi, June 3, 1970, in IBRD/IDA 03-04-09S Box 1; italics mine.

119. PC, November 3, 1969, May 25, 1970, McNamara Papers, President's Council Minutes.

120. World Bank, *World Debt Tables* (Washington, D.C.: World Bank, 1970).

121. PC, August 9, 1971, October 4, 1971, McNamara Papers, President's Council Minutes, Box 1.

122. Memorandum, Shiv. S. Kapur, division chief, LACI, for the record, "Meeting of McNamara with the Mexican Delegation on September 2, 1975," September 3, 1975, 3, in Kapur et al., *The World Bank*, vol. 1, 497.

123. World Bank, "1975- Annual Meeting Briefing-Mexico," August 18, 1975, 3, in Kapur et al., *The World Bank*, vol. 1, 497.

124. McNamara, "To the Board of Governors, Manila, Philippines, October 4, 1976," in *The McNamara Years*, 346.

125. McNamara, "To the Board of Governors, October 4, 1976," in *The McNamara Years*, 347–48, 355.

126. Richard E. Feinberg, "An Open Letter to the World Bank's New President," in Feinberg, ed., *Between Two Worlds: The World Bank's Next Decade* (Washington, D.C.: Overseas Development Council, 1986), 7.

127. PC, May 3, 1977, McNamara Papers, President's Council Minutes, Box 2.

128. Ibid.

129. McNamara, "To the Board of Governors, Washington, D.C., September 26, 1977," in *The McNamara Years*, 455–56.

130. Memorandum, I. P. M. Cargill to Robert S. McNamara, "Riskiness in IBRD's Loan Portfolio," October 25, 1978, in Kapur et al., *The World Bank*, vol. 1, 598.

131. "Board Discussion of World Development Report," undated, 065-1, E-3-B: Motereff, Box 43, Riksarkivet, Oslo.

132. Office memorandum, Ernest Stern to regional vice presidents, "Identification of Country Creditworthiness Issues in CPPs," December 15, 1978, in Kapur et al., *The World Bank*, vol. 1, 598.

133. Helleiner, *States and the Reemergence of Global Finance*, 175.

134. Memorandum, Surinder Malik and C. Doultsinos to Jean Baneth, "Bank Borrowers Experiencing Debt Servicing Problems," October 29, 1979, 2, in Kapur et al., *The World Bank*, vol. 1, 599.

135. PC, November 26, 1979, McNamara Papers, President's Council Minutes, Box 2.

136. PC, December 10, 1979, McNamara Papers, President's Council Minutes, Box 2.

137. Draft Sunday Times (London) Interview with Robert S. McNamara, April 2, 1980, in IBRD/IDA 03-04-12S Box 2.

138. Kapur et al., *The World Bank*, vol. 1, 601 n. 20.

139. PC, January 19, 1981, McNamara Papers, President's Council Minutes, Box 2.

140. World Bank, *World Development Report* (Washington, D.C.: World Bank, 1981), iii.

141. On the debt crisis and its historical precursors, see Barry Eichengreen and Peter H. Lindert, eds., *The International Debt Crisis in Historical Perspective* (Cambridge, Mass.: MIT Press, 1989).

142. See, for instance, Robert Devlin, *Debt and Crisis in Latin America: The Supply Side of the Story* (Princeton, N.J.: Princeton University Press, 1989).

143. Feinberg, "An Open Letter," 7.

Chapter 7. The Birth of Structural Adjustment

1. Robert S. McNamara, "To the United Nations Conference on Trade and Development, Manila, Philippines, May 10, 1979," in McNamara, *The McNamara Years*, 549.

2. Policy-based lending is now called "development policy lending" and, in certain low-income countries, "poverty reduction strategy credits." See World Bank, Lending Tools, http://digitalmedia.worldbank.org/projectsandops/lendingtools.htm#devt.

3. U.S. Department of Agriculture, Economic Research Service, International Macroeconomic Data Set, http://www.ers.usda.gov/Data/Macroeconomics/.

4. *North-South: A Program for Survival: The Report of the Independent Commission on International Development Issues under the Chairmanship of Willy Brandt* (London: Pan Books, 1980), 224.

5. Paul Rosenstein-Rodan, "Problems of Industrialization of Eastern and South-Eastern Europe," *Economic Journal* 53, 210/211 (1943): 202–11.

6. Paul Krugman, "The Rise and Fall of Development Economics," in Krugman, *Development, Geography, and Economic Theory* (Cambridge, Mass.: MIT Press, 1995).

7. Dudley Seers, "The Birth, Life, and Death of Development Economics," *Development and Change* 10, 4 (October 1979): 707–19. See also Albert O. Hirschman, "The Rise and Decline of Development Economics," in Hirschman, *Essays in Trespassing: Economics to Politics and Beyond* (New York: Cambridge University Press, 1981), 1–26.

8. Katherine Marshall, interview with author.

9. World Bank, International Debt Statistics.

10. PC, March 20, 1972, McNamara Papers, President's Council Minutes, Box 1.

11. PC, October 14, 1974, McNamara Papers, President's Council Minutes, Box 1; Ivory Coast official quoted in Libby, "The Ideology and Power of the World Bank," 194.

12. Operations Evaluation Department, "Management Policy Review: Delays in Loan and Credit Effectiveness," July 22, 1975, I:26, Robert S. McNamara Papers, LOC.

13. Richard J. Levine, "McNamara's Leadership of World Bank Draws Sharp Criticism of Retiring Aide," *Wall Street Journal*, November 22, 1976, 3–4.

14. PC, June 26, 1978, McNamara Papers, President's Council Minutes, Box 2.

15. "Staff Association Task Force Report on Forms of Association," cited in PC, July 31, 1978, McNamara Papers, President's Council Minutes, Box 2.

16. PC, August 7, 1978, McNamara Papers, President's Council Minutes, Box 2.

17. PC, February 27, 1978, McNamara Papers, President's Council Minutes, Box 2. Staff occasionally voiced their opposition to Bank lending to specific countries. For example, in the late 1970s, some staff at Bank headquarters staged a walkout to protest a visit by Imelda Marcos, the wife of Philippine dictator Ferdinand Marcos. John Blaxall, interview with author.

18. PC, April 17, 1978, McNamara Papers, President's Council Minutes, Box 2.

19. PC, October 14, 1974, McNamara Papers, President's Council Minutes, Box 1.

20. PC, January 10, 1977, McNamara Papers, President's Council Minutes, Box 2.

21. PC, June 7, 1976, McNamara Papers, President's Council Minutes, Box 2.

22. "Report of Board Meeting October 7, 1975," 065-1, E-3-B: Motereff, Box 42, Riksarkivet, Oslo.

23. "Report on Staff Attitudes and Perceptions," cited in PC, January 17, 1977, McNamara Papers, President's Council Minutes, Box 2.

24. PC, January 31, 1977, McNamara Papers, President's Council Minutes, Box 2. These conclusions were echoed in October when a top-level "Working Group on Operational Monitoring and Control" concluded that the Bank's programming systems were responsible for a wide array of problems in the organization. See PC, October 17, October 31, 1977, McNamara Papers, President's Council Minutes, Box 2.

25. PC, January 3, 1977, McNamara Papers, President's Council Minutes, Box 2.

26. Ibid.

27. Ibid.

28. IBRD/IDA, *Annual Report*, 1978, 8.

29. PC, July 5, 1978, McNamara Papers, President's Council Minutes, Box 2.

30. PC, May 1, 1978, McNamara Papers, President's Council Minutes, Box 2.

31. Babai, "Between Hegemony and Poverty," 282–83.

32. Knapp, WBOH, 77.

33. Stanley Please, *The Hobbled Giant: Essays on the World Bank* (Boulder, Colo.: Westview, 1984), 32. On the early history of policy-conditioned lending, also see Paul Mosley, Jane Harrigan, and John Toye, *Aid and Power: The World Bank and Policy-Based Lending*, vol. 1 (London: Routledge, 1991), 27–29.

34. IBRD, Articles of Agreement, Article III, Section 4(vii).

35. PC, July 25, 1968, McNamara Papers, President's Council Minutes, Box 1.

36. PC, November 8, 1968, McNamara Papers, President's Council Minutes, Box 1.

37. Draft Statement to Follow Announcement of Circulation Today of Pearson Commission Paper on Program Lending and Financing of Local Currency Expenditure, December 15, 1970, in IBRD/IDA 03-04-12S Box 1.

38. IBRD/IDA, *Annual Report*, 1975, 11; Mosley, Harrigan, and Toye, *Aid and Power*, 32.

39. Babai, "Between Hegemony and Poverty," 289.

40. Kapur et al., *The World Bank*, vol. 1, 487.

41. Babai, "Between Hegemony and Poverty," 289. In response to the IMF's moves to make more of its funds available to developing countries, in 1977 the Board of Executive Directors examined program lending at the Bank but failed to come to a definite agreement on whether or how to reform the organization's non-project lending. Instead they agreed with staff that around 7–10% of Bank lending should be in the form of program loans. IBRD/IDA, *Annual Report*, 1977, 10–11; PC, March 28, 1977, McNamara Papers, President's Council Minutes, Box 2.

42. IBRD/IDA, *Annual Report*, 1981, 13.

43. PC, May 1, 1978, McNamara Papers, President's Council Minutes, Box 2.

44. Ibid.

45. See extensive discussion in PC, June 20, 1978, McNamara Papers, President's Council Minutes, Box 2.

46. PC, December 18, 1978, McNamara Papers, President's Council Minutes, Box 2.

47. PC, May 8, 1978, July 5, 1978, McNamara Papers, President's Council Minutes, Box 2.

48. Kapur et al., *The World Bank*, vol. 1, 506.

49. Memorandum, Ernest Stern to McNamara, "Review of the FY 1979 Lending Program," February 26, 1979, in Kapur et al., *The World Bank*, vol. 1, 506.

50. Office Memorandum: Macro-Economic Conditioning, Ernest Stern to Robert S. McNamara, May 16, 1979, I:28, Robert S. McNamara Papers, LOC.

51. PC, April 9, 1979, McNamara Papers, President's Council Minutes, Box 2.

52. Ibid.

53. Ibid.

54. Attila Karaosmonoglu, interview with author; Kapur et al., *The World Bank*, vol. 1, 506.

55. McNamara, "To the United Nations Conference on Trade and Development, May 10, 1979," 549.

56. Memorandum, Ernest Stern to McNamara, "Macro-Economic Conditioning," May 16, 1979, in Kapur et al., *The World Bank*, vol. 1, 507.

57. Staffs of the World Bank and the International Monetary Fund, "Financial Flows to Developing Countries and the Adjustment Process," June 29, 1979, Computer Database, IMF Archives.

58. Ibid., 2.

59. Ibid., 32.

60. PC, September 24, 1979, McNamara Papers, President's Council Minutes, Box 2.

61. Ibid.

62. Ibid.

63. Ernest Stern, interview with author; Kapur et al., *The World Bank*, vol. 1, 508. A preparatory meeting of the G-24 also called for "The establishment in the World Bank of a long-term facility to finance purchases of capital goods should be considered as quickly as possible." Intergovernmental Group of Twenty-Four on International Monetary Affairs, "Outline for a Program of Action on International Monetary Reform, Belgrade, Yugoslavia, September 29, 1979," Computer Database, IMF Archives.

64. McNamara, "To the Board of Governors, Belgrade, Yugoslavia, October 2, 1972," in *The McNamara Years*, 563–610.

65. PC, October 3, 1979, McNamara Papers, President's Council Minutes, Box 2.

66. Ibid.

67. Ibid.

68. PC, February 4, 1980, McNamara Papers, President's Council Minutes, Box 2.

69. Ibid.

70. PC, October 3, 1979, McNamara Papers, President's Council Minutes, Box 2.

71. PC, December 10, 1979, January 2, 1980, McNamara Papers, President's Council Minutes, Box 2.

72. PC, February 4, 1980, McNamara Papers, President's Council Minutes, Box 2.

73. PC, March 10, 1980, McNamara Papers, President's Council Minutes, Box 2.

74. PC, February 4, 1980, McNamara Papers, President's Council Minutes, Box 2.

75. World Bank Archives, "Robert Strange McNamara: 5th President of the World Bank Group, 1968–1981," http://go.worldbank.org/44V9497H50.

76. IBRD/IDA, *Annual Report*, 1980, 111–12.

77. "Background Paper on Structural Adjustment Lending," Background Papers to 1981 World Bank-IMF Annual Meeting, Presidential Papers of Jimmy Carter, Staff Office: Council of Economic Advisers, Box 123, JCL.

78. Knapp, WBOH, 66–67.

79. This account is based on Robin Broad, *Unequal Alliance: The World Bank, the International Monetary Fund, and the Philippines* (Berkeley: University of California Press, 1988).

80. Robert McNamara, "Impressions of the Philippines," November 13, 1971, I:31, Robert S. McNamara Papers, LOC. For instance, in 1969, the Bank approved three loans to the government totaling $71.5 million, almost half the money the organization had lent to the Philippines in its entire history

81. Broad, *Unequal Alliance*, 36–56.

82. Ibid., 59–63.

83. Ibid., 66.

84. World Bank, "Philippines: Country Program Paper, 1978," cited in Broad, *Unequal Alliance*, 68.

85. Broad, *Unequal Alliance*, 68–69.

86. World Bank, "Report and Recommendation, August 21, 1980," cited in Broad, *Unequal Alliance*, 69.

87. World Bank, "Aide Mémoire," cited in Broad, *Unequal Alliance*, 71.

88. Quoted in Broad, *Unequal Alliance*, 72.

89. Ibid., 72.

90. World Bank, "Report and Recommendation of the President of the International Bank for Reconstruction and Development to the Executive Board on a Proposed Structural Adjustment Loan to the Republic of the Philippines, August 21, 1980," 20, i, World Bank, Project Database.

91. Broad, *Unequal Alliance*, 76.

92. World Bank, "Report and Recommendation of President of the International Bank for Reconstruction and Development to the Executive Directors on a Structural Adjustment Loan to the Republic of Turkey, February 29, 1980," World Bank, Project Database.

93. World Bank, "Report and Recommendation of President of the International Bank for Reconstruction and Development to the Executive Directors on a Structural Adjustment Loan to the Republic of Bolivia, May 12, 1980," World Bank, Project Database.

94. Knapp, WBOH, 75.

95. Marshall, interview with author.

96. McNamara, interview with Lew Simons, Smithsonian Institution, August 8, 1980, in IBRD/IDA 03-04-12S Box 2.

97. Lewis in Knapp, WBOH, 17.

98. Stern, "World Bank Financing of Structural Adjustment," in John Williamson, ed., *IMF Conditionality* (Washington, D.C.: Institute for International Economics, 1983), 91.

99. PC, April 6, 1981, McNamara Papers, President's Council Minutes, Box 2.

100. For an introduction to the debate over structural adjustment lending see Lawrence H. Summers and Lant H. Pritchett, "The Structural-Adjustment Debate," *American Economic Review* 83, 2 (May 1993): 383–89.

101. Giles Mohan, Ed Brown, Bob Milward and Alfred B. Zack-Williams, *Structural Adjustment: Theory, Practice and Impacts* (London: Routledge, 2000).

102. Mosley, Harrigan and Toye, *Aid and Power*, 205.

103. See, among many others, Peter Gibbon, "The World Bank and African Poverty," *Journal of Modern African Studies* 30, 2 (June 1992): 193–220 and Michel Chossudovsky, *The Globalisation of Poverty: Impacts of IMF and World Bank Reforms* (London: Zed, 1997).

104. Carl Jayarajah and William H. Branson, *Structural and Sectoral Adjustment: World Bank Experience, 1980–1992* (Washington, D.C.: World Bank, 1995), 173–82.

105. Critical accounts of Bank and IMF adjustment lending include Susan George, *A Fate Worse Than Debt: The World Financial Crisis and the Poor* (New York: Grove Press, 1990) and Giovanni Andrea Cornia, Rolph van der Hoeven, and Thandika Mkandawire, eds., *Africa's Recovery in the 1990s: From Stagnation and Adjustment to Human Development* (New York: St. Martin's, 1993).

106. Nicolas van de Wall, *African Economies and the Politics of Permanent Crisis, 1979–1999* (Cambridge: Cambridge University Press, 2001). Also see George B. N. Ayittey, "Why Structural Adjustment Failed in Africa," in Schydlowsky, ed., *Structural Adjustment*, 108–22.

107. World Bank, Project Database.

108. William Easterly, "What Did Structural Adjustment Adjust? The Association of Policies and Growth with Repeated IMF and World Bank Adjustment Loans," *Journal of Development Economics* 76, 1 (February 2005): 20.

Conclusion

1. PC, June 9, 1980, McNamara Papers, President's Council Minutes, Box 2.

2. McNamara, Announcement of Intention to Retire, Letter to Staff, June 9, 1980, in IBRD/IDA 03-04-12S Box 2.

3. *North-South: A Program for Survival*.

4. Robert McNamara, "Notes on April 15, 1980, Conversation with Vice Premier Deng Xiaoping," I:31, Robert S. McNamara Papers, LOC. Also see "Geopolitical File: China, Trips," I:99, and "China's View of the World Bank and Its Expectations: Extract from Mr. Husain's report, July 27, 1980," I:98.

5. On the origins and consequences of China's entry into the Bank see Harold K. Jacobson and Michel Oksenberg, *China's Participation in the IMF, the World Bank, and GATT: Toward a Global Economic Order* (Ann Arbor: University of Michigan Press, 1990). The event also had important ramifications for China, as the Bank became an important source of financial and technical assistance for the country over the coming years. See Guang Zhang, "Foreign Aid, National Interest, and Economic Development: The Case of China, 1949–2000" (Ph.D. dissertation, Kent State University, 2002).

6. McNamara's disappointment at the pace of development is reflected in Robert McNamara, "Notes and Notebooks: Field Visits, Folders 1–2," I:31, Robert S. McNamara Papers, LOC.

7. Babb, *Behind the Development Banks*, 46.

8. PC, January 14, 1980, McNamara Papers, President's Council Minutes, Box 2.

9. Ronnie Dugger, "Ronald Reagan and the Imperial Presidency," *The Nation*, November 1, 1980, 433.

10. Republican Party Platform of 1980, Adopted by the Republican National Convention, July 15, 1980, Detroit, http://www.presidency.ucsb.edu/ws/?pid=25844. Also see Ann Hughey, "Is the World Bank Biting Off More Than It Can Chew?" *Forbes*, May 26, 1980, 122–28.

11. PC, October 31, 1980, McNamara Papers, President's Council Minutes, Box 2; Memorandum for the President from Henry Owen, Subject: World Bank Presidency, September 5, 1980, Presidential Papers of Jimmy Carter, Staff Offices Counsel Cutler, Box 117, JCL; Memorandum for the President, G. William Miller, Edmund S. Muskie, and Lloyd N. Cutler, Subject: World Bank Presidency, August 8, 1980, draft, in Presidential Papers of Jimmy Carter.

12. "A. W. Clausen Correspondence," I:3, Robert S. McNamara Papers, LOC.

13. Memorandum for the President, From Lloyd N. Cutler, Subject: World Bank Presidency, October 2, 1980, in Presidential Papers of Jimmy Carter, Staff Offices Counsel Cutler, Box 117.

14. Ibid.; Talking Points for President's Meeting with A. W. (Tom) Clausen, Thursday, October 23, 1980, in Presidential Papers of Jimmy Carter, Staff Offices Counsel Cutler, Box 117.

15. Jimmy Carter, draft letter to Pierre Elliot Trudeau, Prime Minister of Canada, Valery Giscard d'Estaing, President of France, Helmut Schmidt, Chancellor of Germany, Arnaldo Forlani, Prime Minister of Italy, Zenko Suzuki, Prime Minister of Japan, and Margaret Thatcher, Prime Minister of the United Kingdom, October 23, 1980, in Presidential Papers of Jimmy Carter, Staff Offices Counsel Cutler, Box 117.

16. PC, October 31, 1980, McNamara Papers, President's Council Minutes, Box 2.

17. Memorandum for the President, G. William Miller et al. On Clausen's tenure at the Bank of America see Moira Johnston, *The Tumultuous History of the Bank of America* (Washington, D.C.: Beard Books, 2000), 79–99.

18. William Greider, "The Education of David Stockman," *The Atlantic* (December 1981): 27–54; Robert Ayers, "Breaking the Bank," *Foreign Policy* 43 (Summer 1981): 104.

19. Ayers, "Breaking the Bank," 106.

20. PC, November 10, 1980, McNamara Papers, President's Council Minutes, Box 2.

21. PC, February 2, 1981, McNamara Papers, President's Council Minutes, Box 2.

22. Ayers, "Breaking the Bank," 105.

23. U.S. Department of the Treasury, *Assessment of U.S. Participation in the Multilateral Development Banks in the 1980s* (Washington, D.C.: Government Printing Office, 1981).

24. Ibid., 56.

25. Ibid., 57.

26. "Reagan Backing Helps Foreign Aid Bill," *Congressional Quarterly Almanac*, 1981, in Babai, "Between Hegemony and Poverty," 375.

27. U.S. Department of the Treasury, *Assessment of U.S. Participation*, 44; Harvey D. Shapiro, "America's Conservatives Close in on the World Bank," *Institutional Investor* (September 1981): 111–20.

28. Armand Razafindrabe, "Statement Before the Board of Executive Directors: The World Bank, June 39, 1981," and Earl G. Drake, "Statement Before the Board of Executive Directors: The World Bank, June 29, 1981," in *A Collection of Farewell Speeches on the Occasion of the Retirement of Robert S. McNamara, President of the World Bank, 1968–1981*, available via World Bank, Documents and Reports.

29. Moeen A. Qureshi, "Remarks at a Farewell Reception, The John F. Kennedy Center for the Performing Arts, June 28, 1981," in ibid.

30. IBRD/IDA, *Annual Report*, 1979, 18–19.

31. "The World Bank's Role in Energy Development," September 16, 1980, Briefing Book: IBRD/IMF General Issues [1], Presidential Papers of Jimmy Carter, Staff Office-CEA (Council of Economic Advisers), Box 123, JCL.

32. Clyde H. Farnsworth, "U.S. Rejects Proposal to Form World Bank Energy Affiliate," *New York Times*, August 13, 1981, D15.

33. See, for instance, the discussions over public and privately managed development finance companies in "Report of Board Meeting September 23, 1975," 065-1, E-3-B: Motereff, Box 42, Riksarkivet, Oslo.

34. Atlaf Gauhar, "Editorial," *Third World Quarterly* 4, 2 (April 1982): xvii; Rogers, "A Comparative Study of the Brandt Commission's Ideology," 270.

35. Ronald Reagan, "Remarks at the Annual Meeting of the Boards of Governors of the World Bank Group and International Monetary Fund, September 29, 1981," http://www.presidency.ucsb.edu/ws/?pid=44311.

36. Toye and Toye, "From New Era to Neo-Liberalism," 177.

37. On the Bank role in managing the international debt crisis see Kapur et al., *The World Bank*, vol. 1, 595–682; Chris C. Carvounis, *The Foreign Debt/National Development Conflict* (New York: Quorum, 1986).

38. Walden Bello with Shea Cunningham and Bill Rau, *Dark Victory: The United States, Structural Adjustment, and Global Poverty* (London: Pluto, 1994). Also see Donald Edward Sherblom, "The Latin American Debt Crisis and United States Hegemony" (Ph.D. dissertation, New School for Social Research, 1992).

39. Toye and Toye, "From New Era to Neo-Liberalism," 178.

40. Guillermo E. Perry, Omar S. Arias, J. Humberto López, William F. Maloney, and Luis Servén, *Poverty Reduction and Growth: Virtuous and Vicious Cycles* (Washington, D.C.: World Bank, 2006), 49.

41. Diana Alcarón and Eduardo Zepeda, "Economic Reform or Social Development? The Challenges of a Period of Reform in Latin America: Case Study of Mexico," in Gustavo Indart, ed., *Economic Reforms, Growth and Inequality in Latin America: Essays in Honor of Albert Berry* (Burlington, Vt.: Ashgate, 2004), 161.

42. Paul Collier and Jan Willem Gunning, "Why Has Africa Grown Slowly?" *Journal of Economic Perspectives* 13, 3 (Summer 1999): 3.

43. On the uneven implementation of structural adjustment programs see Nicholas van de Walle, *African Economies and the Politics of Permanent Crisis, 1979–1999* (Cambridge: Cambridge University Press, 2001).

44. World Bank Group Archives, "Barber Conable: 7th President of the World Bank Group," http://go.worldbank.org/E3LJ89ABX0.

45. On Wolfensohn's tenure, see Sebastian Mallaby, *The World's Banker: A Story of Failed States, Financial Crises, and the Wealth and Poverty of Nations* (New York: Penguin, 2004).

46. Bretton Woods Project, "Success or Failure? Wolfensohn's reforms at the World Bank," http://www.brettonwoodsproject.org/art-15958.

47. Catherine Weaver, *Hypocrisy Trap: The World Bank and the Poverty of Reform* (Princeton, N.J.: Princeton University Press, 2008); Geske Dijkstra, "Supranational Governance and the Challenge of Democracy," in Victor Bekkers, Geske Dijstra, Arthur Edwards, and Menno Fender, eds., *Governance and the Democratic Deficit: Assessing the Democratic Legitimacy of Governance Practices* (Burlington, Vt.: Ashgate, 2007), 269–92.

48. An exception is Robert W. Cox, "The Executive Head: An Essay on Leadership in the ILO," *International Organization* 23 (Spring 1969): 205–30.

49. See, among others, Frederick Cooper, "Modernizing Bureaucrats, Backward Africans, and the Development Concept," in Cooper and Packard, eds., *International Development and the Social Sciences*, 64–92; Uma Kothari, "From Colonial Administration to Development Studies: A Post-Colonial Critique of the History of Development Studies," in Kothari, ed., *A Radical History of Development Studies: Individuals, Institutions and Ideologies* (New York: Zed Books, 2005), 47–66; Jeffrey F. Taffet, *Foreign Aid as Foreign Policy: The Alliance for Progress in Latin America* (New York: Routledge, 2007); Kofas, *The Sword of Damocles*; Bradley R. Simpson, *Economists with Guns: Authoritarian Development and U.S.-Indonesian Relations, 1960–1968* (Stanford, Calif.: Stanford University Press, 2008); David Ekbladh, *The Great American Mission: Modernization and the Construction of an American World Order, 1914 to the Present* (Princeton, N.J.: Princeton University Press, 2010); Nick Cullather, "Research Note: Development? It's History," *Diplomatic History* 24, 4 (Fall 2000): 641–53; David C. Engerman, Nils Gilman, Mark H. Haefele, and Michael E. Latham, eds., *Staging Growth: Modernization, Development, and the Global Cold War* (Amherst: University of Massachusetts Press, 2003); Gilman, *Mandarins of the Future: Modernization Theory in Cold War America* (Baltimore: Johns Hopkins University Press, 2003); Latham, *Modernization as Ideology: American Social Science and "Nation Building" in the Kennedy Era* (Chapel Hill: University of North Carolina Press, 2000); Timothy Mitchell, *Rule of Experts: Egypt, Techno-Politics, Modernity* (Berkeley: University of California Press, 2002); Amanda Kay McVety, *Enlightened Aid: U.S. Development as Foreign Policy in Ethiopia* (New York: Oxford University Press, 2012).

50. An exception is Stephen J. Macekura, *Of Limits and Growth: The Rise of Sustainable Development in the Twentieth Century* (New York: Cambridge University Press, 2015).

51. Paul Hendrickson, *The Living and the Dead: Robert McNamara and Five Lives of a Lost War* (New York: Knopf, 1996).

52. Barbara Ward Jackson to William Clarke, January 25, 1976, I:20, Robert S. McNamara Papers, LOC.

53. For instance, in McNamara's apologia for Vietnam he speaks about his years at Harvard and the Ford Motor Company but ignores his tenure at the Bank. See Robert S. McNamara with Brian VanDeMark, *In Retrospect: The Tragedy and Lessons of Vietnam* (New York: Vintage, 1996).

54. See Steve Berkman, *The World Bank and the Gods of Lending* (Sterling, Va.: Kumerian, 2008).

55. Jessica Einhorn, "The World Bank's Mission Creep," *Foreign Affairs* 80, 5 (September/October 2001): 22–35.

INDEX

ACKNOWLEDGMENTS

Although this book is the product of many years of solitary labor, it could not have been possible without the support of numerous individuals and institutions.

Grants from the UCLA Department of History and International Institute, the University of California Institute on Global Conflict and Cooperation, the Society for Historians of American Foreign Relations, the Lyndon Baines Johnson Foundation, and the Gerald R. Ford Presidential Foundation enabled me to conduct the early research and writing. A fellowship at UC Berkeley's Regional Oral History Office gave me time to work on the manuscript. Harvard Law School was a wonderful setting to conclude the project.

Paul Adler, John Agnew, Michele Alacevich, Ivan Berend, Christopher Dietrich, David Ekbladh, David Engerman, Nils Gilman, Kim Jansma, Kathryn Lavelle, James Lin, Martin Meeker, David Milne, Craig Murphy, Victor Nemchenok, Sam Redman, Daniel Sargent, Aaron Silverman, Richard Webb, and Mary Yeager provided valuable feedback on various parts of the book at different stages of its development. A special thanks to Ellen DuBois for her longstanding commitment to this project.

Staff at the World Bank Group Archives, the Archives of the International Monetary Fund, the U.S. National Archives and Records Administration, the National Archival Services of Norway, the Archivo Histórico de Relaciones Exteriores de Chile, the Banco de la República de Colombia, the Rockefeller Archive Center, the Ford Foundation Archives, the Food and Agriculture Organization Historical Archives, the Hoover Institution Archives, the Library of Congress, and the Lyndon Baines Johnson, Gerald R. Ford, Jimmy Carter, and Ronald Reagan Presidential Libraries helped me track down countless documents. I am particularly grateful to Bertha Wilson at the World Bank for her tireless efforts on my behalf.

Many participants in the events described in these pages took time to speak with me. Thank you John Blaxall, Francis Colaco, Leif Christoffersen

Stephen Eccles, Sakiko Fukuda-Parr, Attila Karaosmanoglu, Katherine Marshall, Eugene Rotberg, Ernest Stern, Greg Votaw, and Michael Walden for sharing your thoughts and experiences. Thanks also to Craig McNamara for filling in some of the personal details about his father.

I presented parts of this project at Aarhus University, Cal State Fullerton, Columbia University, the German Historical Institute, the Graduate Institute of International and Development Studies, the Ohio State University, the Policy History Conference, the annual meeting of the Society for Historians of American Foreign Relations, Syracuse University, the Università di Bologna, and UC Berkeley. Thanks to the attendees for their comments.

It has been a pleasure to work with the University of Pennsylvania Press to bring this book to print. Thanks especially to Bob Lockhart and the two anonymous reviewers, whose insights greatly improved the final product.

My greatest thanks go to my family. My parents, Naresh and Sylvia Sharma, taught me about the world at a young age. For this and so many other things, I will be forever grateful. My brother, Stephen Sharma, has always been by my side. My son Owen, though he does not know it yet, has brought me more joy than anyone could hope for. And my amazing wife, Bitta Jansma Sharma, to whom this book is dedicated, has been a constant source of encouragement. I love you all.

Lightning Source UK Ltd.
Milton Keynes UK
UKOW04n1917200817

307549UK00014B/488/P